Pillow of Grass

Also by Nancy Phelan

ATOLL HOLIDAY

THE RIVER AND THE BROOK

WELCOME THE WAYFARER:
A Traveller in Modern Turkey

SERPENTS IN PARADISE

NANCY PHELAN

Pillow of Grass

With grass for my pillow
Now that I journey...
PRINCE ARIMA, 7th century

LONDON HOUSE & MAXWELL

Elmsford   New York

93275

First published in the United States
in 1970 by The British Book Centre as a
London House & Maxwell book

SBN 8277–0341–4

Printed in Great Britain

For Simon

Contents

List of Illustrations

Acknowledgements

I should like to thank Marie Byles, of Sydney, for helping put me in touch with Dr Ogata, of Chotokuin Temple, Kyoto, and with Ayako Isayama-san, of Itto-en, Yamashina.

I am also very grateful to Ayako-san for sending information since I left Itto-en; to Ayako Yuhara and Masako Endo, who helped me with information and explanations; to John Stocker, of Kagoshima, whose sense of humour introduced me to the real personality of this city; to Simon Virgo, who in return for chaos and confusion in his apartment gave me hospitality, good company, information and endless help in getting the reference books I needed; and to Victor Gollancz Ltd, publishers of *We of Nagasaki*, a quotation from which appears on pages 246–7.

I hope the text shows some of the gratitude I feel to all the Japanese people who were good to me.

NANCY PHELAN

Glossary

anoné	well; however
benjo	W.C.
bento	lunch box
densha	local train
domo	contraction of thank you; should be *domo arigato gozaimasu*
dozo	please
eki	station
eta	outcast
e-to	well . . . let me see . . .
furoshiki	large handkerchief-scarf in which things are wrapped
fusuma	sliding screen between rooms
futon	mattress
gaijin	foreigner
geta	wooden sandal
gohan	rice . . . used for food
hai	yes
haiku	Japanese poem of seventeen syllables
hakama	divided skirt
haniwa	proto-historic clay figure
hoteru	hotel
ishidoro	stone lantern
jinja	shrine
Kami	'superior being' . . . god

kisha	main-line train
Komban wa	Good evening
Konnichi wa	How do you do
maiko	Geisha in training
miko	shrine maiden
mingei	folk art
mompei	working trousers
noren	decorated squares of material hung across restaurant doors
obasan	old woman
obi	sash
o-cha	honourable tea
odori	dance
o-furo	honourable bath
ohayo gozaimasu	good morning
onsen	hot spring
ryokan	Japanese inn
sashimi	raw fish
sembei	a kind of biscuit
shamushu	shrine rest-house
shoji	sliding paper door
shoyu	soya sauce
So *desuka!*	Is that so! Really! etc.
sushi	cold rice balls and fish
tabi	socks with split toes
tanzen	a padded gown
tatami	straw mats
tempura	fried fish or vegetables in batter
tenugui	head towel
tokonoma	alcove in Japanese room
torii	gateway to Shinto shrine
yukata	summer cotton kimono
yushoko	supper
zabuton	flat cushion

SEA OF OKHOTSK

HOKKAIDO

Wakkanai
Rebun
Rishiri
Shimo
Yubetsu
Abashiri
Engaru
Lake Kutcharo
Asahigawa
Kushiro
Otaru
SAPPORO
Shamani
Shiraoi
Hakodate

SEA
OF
JAPAN

Aomori
Hachinohe
Kuji
Omoto
Miyako
Lake
Towada
Akita
Kamaishi
Ofunato
Ishinomaki
Kinkazan
Sendai
Matsushima
Ryotsu
SADO
Niigata
HONSHU
Nikko
Matsumoto
TOKYO
Takayama
FUJI-SAN
Hakone
Gifu
NAGOYA
Yokkaichi
Matsue
KYOTO
OSAKA
Nara
Ise
KOBE
Muroji
Shodashima
Haseji
Matsunaga
Kôya-san
Onomichi
Hiroshima
Miyajima
Innoshima
Iwakuni
Imabari
Aki
KITAKYUSHU
Matsuyama
Kochi
SHIKOKU
Kubokawa
Beppu
Uwajima
Hirado
Sasebo
Takachiho
KYUSHU
Ninety-nine
Islands
Nagasaki
Kumar
Miyazaki
Amakusa Islands
Yunomae
Sakurajima
Kagoshima
Ibusuki
SATSUMA PENINSULA

PACIFIC OCEAN

EDGAR HOLLOWAY

1

Narrow Road to the Deep North

THE LINE between Tokyo and Sendai is all inland, through rich domestic scenery with far-off watching mountains. It is England moved to the tropics... England's freshness and order, no longer virginal; English purity replaced by a deep knowing lushness; maiden green tarnished with gold; cool northern forms injected with intensity, a hint of violence; and in this enriched uninnocent England, un-English sights ... the froth and feathers of young bamboo; tiled concave roofs of charcoal or gunmetal grey; high gables of mouse-coloured thatch without chimneys; shrines; scarlet *toriis*, rotating scarecrows with a lantern in each hand; graveyards on hillsides where barren land can be spared for the dead; and below the deep shady woods, round the dark peninsulas of trees, the land-locked islands of trees, the farmhouses moated with trees, the piercing almond-green rice-fields, and beyond all, distant wheeling-back mountains smoking with mist.

The usual way to go to Hokkaido, the most northern Japanese island, is to fly from Tokyo to Sapporo, especially if you are a foreigner, or take a sleeper to Aomori, at the top of Honshu, and a boat across to Hakodate; but after studying the map of Japan I felt it might be better to go by train to Sendai, two hundred and twenty miles north of Tokyo, then make my way east by local train, bus or boat, out through Matsushima to Ishinomaki, round the Ojika Peninsula and on up the coast of Iwate Prefecture and finally inland to Aomori.

When I asked the Japan Travel Bureau about local transport in this area they said I couldn't go there at all because I didn't speak Japanese; then they said I was mad; finally they shrugged their shoulders and said I'd have to find out when I got there. They spoke as if I were going to completely unexplored country full of hostile savages. The best I could get was a kind of blanket ticket for the main railway routes through *Tohoku* (north-east Japan) and Hokkaido, and even in this they managed to make mistakes. J.T.B. are misnamed; they cater for tourists, not travellers; yet I sometimes wondered if their weird behaviour is true Japanese or, as I often suspected with others, what they think we expect of them.

In summer travel is easy, if hot. I took only a nylon dress, nylon raincoat, nylon trousers, a shirt, a sweater, a pair of thongs. Japanese inns supply *yukata*, a cotton kimono, for sleeping. Each time I left Tokyo I went light as a bird; each time returned weighted down with pottery, folk toys, *presentos* from people encountered on my way.

At Ishinomaki I waited till the other passengers had gone, then approached the ticket-collector and said, '*Dozo ... ryokan?*' which is shorthand for 'Could you please direct me to an inn?'

He said 'Ah!' and pushed back his cap, smiled, asked me to wait and rushed off. I stood on the hot station wondering if he would come back, if he had understood me. This was really the start of my journey. Sendai is a city; Matsushima, though beautiful, crawls with Japanese trippers. Ishinomaki, a big fishing town, seemed populated mainly with locals getting on with their lives.

12

The ticket-collector returned with a cheerful disarming youth who picked up my bag and led me out into the narrow streets. As we sweated through crowds of workers with baskets and jumped to and fro to avoid cars and buses, he asked me, in English, if I liked *sashima* for which Ishinomaki is famous, and told me the town's population is one million, maybe.

The *ryokan* was old and high, with a garden of pines and stone lanterns and when the plain kind-faced maid opened the *shoji* of my upstairs room I saw that we were on the quay. A wide river, the Kitakami, flowed beneath my balcony and rowing boats were tied up at the bank. At night from my bed on the floor I could hear water lapping, the creak of rowlocks and voices of people alighting at the little steps. Across the river, hills rose behind low houses and down-stream was a long red arched bridge and deep-sea trawlers tied at the harbour quay.

It was a Japanese room with straw-coloured *tatami* (mats) smelling of dried grass, a low red-lacquered table, a pile of flat cushions, called *zabuton*, a lacquered kimono stand. In the *tokonoma*, or alcove, an arrangement of pine branches, a scroll with a carp...all simple, clean, extraordinarily restful.

Apart from the smiling boy, Hiroshi, no one spoke English. The inn was homely and comfortable, with splendid fish meals. My only complaints were the size of the indoor slippers, which fell off when I walked upstairs, and the way the maid sealed me in at night after lighting mosquito-incense in a clay pig burner. When she had gone I could open the *shoji* and move my bed, which was spread on the floor; but I had to put up with the slippers.

There is a good deal to know about footwear in Japanese houses. You may walk on corridors with indoor slippers but not on the *tatami*, on which you sit. Stepping on *tatami*, even in slippers, is the one thing that makes Japanese women shriek. It is the equivalent of standing on tables and chairs with one's shoes on.

Indoor slippers are changed for special scuffs or clogs for the

13

benjo or lavatory. The Japanese *benjo*, which sometimes has an *o* before it, making it 'honourable', is a bidet-shaped hole in the floor. It may have white tiles and water laid on, as at Ishinomaki, or be a primitive earth model. There is a goddess of *benjos*, in whose honour flowers are put on the lavatory wall. Sometimes straw sandals are tied, one each side of the aperture, so you don't drop them down during difficult athletic proceedings.

At Ishinomaki my *futon*, or mattress, was set out on the floor each night by the maid. I was quickly in love with Japanese beds. Trained to relax on the floor, I found them physically restful, but there is something else just as important. In travelling, lying night after night in strange western beds you soon find each has its own character. Sometimes they are innocent, welcoming you to peaceful sleep; sometimes formidable, stark and cold as though kept exclusively for laid-out corpses; sometimes smotheringly full of voluptuous goings-on, sometimes plain sordid, or terrifying in their misery, accumulated torture, nightmares, despair and decay. But no matter what happens in Japanese beds, it all goes with the morning. When the *futon* is rolled up, stowed away in a cupboard, there is no chance of emanations lingering on.

On my first morning at Ishinomaki the sunlight fell on my face and woke me at dawn. I lay watching reflected water glittering on the ceiling. The smell of mosquito-incense persisted pleasantly; under the balcony the river rustled and from down at the port fragmentary voices and hammering sounded from people at work.

At seven came the gentle knock, the sliding *shoji*, the kneeling figure, the murmur…'*Ohayo gozaimasu*…' Blue and white bowls were carefully set on the red lacquer table, each item produced with a modest pride that complimented receiver more than offerer; then with the air of a special treat, a small narrow dish with a dark sliver wrapped in cellophane, light, brittle, shiny, like sliced green mica. Seaweed. But how did you eat it? The maid showed me, delicately extracting a slip

14

with chopsticks, then presented an egg, raw, glaucously glaring up at me like a jaundiced eye. Most Japanese break their eggs into their rice and slosh them round, but here, apparently, I was to swallow it down with nothing but *shoyu*.

I swallowed it.

The maid sighed with the brooding affection of a mother for an afflicted child. This maternal tenderness seems to be part of a *ryokan* servant's work, along with the washing and scrubbing and fetching and carrying that goes on from pre-dawn to late at night.

Then she noticed I had moved my *futon*. Her concern and distress seemed out of all proportion and quite inconsistent with her general air of indulgent benevolence. It was not till later I learnt that I had slept in the position reserved for the dead, with my head to the north.

When Hiroshi heard I was going to Kinkazan, a sacred Shinto island several hours from the coast, he took me down to the fish-smelling harbour, bought my ticket and stood with me till it was time to embark. The quay was hot, busy, cheerful. Steaming mist rose from the mountains, the water had the dull glint that presages great heat. Chequerboard flags and bright streamers hung limp on curved coloured fishing-boats moored in the river-mouth.

Although I was coming back to the *ryokan*, Hiroshi *sayonara*'d me as though for ever. In the cabin, smelling of *benjo*, sardines, seasick and engine oil, people were lying down on the floor with bottles. I went on deck where a loudspeaker gratingly gave forth melodious Japanese wails, and soon we moved down the river-mouth to the sea.

Ojika Peninsula is scalloped all round with long pale beaches. Rib-roofed villages cluster like shells; the hills leaning back into the sky are blocked-out in solids and lines of dark green and light, blue-green and almond, forests and rice-fields and gardens. All is worked upon, nothing is wasted; and in the foreground, attended by gulls, fishing-platforms, fish-traps, fishing-boats harvest the blue ruffled sea.

15

Far away, the island of Aji was low on a smudged horizon; then we turned past a black rocky headland and I saw a mountain rising from the sea, its heights hidden in cloud. It looked rugged and not very welcoming.

'Kinkazan,' said a friendly man who sold *bentos*. '*Hoteru?*' he asked.

I said I was going to stay at the shrine rest-house. He said, 'Ah so! *Jinja!*' and pointed up into the clouds.

Kinkazan's name comes from 'gold flower'. The rocks are said to glitter with gold mica, but from this distance all was sombre.

The boat hooted, the loudspeaker gave out a cheerful tune, people gathered their bundles. Immediately we touched the quay they were ashore, and by the time I landed, were plodding up the wide mountain road, bent double under their boxes of food and drink. Were they all going to stay at the shrine?

'No, no,' said a friendly student, eager to practise his English. 'Tonight they go home.'

He carried my bag as we trudged up the steep path, through great trees with writhing roots and mossy trunks. Below were glimpses of dark rocks and clear water where families were gathering shellfish.

When we came out on an open grassy space the crowd had gone. Chestnut deer, antlered, melting-eyed, watched from clumps of red-trunked pines. Curious, eager yet timid, they gently snuffled the air, stretching forward satiny noses.

'Ah!' said my student, digging into his pocket for biscuits.

I sat down.

A few minutes before I had been in the twentieth century, among Japanese trippers with cameras, transistors, binoculars. Down in the bay was the ferry, the fishing-boats out at sea carried radar, no doubt the hotel below the hill had television; yet here was a world I had thought no longer existed. Up the worn stone steps beyond an immense scarlet *torii* an old woman toiled in dark kimono – the ancient nurse. Lining the grassy

16

avenue, red-painted lamps, little houses on scarlet posts, stood among softer stone lanterns with square Chinese hats; and on the lawns enchanted princesses turned into deer awaited the valiant *samurai*, the noble prince. What would this island be like in the snow...with the scarlet, the lanterns, the captive princesses among the red-trunked pines?

But the twentieth century was very much present in the shrine courtyard. *Bentos*, Kinkazan *sembei*, chocolates, Pepsi-Cola, cakes, bread-rolls and milk drinks, dolls, *tenugui* (head-towels) printed with deer, coloured postcards were on sale. People shouted and laughed, dipped long-handled ladles into a tank where water ran from the mouths of dragons and turtles. Old ladies in kimono, middle-aged ladies in suits, jovial working-men kicked off shoes and thongs and clambered up the steps of the shrine rest-house, commandeering patches of *tatami*, opening *furoshiki*, spreading out *bentos* and bottles, padding to and from the kitchen with kettles of *o-cha*.

In a cage that smelt of decayed fish and *benjos*, monkeys swung and scrambled, intently watched by little men who might have been their brothers. In another cage golden pheasants flashed to and fro. Every kind of camera, tripod and lens was in use. People posed alone, in pairs, in rows like school teams, before the monkeys, by the dragon water-tank, with a tame deer, before the rest-house. They crowded round, tying little white paper prayers to the branches of what already resembled a snow tree; others plodded up the long flight of steps, between lanterns and cypresses to the Koganeyama Shrine at the top.

At the shrine young men and their girl-friends jerked at the thick twisted rope to jangle the bell, threw an offering into the box, clapped hands, bowed, then took photographs on the steps. Children tugged at the rope, scrambled up the shrine steps and slid down on their bottoms. No one looked over-awed, guilty, oppressed or wore a long face. It was a courtesy call on the gods before the picnic; perhaps to ask a favour or give thanks for one received.

It was surprising and very attractive. The colour, gaiety, vitality, homely informality of popular Shinto are always beguiling, its visual excitements and beauties blot out the black side of its history. The Shinto seen at Kinkazan was not the official state religion, the political weapon that helped bring Japan into war, using imperial divinity for sinister ends, but a poetic cult that sees gods in trees, mountains, rivers, that requires mainly purity from its followers, whose deities are satisfied with apples, cakes, *saké* and cups of tea.

From between the bronze lamps at this Gold Mountain Shrine is a Capri-like view across a Prussian-blue strait to the mainland's rich crumpled hills and deep fan-shaped beaches. Squirrel-grey roofs of shrine gatehouse and office merge into cypress and pine. Though the present building dates only from Meiji times, the trees on the sacred island are ancient and have never, they say, been touched by an axe.

My student friend guided me to the shrine office where a young priest in starched white sat at a window. Round the corner a beautiful porcelain-faced shrine maiden with a long black plait and scarlet divided skirt sold charms to the multitude.

'*Hai-hai-hai . . . Sah!*' said the young priest sucking in his breath; then quickly murmured a warning.

'Only Japanese food and bed,' translated my student.

I said I could eat Japanese food, sleep in Japanese beds. I would have agreed to anything. For £1 sterling I was to get supper, bath, bed and breakfast. I tried to find out if there would be a morning service in the prayer hall and if I could go but in Japanese the word *service* has a different meaning. The priest, looking slightly put out, assured my friend there was no charge for *sarvus*.

I tried again, putting hands together in prayer, saying '*Odori?*'

'*Hah! So! Hai hai. Odori!*' All smiles, he waved at the prayer hall and held up six fingers. I hoped I would wake in time.

*

Inside the rest-house the picnickers were approaching saturation among their empty bottles and *bentos*. Faces were flushed, voices loud, laughter blurred; then bodies slumped down and contentment, benevolence, finally silence sank over the building.

I lay on the hillside under a tree by a stream and looked up through the leaves. Immense stately ants paraded, purple-lustre beetles crawled over me. By the path through the woods was a small stone Jizo with red cotton bib round his neck, red cotton ice-bag on his head and on this again a high pile of stones. These little wayside figures are all over the countryside, usually with cotton caps, bibs or piles of stones. Jizo is not an historical character; he is a personification of benevolent forces, specially protective towards children, pregnant women and travellers. Sometimes he is plump and well defined, sometimes almost worn away, but his expression is always calm and amiable.

The bibs and caps come from mothers of sick children, from people wishing a cure or a blessing or giving thanks for one received. When I asked about the stones I received mixed answers.

'The stones are piled for good luck,' said a Christian missionary. 'The people believe if they can add one more without knocking over the pile they will get their wish.'

'Jizo is deaf because he is made of stone,' a Kyushu countryman told me. 'So if people are going deaf they put stones with holes in them on special Jizos, for a cure.'

'They are simply piled there because someone is tidying up,' said a Japanese student, looking ashamed and embarrassed; but a Buddhist nun said compassionately, 'Ah, the caps and bibs belonged to dead children. The parents put them there to ask Jizo to help their departed spirits, and the stones for the same reason. It is not Buddhist teaching, it is not consistent with the Buddha, but some people believe that while dead children are awaiting rebirth they must work at piling up stones. As soon as the pile is finished a demon knocks it down, so the

19

child must start all over again. It goes on endlessly. The parents think if they pile up the stones by the Jizo it will help their poor children.'

I dozed and woke at the sound of a rhythmical drum, deep, slow, immensely compelling. The courtyard was full of reeling, red-faced men, dishevelled women with bundles and children, all jovial, all on the move, shouting, laughing, scrambling down from the rest-house into their sandals. As quickly as they had left the boat they were now leaving the island. At the port where the white *vaporetto* waited with its banners and flags, a loudspeaker summoned and urged between sexy tangoes ... *Dozo ... dozo ... Onagawa ... Onagawa ...* Then, with a farewell hoot and blaring band they set off towards Onagawa, on the far side of the Peninsula. Music floated back to the quiet island, grew fainter, fainter and died as the boat rounded the distant headland.

Now I could hear the island's own sounds ... cicadas, the strange cough and bark of crows. The change was immediate and complete. Free of invaders, Kinkazan began to reveal itself.

The coast road round the island was sweet with scents of hay, of summer dust and flowering bushes. In the deep rich forest I rested on moss and immense twisted roots. Each bend and headland revealed the shining sea. At one great gap in the cliffs, they say, a thousand men fell over, hunting with their lord, Date Masamune. It is one of the ominous roaring-sea places the Japanese greatly admire.

Though there is a hotel on the island it is far away from the shrine and whoever was staying there never appeared.

In the shrine courtyard men were sweeping up the trippers' leavings. Stags, great sombre birds overturned rubbish tins, nosing out scraps. In their cages the monkeys pounded, the golden pheasants swished; in the forest the crows barked.

A thin rain cobwebbed my hair as I climbed the rough mountain path. Two students with misted spectacles and hob-nailed boots crunched purposefully behind, alongside, then ahead, eager to reach the top before dark, to see the view.

At the rest-house an *obasan* (old woman) in dark brown kimono beckoned me in from the rain, holding out slippers, stowing my thongs in a plastic bag. Inside, men were still cleaning up after the picnickers, sliding out screens that divided the great hall into separate rooms. The old woman said *Dozo*, pointed down at my slippers and pushed open the *shoji*. I bowed, stepped out of the slippers and entered. She closed the *shoji* and left.

Muddy, sticky, hot, dying for a bath, I sat down blissfully on the *tatami*. Expecting to sleep in a dormitory, prepared for roughness, even squalor, I found a restful beautiful Japanese room with a heron scroll, a hollow stone holding flowers and, astonishingly, a streamlined telephone. Outside was a little interior court with small twisted pines, a *bonsai* in a pot, mossy stones and *ishidoro*, from which you looked up over grey-tiled roofs to mountains wreathed in mist.

The bathroom was large, tiled, clean and deserted. I soaked in hot brown water, listening to the men splashing next door. As I came out, feeling warm and refreshed, I met the handsome young priest of the morning. He was leaving the *benjo*. He gravely bowed and said 'Konnichi wa' as he finished adjusting his dress.

Supper was served in a big hall where low black and orange tables were set end to end, making oblong checks. The fish and vegetarian meal was good and well-cooked. I was the only foreigner among twelve boy and girl hikers, the only one in *yukata* with long hair. The Japanese girls wore sweaters and jeans and short Beatle haircuts.

In the twilight I walked up the steps past the pheasants, towards the shrine. Something was going on in the prayer-hall. I hovered but could not see, though I heard a strange measured reverberating drum. Then came a flat, light-brushing metallic tasselling... *shay-shay-shay*... and again the circling-out-and-back searching drum. Now a pipe or flute, weird, husky, tentative, and a droning atonal chant. Again the *shay-shay-shay*, the light-shaking harness on the fast-moving horse; then a long silence. Waiting in the fine rain I thought I heard movements and murmurs, but no one appeared. As I started back down to the *shamushu* (rest-house) the drum spoke again, muted, and again came the soft answering shuffle of anklets or bracelets, the rusty mournful pipe.

In the trees of the courtyard cicadas still drummed. A little sad cheeping bird sang alone in the twilight.

I was dozing when a maid padded down the passage and started to shut my *shoji*. Though the mist had come down and sealed us in so that even the little courtyard had vanished, I begged her to leave them open. With an incredulous stare she shrugged, muttered and made off.

In the night I woke to strange sounds...thuds, animal cries ...a sudden scream. *Things* were on the move. I thought of creatures come down from the forest, of great vengeful birds, of *kami* (gods) resenting my presence, of living sacrifices dragged to the altar. In the depths of the night these inhuman cries were part of my drugged half-sleep, part of a frightening grey twilit world in which I was caught, paralysed as in a nightmare. I lay sweating, and finally dozed, to wake again, chilled, confused. People were guardedly gathering on the veranda outside my open *shoji*; there was an impression of late-comers hastening, even tripping up the little staircase that led from the priests' sleeping quarters; a rustling of robes or kimono, a whispering as they lined up and shuffled away. The sinister stealthiness was informed with authority, like the little processions that come down the hospital ward in the night to move the still body behind the screens. It was their right. Intruders, eavesdroppers must take the consequences. Did I dream it? Were priests going off for a midnight observance? Or was it something horrible from the past that lived again at this hour? Who were they coming for? Who were they carrying away?

When I woke the courtyard was still invisible. Mist enclosed the shrine buildings. In the forecourt the paper twists on the snow tree drooped, dejected, their sodden weight bending the branches. Invisible crows made their strange harsh bark on the mountainside.

Then I heard the slow drum again, still muted, still measured and spaced-out, and presently with a gentle rush and rustle priests in starched white and lacquer-black caps began filing up a dark covered stairway towards the prayer hall. I pattered through the rain to the open balcony where an elderly priest invited me in.

In the dark hall, beyond the banners and huge pallid bales of *saké*, a priest sat at an immense drum, gold, with a dragon and blue, yellow, green, orange swirls and trails. On the shadowy altar blond wooden trays were piled with apples, vegetables, white china *saké* jars. *Nusa* – purification wands – hung with paper strips like New Guinea witch-doctors, stood in the altar alcove, one white, one silver.

Visually the service was exciting, but nothing much happened. There was a great deal of bowing, clapping, swishing of the witch-doctor in ritual purification. The drum sounded; the priests chanted in harmony, changing key, rising slightly in the scale and at the end trailing off like a disc running down. Bow, bow, clap. Bow again. Then it was over. Slightly disappointed, I returned to my room. On the way I saw monkeys on the roof. Were they the nocturnal screamers?

But now a priest came and bowed, gesturing so intensely I wondered if I were being asked to leave. With immense effort and embarrassed smile he finally said, 'Dan ... sing!' and jerked his thumb over his shoulder towards the prayer hall. 'Many boys come.'

I rushed at once up the steps in the rain, to the prayer hall veranda. Again the priest at the drum beckoned me in, waving to the best position.

Two very young camellia-faced girls entered gravely, in pure white robes beneath scarlet, high-waisted, divided skirts of incredible elegance. They knelt at the altar and prayed. Then the golden dragon drum sounded and in came the 'many boys' -- workmen perhaps, from their clothes, or fishermen put in from a boat for a blessing service. They were chatting, smiling, doing up their flies, ruffling back their hair, like Turks coming into a mosque late for prayers. Their leader held a large *saké* bottle and one of whisky which the priest set on the altar among the apples and pumpkins. As the men arranged themselves for the service they bowed and grinned at me in the corner.

The shrine maidens now reappeared in white kimono decorated austerely with dark-green trees and flowers. They carried fans and wore golden crowns surmounted by stiff gold sprays of chrysanthemum. They sank down opposite the kneeling priests. The priests' dress had the chill harmony of fish or wet forests, black Mikado caps tied under the chin, starched white or green robes, pale turquoise *hakama* or divided skirts – a perfect background for the ritual; for after the bowing and handclaps and chanting and purification the maidens lit incense fires in great cauldrons and little orange tongues of flame shot up against the sombre background. Then the maidens danced to the flute and drum, their fans replaced by sticks with rattling bells, trailing scarlet ribbons. When they moved, scarlet showed beneath their gold-coloured kimono skirts and small frost-white *tabi* (socks). Slow, graceful, exquisite, gravely turning, venturing a foot, sliding forward, turning again, slowly, slowly, while the little bells *shay-shay-shayed* and the weird music wailed and against the shadowy altar the incense smoked and candle-flames wavered, and blue-and-white banners and great red lanterns and splashes of colour from drums and robes made moving reflections on the glassy floor.

Then the priest summoned the workmen's leader to the altar steps and handed him a green branch of *sakaki*, the sacred Shinto tree, for offering to the gods. Carefully, skilfully, the leader turned the branch, presenting its stem to altar. He placed it on a stand, knelt, clapped hands, bowed, murmured, backed away. Everyone got up very cheerfully, rubbing their knees, and stamped out to a counter beside the prayer-room where

24

the maidens, now out of their dancing kimono, were dispensing *saké*. The wood of the counter at which they stood was pale butterscotch, the *saké* vessels stark-white. Shining black plaits, scarlet *hakama* showed sharply against chalk-white robes.

I went away marvelling at Shinto's magic. Though the colour and movement, incense, rhythm and sound of this ritual appealed to all the perceptionary senses, the impact was completely unsensual. The whole impression of Shinto is one of purity and austerity. Even banners and candles and dragon-drums cannot create the dark gorgeousness, the almost voluptuous splendour of certain Buddhist ceremonies or temples. These are descended from China's and India's wealth and magnificence; Shinto shrines are bred of Japanese poverty and simplicity. It is the difference between a rich brocade sofa and a scrubbed table. Yet in sometimes sombre mysterious Buddhist temples one feels safer than in light, wide open Shinto shrines. For all their shadows, the temples evoke the thought of human compassion, but the *kami*, the Shinto gods, are everywhere and not always benevolent.

At first I would wait for the jarring note, the aesthetic mistake in this superlative theatre, but it never came. Setting, costume, colour, choreography remained perfect. It did not pall because there is always contrast, even comic relief. The merry picnickers, the *saké* drinkers, the young men photographing their girl-friends do away with preciousness; the gimcrack souvenir stalls at the entrance heighten the purity and austerity of buildings and ritual. And against these pure austere buildings, colour is used with nature's own innocence and lack of prejudice, yet with enormous subtlety – a hint of faded coral against dried-ink blue, cinnamon gauze over white, black against smoke grey – and textures and materials the tepid west considers garish or cheap are united with triumphant audacity.

Unlike its architecture, Shinto mythology is a long-winded confusion, as full of hyphenated names as any Polynesian legend. In one creation story the Sun Goddess, Amaterasu, retired to a cave in displeasure and though the world had grown dark and cold, refused to come out. Then one of the gods did a dance so obscene and hilarious all the others roared with laughter and Amaterasu came out to see what was going on. The dance I had just seen, the ancient Maiden *Kagura*, is said to descend from this, but I could see little connection between the god's bawdy dance and the grave sliding movements of the Kinkazan shrine maidens.

It is not hard to see Maiden *Kagura*. It is performed on certain days at the shrines, and will be done specially if you make a suitable offering; but for me it never again had the beauty and power of the first time. Nor could any other setting compete – the slight early-morning chill, the background of imprisoning rain, the mists that rose reluctantly, leaving trails in the trees, the spotted deer and golden pheasants, the bark of the crows in the sacred island's dark forests.

2

'No Good Ofunato'

WHEN I left Ishinomaki, after exploring Ojika Peninsula, Hiroshi gave me two *kokeshi* dolls. These sad sweet-faced wooden cylinders are folk-toys of *Tohoku* district and were the first of the collection of *mingei* or folk art which was to swell my luggage so disastrously.

He also took me to the bus depot, got me the best front seat on the side with the view and instructed the driver to point out the main sights; and since the bus-line ends at Kesen-Numa, several hours up the coast, to get me a taxi from the terminus to the railway station.

All these instructions were carried out, though the driver, conditioned to keep to a timetable, rushed me ruthlessly through beautiful villages and enchanting coastal scenes where I longed to get out and explore. Towards five o'clock, in intense heat, I reached Ofunato, a fishing town, in Iwate Prefecture. I hoped to find a bus here, to take me on to Miyako, where sometimes you may find little coastal boats.

Waiting to pass through the exit at Ofunato I rehearsed my enquiry about *ryokans*. When my turn came the young man at the gate studied my ticket rather closely, turning the pages back and forth, then settled down for a good read. I waited patiently, but just when I thought he had finished he quietly put it into his pocket.

I knew I must not lose sight of my ticket. The whole of *Tohoku*, Hokkaido, the west coast were on it. I said, '*Dozo . . .*' and held out my hand.

He said, '*Chotto matte, kudasai*' (Please wait a minute).

People were gathering. They peered round me, asked each other what was going on. The ticket man, again telling me to wait, started off for the office but made no effort to stop me following. The Japanese public are so well drilled that officials are often nonplussed by foreigners' disobedience.

In the office, several young men were passing my ticket from hand to hand, turning over the pages, nodding gravely and saying '*So!*' and '*E-to!*' Then one said slowly in English, 'Ticket no good.' He courteously drew out a chair for me. Another young man offered tea.

'But it must be! It was issued in Tokyo by J.T.B. and cost many thousands of yen. They told me it would last for weeks and take me everywhere I want to go.'

'No good Ofunato.'

'But why not?'

He could not explain why, his English had run out. He said, '*E-to*,' then '*Anoné*,' finally, 'No good Ofunato.'

A round-faced heated young person had gone to the telephone and was shouting '*Moshi-moshi*' which is Japanese for 'Hullo'. After banging the receiver up and down and crying '*Mush-mush*' he was now smiling into the mouthpiece, saying '*Anoné*' and '*So So!*' and '*Sah!*' and '*So desuka!*'

The others had started to argue. The majority seemed in favour of closing a blind eye and letting me go, but not the young man who had spoken in English. Tall, slim, with a long thoughtful face and many gold teeth, he emanated a gentle

28

persistence far more sinister than blustering threats. This type cannot be got round; so I turned to the weaker section and looking helpless repeated '*Tokyo kippu* (ticket) *okay*' so earnestly that quite soon they began to smile and say soothingly '*Hai hai hai*'.

'Ticket no good,' said the pensive young man.

'But *why*?' It was absurd, no other station had made such a fuss; I would complain to the railways – yet I felt slightly uneasy. This stubborn young man did not look stupid. I was relieved when a European voice said, 'Can I help you?' and a sunburnt man in a green shirt came in, wiping perspiration from his forehead.

The railway men all began talking at once, explaining, turning the pages of my ticket, pointing out words and numbers. He listened, smiled, nodded, said, '*Ah so! So desuka!*' then turned to me.

'There has been a mistake on your ticket. It has not been made out to include this station. You should have taken a slightly different route.'

'I understood I could go anywhere on this line.'

'Not here, apparently. It is a matter of paying another Y200.'

The tall young man spoke urgently. My interpreter added, 'If you do not want to pay you must go all the way round by the other route.'

I laughed. He laughed; the others laughed; even, eventually, the serious one. I said, 'Oh no no no! I'll pay the Y200!'

The man in the green shirt, a Swiss Catholic Father, had been summoned by the heated plump telephoner, one of his parishioners. He seemed surprised at my presence in Ofunato, where he said Europeans never came. He had only seen two, male photographers, four years ago. When he mentioned a resthouse attached to his church, for Japanese hikers and students, I said I would like to go there, and after bows, thanks, apologies and farewells, he took off on his motor-scooter and I followed by taxi.

❋

The Catholic church, on a hill on the outskirts of Ofunato, was hung with coloured lanterns. This was for *O-Bon*, the Buddhist festival when for three days the dead come back to this life. From train and bus I had seen lanterns in country cemeteries and noticed flowers and fruit piled by graves. After cleaning their family tombs and making these offerings, people go to the cemetery on the first day of *Bon*. They light a candle on the grave and bring it home in a lantern, which is put on the family altar. At the end of the third day another candle is lit on the altar, taken back to the cemetery and left on the grave. The spirits travel in the candle flame.

Fires and lanterns are also lit to help guide and welcome the dead, for this is a happy time of loving reunion, without fear or sadness.

The Father's house, in a green garden, was next to the church. Behind was a little school and the rest-house, a low building with bare Japanese rooms, kitchen, *benjo* and wash-room. It was wonderfully, beautifully, peacefully empty.

On my way down to Ofunato I stopped for a beer in the Father's cool pleasant sitting-room. Of his seventeen years in Japan, all have been spent in the north. He rarely sees Europeans, even Japanese tourists. Iwate Prefective, he said, is considered too primitive, without convenience or culture. Besides, transport here is difficult and most Japanese have only one short holiday a year, so must go where they can move about easily.

The Father was kind, cheerful, tolerant, eager to help and when I described my frustration at being whirled past fascinating scenes, suggested local buses and villages along the coast. Then he took me down the hill, put me on the bus and gave me his card on which he had written, in Japanese, a request for the bus home.

Ofunato's main attraction is the beautiful swordfish-nosed fishing fleet. When I had seen it I produced the Father's card at a little hardware shop. The proprietor read the address and instantly crossed himself, rolling his eyes piously with an en-

30

quiring grin, so quickly, so wittily that I burst out laughing. He laughed too and, beckoning gaily, pranced out of his shop and away on his short bandy legs to the bus stop.

At the top of the hill the *O-Bon* lanterns glowed in the church entrance. When I knocked at the Father's door to say good night he looked out and said, 'Come in. The young man from the railway is here. He's been trying to get in touch with you...'

I was appalled; but he reassured me.

'No no... it's not the ticket this time. Come on in.'

The grave young man with the gold teeth was now all in white and dazzlingly clean. His hair gleamed as he stood up and bowed. He had telephoned several times while I was out, the Father translated. He wished to apologise for any inconvenience caused over my ticket. He felt responsible... was afraid I might be annoyed.

I protested I was not annoyed, had forgotten the incident. He had only been doing his duty. I was longing for bed and wished he would go; but the Father, smiling in the Japanese way, continued interpreting. He gave no hint that he should at that moment have been somewhere else at an urgent appointment. It went on and on, smiles, *So desuka!* smiles again. I found it hard to keep my eyes open.

'...to atone for the inconvenience he caused you...'

'But...'

'I have been telling him how frustrated you were when the bus wouldn't stop in the villages. He says that he has a car and it is his day off tomorrow. He would like to take you along the coast...then you could pick up your bus to Kamaishi.'

'That is terribly kind. But really he needn't...'

'It's not that,' said the Father. 'But Japanese people are very kind to visitors. He would like to offer you hospitality. If you want to see fishing villages this is a wonderful chance. He can take you to one never seen by Europeans, not even Japanese outside the area, where life has not changed for fifty years.

31

He knows the president of the local Women's Committee;* she will arrange lunch for you there. They will show you everything, fishing, village life, and the scenery is beautiful. Then he will drive you on to Kamaishi.'

My now eager acceptance seemed to inspire young Mr Izumi-sawada. He began making expansive gestures. If I would like to sleep in a Japanese house he and his wife would be happy to welcome me. I could come back after the drive and spend the night with them and he would drive me to catch the Kamaishi bus early next morning.

At the rest-house I spread a *futon* on the floor and finding no bedclothes covered myself with my raincoat. A climbing rose brushed the wide open windows and sweet scents came in from the Father's garden. I fell at once into a deep well of sleep.

Sometimes in travelling there are memorable nights of perfect rest. They often come in very simple surroundings – a Samoan *falé*, a country inn, a fishing village – after sustained exertion. It is as though sleeping body and mind absorb surrounding vibrations of peace and harmony. I woke in the bare rest-house room completely refreshed, tranquil, feeling healed and with a sense of lightness and freedom. It did not seem strange to hear music; it was part of the grey shadowless light, the rose in the window, the cool dewy air. I fell asleep again to the sound of church bells and woke with the sun in my eyes. The music had gone, the air was steamy. I took a cold shower from a basin and ate some fruit.

The Father was waiting at his house. I had not imagined the music; he had been in his church at dawn.

At eight o'clock representatives of the local paper arrived. They were very polite and asked my purpose in coming to

* There are now thousands of Women's Clubs all over Japan. Many are mainly social . . . for companionship and joint outings, but others do much good work, specially in the country, where they look after local health and domestic education and infant welfare. They can bring pressure to bear in the form of blacklisting or persecuting employers if they feel one of their members has been wrongly used or dismissed.

Japan, my impressions of Japanese people, my views on Japanese culture, my age, my husband's occupation, his age, my daughter's age, how many books I had written. In the garden, pictures were taken, instantly printed and shown to me; then we all bowed, smiled, bowed again and I went with young Mr Izumisawada to the car where one of his friends waited.

Outside Ofunato, when a heat-haze covers the bay, the islets are irregular green woollen cones, the fish-traps enclose grey silk. Mole-coloured houses look down from rice-patterned slopes upon dark shallow boats drawn up on charcoal beaches. The scene asks nothing from colour; it is so poetic, so Japanese I begged to stop; but the young men assured me it was nothing; there was something better in store.

Colour began as we turned inland between the hills – vivid rice, yellow tobacco leaves drying, and like tents and marquees, brilliant *futons* and bedcovers spread out to air on roofs and balconies – red, yellow, purple, orange, blue. The air smelt of green crops and human manure that has turned to earth again.

I was driven, far too quickly, past farmhouses where moss, grass, ferns, even little trees grew on the thatch; past wayside Jizos and old women in *mompei* (work trousers) or kimono, tottering, pigeon-toed, under enormous loads, or mopping their necks in the shade of pawlonia trees. Humidity rose from lush fields and hedges, but beyond the hills the haze had lifted. The coastline blazed; sparks flew up from a flashing sea, dazzling the eyes.

I sat in the back with the cakes brought as *presentos* for my lunch hostess and for Mr Izumisawada's wife. In the front, half-turned, he explained the scenery, in limited English, while his dashing impatient friend drove the car. Difficult surnames were quickly discarded. I was Nassi-san; he was Keiichi, though his friend remained Mr N.

The promised 'something better' was a view from a cliff with a horrible blow-hole, where water rushed in and roared and swirled about menacingly. This was *Scenic Ofunato Number*

33

One, Keiichi said proudly, harking with respect to the sinister din. 'Boom! Boom! Booooooom!' he said with satisfaction.

Mr N. was busy with tripods and range-finders. Both boys had elaborate cameras with filters and metres and flash-guns and extra lenses and both took pictures incessantly... of me, each other, the scenery. The Japanese are wild and indiscriminate photographers, they lose all sense of restraint when exposed to a view. The boys photographed wide-open tracts of featureless ocean and far-off blurred headlands and ill-lit crevasses and over-lit surf. They seemed surprised that though I admired the colour and splendour I made no attempt to record it. I shot off a few frames, to be friendly, but felt slightly diffident before the display of professional equipment. I have only a Rolleiflex which does what I ask it, however unreasonable, but is not spectacular.

The village of Yori, to which we were driving, is built at the head of a deep-set, almost land-locked bay. There is a harbour inside a breakwater and a flat marshy stretch where boats are built, nets made and fish prepared for market. Great iron doors and a high sea-wall protect the inner harbour from flooding storms, but most of the houses are built up the hillsides. The fishing fleet anchors out in the bay.

Keiichi's friend, Mrs Nonomurta, lives in a high-up house with windows looking down upon roofs and terraces in a Mediterranean manner. She is an important woman in Yori but had set aside most of the day, at short notice, to show me the life of the village.

She greeted us on her knees at the door as we took off our shoes. We presented the box of cakes. She bowed again and led us inside. We sat down. She bowed and withdrew and presently bowed her way back with a tray of cold drinks and fruit salad. We sipped, perspired, smiled, bowed, exchanged compliments. My age and personal history were discussed. My hostess, plump, motherly, with gold teeth and glasses, denigrated herself to flatter the guest. She was four years younger,

34

she said, but looked like my mother. She joined in the laughter.

There was all the time in the world and it was all familiar, it had happened before. I had often sat like this in a cool house, in the best room, with cold drinks and fruit salad while heat glared outside and quiet voices talked in this leisurely way. It was hard not to sink into a dreamy trance and forget why one was here.

But this was not the South Seas or rural Turkey. Keiichi looked at his watch. Mrs Nonomurta took up her basket and conducted us through the village to the house where we were to lunch. In a cool upstairs room we sat on *tatami* round a low table and ate beautiful sea-food and salads. I still do not know who my host was but suspect Keiichi. Later, money changed hands discreetly, but I was not permitted to pay. Keiichi is not rich, he works on the railway and has a wife and two children, but to him, as to most Japanese, money is servant, not master.

While we ate and laughed and talked, the brilliant morning changed. Clouds hid the sun. I knew I must not show impatience but could not help whispering to Keiichi about the light. At once he began the long preliminaries of polite disentanglement; but I seemed to be in a web of courteous misunderstanding. I did not want V.I.P. treatment. I only wanted to walk in the streets, on the quay, smile, bow, look at houses and boats and nets, and if no one objected take pictures of people at work in their ordinary everyday clothes; but kind Mrs Nonomurta, eager to help, led us straight to the village school.

Schools in any land are the biggest hazard, even worse than hospitals. You have to start at the top with the headmaster and work your way through to the smallest junior, be introduced over and over again, explain (or invent) your mission, drink tea, ask interested questions, give intelligent answers about education in your own country, of which you know next to nothing. In each classroom you must say *Good morning* in the appropriate language, and *Please sit down*, when they stand up to greet you; and all the time you know that these smiling people, who show no sign of strain at the invasion, are really overworked, flat-out, with no more time to spare for visitors, tea, chats and compliments than you have for inspecting schools.

I expressed all the gratitude and appreciation I could command; but when, driving away, Mrs Nonomurta suggested the hospital, I cried, 'Oh please...Can't we go to the harbour? The village?'

She looked startled at my desperate tone, but when Keiichi, whose English was hourly improving, translated, smiled tolerantly at my eccentric preferences.

Though it had started to rain, people were out of doors working. Men with blue and white *tenugui* or wide straw hats tied under the chin were building or painting boats, making or mending nets. They might have been anything but Japanese ...Mexican, Turkish, Italian. Every face was different, thin or broad, long or short, smooth or wizened, plump or monkeyish, thick-lipped, aquiline, snub-nosed. Their one common feature was the gold teeth revealed by the humorous grin. The women were another race from the waxen dolls of the south. Slim, strong and robust, with broad rosy cheeks, their laughter was jovial, their wit apparently bawdy. They were heaving loads, carrying packs on their backs, dragging heavy carts, hacking at wood or packing stones into walls or roads with gusto and good humour.

All these workers, in their working clothes, had an air of dash and character. The men tied their head-towels with a flourish, the women's gloves and long rubber boots gave an almost swashbuckling touch. Others wore their blue-and-white *mompei* and bonnet-like head-cloths with chic, and the slender figures, small hands, sure controlled movements were graceful and dignified.

In a tin shed young women were packing seaweed. Yori seaweed was Number One in Japan, Keiichi said proudly.

The girls worked in a hot twilight beneath an iron roof, rolling the dried weed in straw mats, hoisting heavy roped bales on their shoulders, stacking them out in the yard for the truck. They wore protectors over their sleeves and bare arms. The teenage girls still looked youthful, but others, who seemed middle-aged, I discovered were also young. They were nearly all married, with babies at home being minded by *obasans*. I asked how much they were paid and was told 'about Y1,400 a month with extras' (less than thirty shillings sterling).

I don't know if this rough monotonous work influences the workers or if only certain types take to it. Though pleasant, these girls were much more stolid than the merry women outside, whose rakish boots and gay bonnets, cheerful laughter and uninhibited shouts enlivened the village.

The men loading floats into fishing boats at the quay might also have been a different breed from the boat-builders and net-makers. Some were very strange, with long narrow faces and heads, wiry tousled hair and Mandarin moustaches that drooped round the ends of the lips. In rubber trousers and gloves, like creatures from science fiction, they held their heads and backs very straight and seemed extremely strong, easily lifting great glass balls in rope nets, encrusted with marine growths.

Now that Mrs Nonomurta realised what I wanted she was eager to help me get pictures. Everyone knew and respected her. The boys, who saw nothing interesting in village life, had given up their photography. In my rubber thongs I slithered about in rain and mud as she gestured, waved, called, beckoned people, commanded them to raise head or turn away, arrest hatchets or knives, smile or refrain from smiling. She understood quickly, despite lack of English, and after I once said 'Oh no...just natural,' forbade studied poses. The Japanese, who like being photographed, really prefer to pose but are very obliging, falling easily into natural positions, like Polynesians; so now they went on placidly making nets, loading their boats, spreading seaweed on the quay.

Fish is the life of this village, and all existence comes from the sea. In the open, red-cheeked women were cutting up fish for *sashimi*, trimming squid and octopus; indoors, pallid old crones packed dried *bonito*, hard as wood. In some houses whole families were working together, smoking, curing, preserving, preparing fish for market; and those not handling the sea's harvest were on or in the water – the men in their boats, the children swimming with splashes and screams in the harbour, agile, slithery, quick as fish.

Outside Yori, male and female roadworkers were coming home with their tools on their shoulders. I stared at women loading logs on a lorry, at a man winding silk. Two ancient *obasans*, trudging along with kimonos tucked high above their withered knees, shrieked as we passed and began a grotesque obscene dance on the roadside, toothless mouths stretched with malicious delight.

Obasans did as they liked, Keiichi said sheepishly. In Japan, old people do not worry about appearances.

Compared to his friend, who when not gay looked sulky or bored, Keiichi seemed a sad young man, calm and deliberate, but his face was thoughtful, intelligent and very kind.

Mr N. had begun to drive very fast, hurtling up and down roller-coaster slopes on an atrocious road, now through a forest, now by the sea again. Dusk was falling and I wanted to know where we were going, but Keiichi either could not or would not explain. He just made *Chotto matte* (Wait) gestures and murmured in Japanese.

On the sheltered side of a cliff we turned into a *ryokan* garden where flowers grew among cabbages and shaped trees. Blue-and-white *yukata*, patterned with fish and waves, hung out in rows with poles through the sleeves and in two ponds, joined by a waterfall, *sawara*, a kind of mackerel, slowly cruised. There was peace; the sunset was reflected on the opposite hills and soft mists were gathering.

I wanted to get out and stay the night. Already rosy-cheeked girls had come to welcome us, but the boys had just called to pick up a friend. He emerged from the inn swinging a bucket, a schoolboy in black high-necked uniform.

'But where are we going?' I asked plaintively, as we hastened on round the steep narrow serpentine road, as though hurrying against the light.

'Surprise,' said Keiichi. 'Surprise, Nassi-san.'

We stopped above a quiet bay. The air was still warm as we picked our way down the track to the beach, but the sun's ferocity was already muted by evening mists. The last flare had faded out on the hills; the world was blue-grey. In the sheltered cove boats were pulled up on the shingle and dark trees leaned over the rocks to see themselves in the depths. The blood had gone from the day, all was turning to spirit. The squeals of little boys swimming offshore were delicate insect cries; isolated sounds from across the calm water came clear, flat, fragile, fragmentary. Relief, refreshment crept into the air. We moved in an almost tactile serenity.

The boys dragged a boat down the beach and into the receptive shallows. Wading out, I stood in the water, conscious of all the times I had done this, on just such an evening. Only the setting was different; the essence is always the same.

Upright, with a long oar over the side, the schoolboy sculled us out into the bay. All round, square enclosures brimmed, like small liquid fields in picket fences. We tied up at one and the boys, standing in line so the boat canted steeply, cast with rods into the fish-trap. At once the water thrashed, a silver leaf twisted up through the air and fell on the floorboards. Another, then another, line after line, all three together, as though the fish could not wait to die. Soon the bucket was full of convulsive movement.

I watched the cool grey evening, trailing my hand in the sea. Sleek as oil, threaded with steely bugle-beads, the water gleamed round the narrow boat, reflecting the gunmetal sky. Neighbours were out emptying their traps. Their voices, disjointed words, clatters and splashes echoed quietly up to the high slopes and blue-green pines. Across the bay, dark-patterned peninsulas, dove-coloured villages rose from the sea, and above the Welsh mountain mists waited to close in with the night.

3

Ofunato Nights

Since Mr N. showed no signs of turning off to the church I asked were we not going to see the Catholic Father before we went to Keiichi's house.

'Father in Morioka,' Keiichi said. 'Come back my home now.' It was not till next day I learnt he meant his own father.

At a garage he drafted me from the car to a taxi and off through the darkening streets to Shinofunato, on the far side of the town.

It was dark when we got there. He led me up a small lane to a row of houses along the train line. People sitting beside their *shoji* or out in their gardens bowed and called 'Konnichi wa' and asked questions.

'My home,' said Keiichi at last.

At the entrance a pretty girl knelt with two living Japanese dolls. 'My wife, Kimiyo; my daughter Yoko, my daughter Michiko,' Keiichi recited, as Kimiyo murmured her greetings. We bowed, smiled, kicked off thongs, slid into slippers. The

40

box of cakes was presented; I was besought to enter. The larger doll bashfully stood behind her mother but the little one, Michiko, flung herself on Keiichi, who lifted her up in his arms.

I was sticky and dirty and tired; I longed for the silent resthouse up by the church. Keiichi's house, which seemed to consist of two rooms, lacked the bare simplicity of Japanese interiors. The room where we sat was hot and crowded with a large sideboard and television. I sweltered as I sat on the floor drinking beer, which I do not like; but the young couple's kindness made me ashamed.

Keiichi had changed to a grey kimono with a black sash tied low round the hips. In western clothes he might have been any slim Asian young man; now he was subtly transformed, older, more dignified, completely Japanese.

The children were also in kimono. Michiko had got over her shyness and screamed with excitement at the Hong Kong rings and kangaroo pennies I produced from my bag.

While Kimiyo prepared supper – with which I was not allowed to help – Keiichi showed me his treasures. They included souvenirs from Hokkaido and trips to the south and astonishing photograph albums. Where were the brilliant and subtle fruits of that splendid impressive equipment? Page after page showed slightly off-focus views with Keiichi himself in the foreground. He intoned the commentary: 'Sapporo; Tokyo Airport; Nikko; Sendai; Morioka; Kyoto ...' Then he brought out a thread ball embroidered exquisitely in brilliant silks, with a long tassel.

'I make,' he said.

These balls, made of paper, were originally for amusing court ladies, but are now mainly found in folk art shops and museums. I could not imagine an Australian railway man embroidering in his spare time.

After supper Keiichi asked if I would like o-furo (Japanese bath). Kimiyo brought out soap, a towel and clean starched yukata with blue and red butterflies. I was led to the bath-house across the garden where a large wooden tub, like a copper, simmered in a cloud of steam. There were two entrances. On one side you climbed up to a platform where you washed, before sliding down into the copper; from the other, presumably, you stoked the furnace that roared away underneath.

The earth *benjo* adjoined the back veranda of the house. It was spotless, with lavender-scented airwick, a vase of flowers and squares of tissue in a little basket.

When I came back from the bath Kimiyo, entertaining a friend, shrieked with horrified laughter. Both girls rushed forward and began to tug my *yukata*, as though to tear it off.

Keiichi tried to translate.

'No good.' He demonstrated how I had wrapped it, left side under right. 'This way no good.' I said, 'In my country, okay for women this way, but not for men.'

'In Japan no good, man or woman. Only dead people. Bad luck.'

When the girls had rewrapped me correctly, right side under left, they began nodding and murmuring and shaking their heads. They disappeared and came back with arms full of clothes. Keiichi was sent away, I was taken from the *yukata* and given a long half-petticoat. The *yukata* was then replaced and properly wrapped and, since it trailed on the ground, hoisted up at the waist with a huge tuck. This is the usual way to adjust kimonos, which are all made the same size.

The manœuvres took a great deal of measuring, discussion and shaking of heads. I stood meekly, stupefied with fatigue, while the deft clever fingers dressed me.

When the length was right they began on the waist, quickly building it up to the size of my hips. Several cords, bandages, stomachers and stiffeners were lashed round, drawn so tightly I could not take a deep breath. A wide board-like band with a pocket cut into my bust, kept me upright and prevented exhausted slumping. A broad stiff yellow *obi* (sash) was arranged

42

with a clip-on pre-fabricated bow the size of a bustle, then another cord tied round the *obi*.

'What is this for?' I indicated the final cord.

'Keep in place,' said Keiichi, summoned to see.

Keep in place! It would be impossible to remove the construction by force.

Keiichi sat watching in a corner with the spellbound children. From time to time they squeaked and he gave an appreciative moan.

'Wonderful! Wonderful in *yukata*!'

But the girls were less easily satisfied. They stood back and viewed me with half-closed eyes, then pounced on my hair, tore it down, dragged it up, scraped, twisted it into a Japanese coiffure. Excited by its length they handled it like children with a special toy.

Keiichi moaned on.

'Wonderful! Wonderful Japanese hair! Wonderful in *yukata*!'

I was given a glass and invited to admire myself. I thought I looked a sight but they assured me it was perfect. Kimiyo brought out a pair of embroidered shoes, seemingly made for a doll. I got my feet in but doubted if I could walk. I was appalled when, handing me a fan, the two girls bowed and wished me God-speed.

I wanted to go to bed, not out, clamped in the Iron Maiden of Nuremberg, in Chinese torture boots; but Keiichi had risen and stood waiting to show me the night life of Ofunato.

He had a very free way with taxis and seemed to know many local drivers. He would stop a cab rushing past, usher me in, and the driver, abandoning any previous plans, would turn round obediently and take us wherever instructed.

I was first driven up to the heights to look out on the lights of Ofunato; then to call on Mr N.

A sad-faced young woman invited us to sit at a low table covered with plastic, with our legs dangling in a square hole cut in the floor. In winter this hollow contains a charcoal fire.

It is covered with a cage and a heavy quilt and people sit round with their legs underneath and the table drawn over.

Tonight, in sticky heat, we sweltered round the empty *kotatsu*. Beer and fruit were produced; the host brought out his photograph albums. Like Keiichi's, they were full of blurred pictures of himself posed before famous views. Mr N. was already a little drunk and wild-eyed.

The louder he talked the sadder his wife looked. Her plain face was patient, her eyes meek, her head drooped humbly.

'She is sad,' Keiichi explained later, 'because my friend is bad boy.'

She had nothing to say, even in translation, and sat offering fruit and beer in a rather crushed way, fetching and carrying for her handsome young husband and for an ancient parent or in-law off-stage who communicated in peremptory grunts. When, against all my protests, the gay Mr N. thrust upon me a prized wooden *Tanuki*, she obediently fitted it into a box and wrapped it most beautifully in coloured paper, handing it to me on her knees. I felt in my bones she regretted this wild generosity but I could not reject the gesture.

Tanuki is a legendary badger, a kind of minor god, who comes down from the mountains and gets into all kinds of trouble. He is fat and jovial, with a mushroom hat, and carries a *saké* bottle. He is a good luck charm for boys, believed to give them male strength. Poor young Mrs N., being childless, had perhaps not lost hope while *Tanuki* was in the house.

When we left with Mr N., she farewelled us humbly. She would clearly wait up, by the empty *kotatsu*, to welcome her drunken master and put him to bed. Without children as compensation, she seemed an unhappy, unloved, unpaid domestic drudge.

I hoped we might now be going home to bed, but the boys hailed a taxi.

'Night club,' Keiichi said, ushering me in through a discreet door, to a murky room throbbing with sexy music.

An expanse of gold teeth advanced through the dusk, Mr N. was clapped on the back and we were bustled and bowed to a table. The toothy host waved his hands and instantly two females leapt up as though conjured from the ground. They wore extravagant kimonos and elaborate Japanese hair full of knitting needles and flowers. Their faces were dead white and they had many gold teeth.

As though the hostesses had pressed a button, waiters converged with drinks. Baskets of green soya beans were put on the table and the girls began shelling and eating them, from time to time pushing them into the boys' mouths. A menu was flapped at us; snacks appeared and more whisky for Mr N.

If I was fascinated by the hostesses they were intrigued by me. They peered and pulled at my earrings to see how I kept them on, marvelling to find my ears pierced; and made guesses at my age, which due to the twilight were twenty years off the mark. I longed to know if they wore wigs.

They talked incessantly, in high parrot voices. This rapid chatter, combined with ceaseless movements – peeling beans, hand-feeding the boys, filling their glasses after each mouthful – created a restless disturbing atmosphere. The band's jungle rhythm increased the strain. My interest in Ofunato's night life was waning.

'Too much talk,' Keiichi said. 'Too much drinking.' He looked very grave, rather careworn. He suggested we join the twitching forms on the tiny floor but I could not dance in Kimiyo's shoes. I had got them off under the table and doubted if I should ever get into them again. Mr N. had gone to the bar where he was noisily being a jolly good fellow. The hostesses, who found Keiichi a rather poor customer, were displeased.

'Too much talk,' he muttered. 'Too much whisky. No good.' He stood up to go. Before we had reached the door the girls were fluttering round another table.

As we drove off Mr N. emerged and jumped into the taxi.

On his direction the driver took us, in the usual Japanese frenzy, to another bar.

I tried to think of it as research as I limped, tired, hot, bored, with sore feet and aching head into the dark narrow room. The bar, little more than a corridor, had a counter along one side where a stout ruined beauty in kimono stood watching with Medusa eyes.

'*Mama-san*,' Keiichi explained, and led me upstairs to a tiny gallery. Mr N. stayed at the bar where he could drink with more speed and freedom, laughing and shouting at the *Mamasan*.

Girls appeared and the basket of pea-pods. Keiichi looked increasingly lugubrious as he sipped his drink. I felt he had not much heart for this sort of thing and was doing it to please his friend, to entertain me. Prevented by politeness from saying openly that I'd had enough, we sat on, sweating, trying to keep our eyes open. At least there was no jungle band, only discs.

Apart from *Mama-san* and the hostesses in kimono the bar was not particularly Japanese. It could have been anywhere in Europe, specially Paris. There were French similarities I had noticed in Tokyo – the choice of music, the intimate air, the simple elegance of the girls in western dress. Behaviour was fairly free; couples were holding hands, gazing into eyes. At one table a rather drunk young man sat with a girl who might have been French, slim, chic, with black fringe and creamy skin. She was working hard on him, holding his eyes in long looks, passing the tip of her tongue round her lips.

'Bad girl,' Keiichi said severely. 'No good.'

Immensely attractive, her beauty was already tinged with rottenness. She was poised above the abyss. Another few years, months, even days she would fall over into decay. In repose her face was perfect; when she smiled, blackened teeth gave a chill premonition of what was to come.

'Let's go,' Keiichi said.

Mr N. preferred to stay. Eyes and hair now very wild, he

46

was arguing noisily at the bar. Keiichi shook his head as we left.

'My friend drink too much,' he said in his low sad growl. 'Bad boy.'

Though long after midnight, Kimiyo was waiting. She looked tired but brought out coffee and cold drinks, rich cakes and pastries. While I did my best to swallow, Keiichi gravely took from a glass-fronted cupboard his souvenirs of past holidays, and despite my protests presented them solemnly, inscribing each one with my name and the date.

I did not want to take his treasures, any more than Mr N.'s *Tanuki*, nor could I fit them into my luggage; but to refuse was unthinkable. Though I had come prepared with reciprocal *presentos*, nothing lessens the generosity of giving away these family treasures.

Then Keiichi got to work on my ticket so the incident at Ofunato should not be repeated. Pale and drawn, he carefully made out my future route, writing in English and Japanese, translating place-names on my ticket into Roman characters. He wrote a series of little notes in Japanese to the ticket collectors at Miyako, Hachinohe, even Wakkanai on the far northern tip of Hokkaido. These notes, he explained, asked the recipient to look after me, to direct me to a suitable *ryokan* and see that I caught the right train for the next step of the journey.

I slept on the *tatami* in the main room while Keiichi and his family sweltered together next door. Despite the heat we were all sealed in behind tightly-closed *shoji*. It was dark when I got up and dressed and presently Kimiyo came sleepily through the *fusuma* with the children.

Out in the village people were sprinkling and sweeping before their houses. In little gardens of phlox and sunflowers grandmothers played with babies while housewives prepared breakfast. The air smelt of wood-smoke and mosquito incense.

47

Though fresh, the morning was moist and grey, undeclared but suggestive of heat. Already women were down at the seaweed factory, making straw bales, and at the fish-market the night's catch gleamed on the wet floor. The fleet lay alongside, bright medieval flags limp in the unmoving air, great coloured reels for nets standing out against white hulls.

Above the tranquil bay the night mist was already separating into bands of smoke, through which the dark islets showed as through slatted shutters.

It was quiet away from the noisy fish-market; only distant voices from over the water, from the hills behind the village, the engines of little boats setting out, the splash of oars, the creak of rowlocks.

At the house Kimiyo had removed my bed and prepared breakfast – cold fried egg, white bread, cold sausage, potato salad, cream-and-chocolate cakes. She had gone to much trouble to provide it so I must eat it. The others had rice. The TV provided morning exercises while we ate; then it was time to leave.

'*Sayonara, sayonara,*' the little girls cried, bowing.

'*Sayonara,*' said Kimiyo bowing and waving.

'*Sayonara,*' cried the neighbours as we picked our way through their gardens to the waiting taxi.

'*Sayonara Nassi-san,*' said Keiichi when he had put me into the Kamaishi bus, told the driver to look after me, been forestalled in trying to pay for my ticket. He stood in the muddy street gazing sadly in through the door.

The bus began shuddering. The driver hooted; Keiichi bowed and stood back; then a man rushed shouting from the ticket office.

'*Telefono! Telefono!*'

The bus stopped. I hurried to the telephone.

'Bon voyage,' said the good Father at the other end of the line. 'Enjoy your journey. *Sayonara.*'

Boatbuilder of Yori

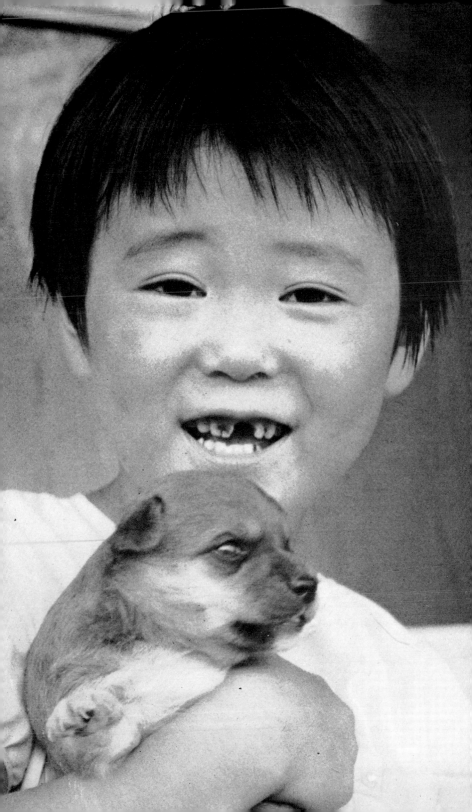

People of Ojika Peninsula

Keiichi and Mr N.   Medieval flags

Iwate coast

Working women

Making sashimi

In Yori village – making nets

Oshidomari, Rishiri

Left and above: *Rishiri women*   *Mountain climbers*

Chief Tolstoy

4

Peacock Coast

THE FISHERGIRLS opened their *bentos* and began to eat breakfast, selecting grains of rice carefully with their chopsticks, as though each had a subtle difference.

As the morning passed the bus became very noisy and jolly. Country men wearing jodhpurs and wide straw hats, red-cheeked old women with small wicked humorous eyes clambered in spryly, with immense loads, cackling and chattering. Poor, overworked, prematurely aged, often shrivelled like monkeys, all had enormous vitality. Most of the *obasans* smoked, some with incongruous cigarette-holders; many had dyed their hair, then offhandedly let it grow out to show inches of white round the roots. The majority, men and women, had little fans.

There are two kinds of Japanese smiles...the polite exposing of teeth that has been taught from birth, and a whole-hearted merry grin that flashes out, in which the eyes disappear and the mouth becomes a watermelon slice. I do not mind the disciplined smile that often enrages westerners, but infinitely prefer the grin, which I saw constantly, bouncing with noisy, garrulous peasants and fishermen over appalling roads or in hot crowded trains, and which recalls the Micronesian Gilbert Islanders.

The faces in this Iwate bus were engraved with cheerful good nature. Creases round mouths spoke of frequent laughter, twinkling eyes of well-being rather than mere manners. I was astonished and shocked at the terrible teeth and all the gold and amalgam. Is it a status symbol? or sentimental refusal to part with even a rotten tooth? Sometimes there is little more than a splinter of the grey original, set in gold like a saint's bone in a reliquary, or Renaissance jewellery in which gold and enamel round pearls create dragons, dolphins and fabulous creatures.

Only our driver did not laugh and talk. Brilliant, skilful, daring, in immaculate white gloves, he navigated hairpin bends, zig-zagged round pot-holes and with imperturbable good humour pulled up short to avoid head-on collisions, or reversed along razor-edge cliff-roads to let others pass. My faith in him was complete; in any case I was too taken up with the scenery to think about accidents.

'Like Norway,' Tokyo friends had told me, 'the Rikuchu coast. The sea comes into the land'; but these fiords are softer and richer, though the rocks are black and the cliffs high. Creepers and vines give tropical luxuriance, the purple-stained peacock sea is the Pacific. Crooked pines overhang white beaches, cliff-tops are lush. Heavy stones on roofs suggest wild weather but in these summer days all is brilliant, the air clear and glowing above a contented ocean. Towards midday the turquoise sky pales with heat, then flares into slow evening fires that draw blue shadows out from the feet of the trees.

Whenever a clear landward view opens up, coloured rice-fields bring a domestic touch to the grandeur. Man's work is everywhere. From the loneliest headland a deep-sea fisherman is seen far out on the horizon; in almost invisible coves grey villages crouch behind crescents of drawn-up boats. White

50

caiques lie at anchor in hook-shaped bays, tarred ropes are coiled on the quay. The fields are alive with scarecrows and coloured flags, the houses with washing hung out on poles and bright *futons* airing. In the forests, like northern jungles, logs lie in orderly piles and along remote cliff-roads women work in tin hats and gloves. The further you go the more magnificent it becomes, until, when it ends at Kamaishi, with industrial smoke, chimneys, a long wait at a hot crowded station, there is almost a sense of relief. Extreme beauty demands contrast. Kamaishi, which has mines and iron works, is just what is needed.

Rain pelted down at Miyako; the streets were full of traffic and mud. At the station I presented the first of Keiichi's notes to the ticket-collector.

He was a handsome young man with humorous eyes. He read, said '*E-to!*', laughed, pushed back his cap and scratched his head, set his cap straight, laughed again, drew a deep *Sss* breath and asked me to *Chotto matte*.

There was a dash to the station-master's office, chair drawn out, *o-cha* poured, the note handed round and inspected by colleagues; then someone took over at the barrier and off we went into the town.

I had expected only directions, not personal escort, but when I suggested a taxi Keiichi's friend Tetsuya smiled. Carrying my bag, he guided me through puddles, shielding me from on-coming traffic. Miyako seemed very full, very touristy, though I saw no Europeans. Keiichi had said it was beautiful. This was not noticeable.

'*Ryokan!*' Tetsuya waved, flashing his handsome black eyes and I saw the familiar signs – crooked pine, stone lantern, brown *shoji*, rows of shoes at the wide entrance.

The host, in kimono, spoke only Japanese. Tetsuya booked me in, explained my plans, found out when my boat left next morning and where I must catch it; then he was off, smiling, bowing, raising his cap.

The incredible peace and comfort of good Japanese *ryokans*! Hot *o-cha* and bean-jelly cakes ... wet clothes off ... *o-furo*, a clean *yukata*, a rest on the *tatami* listening to rain beating down on bamboos and stone lanterns; then a perfect dinner of sea-food, exquisitely cooked.

I yawned, stretched, lay down on my *futon* and began reading *haiku*.

The telephone rang at my head.

'Nassi-san?'

'Keiichi! What on earth are you doing?'

'Telefono Nassi-san. Okay? Lettra okay? Miyako *eki*? *Ryokan* okay?'

I said yes yes, everything was okay, Miyako station okay, good *ryokan*, good supper, tickets okay.

'I come Miyako maybe,' said Keiichi. 'My father Morioka. Tomorrow my Sunday. Maybe drive Miyako tonight, see Nassi-san okay, see my father Morioka, come back my home.'

'But Keiichi, it's nine o'clock and pouring with rain. You can't drive eight hours in the dark along that terrible road. It's suicide.'

'Maybe.'

When people say 'maybe' like that it means they will not be dissuaded. I said, 'You're a lunatic.'

I might have paid him a compliment. He said he would bring photographs taken at Yori.

'Have some sense, Keiichi. Drive tomorrow morning to see your father. Go home now to bed.'

'Maybe. Maybe see you. Miyako.'

At 6.30 next morning the telephone rang again.

'Nassi-san?'

'Keiichi! Where are you?'

'*Ryokan*. Hurry. Come down.'

I was crossing the landing when he appeared up the stairs.

'Hurry,' he said. 'Big fish-market is NOW. Number One Iwate Prefecture.'

I was not in the mood for fish-markets however big. I had

52

to pack up, eat breakfast, pay my bill and catch an early bus to Jodohama for the boat up the coast; but Keiichi, though haggard and pale, with dark-circled eyes, remained dedicated to my instruction. I had expressed interest in local life; I was going to get local life if it killed him.

'When did you come?' I asked.

'Now. Just now I come. Eleven o'clock leave my home. Drive all night. Miyako six o'clock.'

'But why? You must be dead. Why not wait till the morning?'

'But,' he said, surprised. 'I had to bring photographs!' He held out a sinister wad.

A strange, rather beat-up car waited in the garden.

'My friend Mr N. bad boy,' Keiichi said in his slow sad growl. 'Take my car not come back last night.'

The rain had stopped but Miyako was drenched. We drove to the fish market, then round the town viewing local sights, none of which made me wish to stay in Miyako the Beautiful. Keiichi's air suggested unlimited time and when I mentioned my early bus said he would drive me to Jodohama. Plenty time.

The car gave a high helpless whine and began to shake. Keiichi groaned.

'Aah. This car no good. My friend no good. Take my car. Not come back.' He groaned again, looking baffled.

'Maybe petrol?'

He shook his head glumly but guided the faltering vehicle to a garage across the road. He seemed surprised to find the tank empty; but even when filled the car would not go. It strained, roared, collapsed in frustration. Keiichi stared blankly at the dashboard.

The garage boy, with a gay smile, stuck his head in the window and suggested the hand-brake. Released, the car shot out into the road.

I wondered how Keiichi had driven himself through the night and the rain round the hairpin cliff roads of Iwate.

At Jodohama, a scenic beauty spot mainly composed of

rocks, people were hurrying to the quay. Before I could join the queue Keiichi had elbowed his way to the front and was buying my ticket. The others stood back watching meekly. Japanese queue-jumping always succeeds. The one who is serving, taken by surprise, drops what he is doing to attend to the newcomer. No one ever objects or says it is unfair.

We ran to the quay and I jumped on the boat as it drew out. Several cheerful young girls clustered round, laughing, to pull me in. The little boat chugged round the headland; then the girls tugged my arm, pointing; Keiichi was scrambling across the rocks, waving distractedly.

'You are American?' asked the girls.
'No; from Australia.'
'Ah so! Australia! Excuse me please, where are you going?'
'Kuji...Hachinohe...Aomori...Hokkaido.'
'Ah, *Hokkaido! So desuka! Hokkaido!*'
It was always the same when you mentioned Hokkaido. People looked awed, impressed, envious, longing. It was a strange land, almost like going abroad; big, empty, beautiful, foreign, exotic.

But Hokkaido could not be more strange or beautiful than this northern Iwate coast. The little white boat with its valiant flags took us past lonely headlands and bays so secret, beneath slopes so steep that no roads existed. Here, on the crowded island of Honshu, were empty beaches where none came but gulls and transient fishing boats; but the sea was farmed everywhere; on its cobalt surface boats, nets, fish-traps waited patiently.

'Your friend ask,' said the girls. 'Masaki, buy ticket. Change Omoto.'

How Keiichi had organised them to help me buy tickets and tell me where to change buses I never knew; but somehow they got me a window seat on the crowded bus at Masaki, took me off again at Omoto, showed me where to get tickets and catch the Kuji bus.

Now the tremendous landscapes began again, yet without satiety for they constantly changed – rural; coastal; a forest; a rough stretch with timber camps; a vast panorama; an intimate sylvan vignette with shabby fox shrines and faded *torii*; deep rich Devon country lanes; aerial views across volcanic hills like arrested waves, smooth as moss, with rivers of dark trees cascading down to bays so deep, landlocked and silent they might be crater lakes; and beyond white crescents embraced by headlands, a dreaming ocean dusted with sequins and sleek oases without current or tide. Black Cornish needles, pinnacles, arches, Faraglioni rocks were set on paper-lace doilies in a blue-bag sea, and cliff bases stood in a sliver of white, like the fold at a kimono neck. On the horizon, celestial Alps bleached the summer sky. The ocean was in *samadhi*, suspended, at one with the universe.

Because our bus was informal and rural the driver kept stopping to let the few hikers photograph each other against the scenery and even drove to the edge of cliffs so we could admire the view; but soon the hikers got off and I was the only passenger. In the front seat, I had grown close to conductor and driver, sharing *sembei* and sweets, admiring the scenery they eagerly pointed out.

The country was becoming strange, less Japanese. Piles of firewood against walls hinted at bleak winters. On the highland roads, Mongolian-looking *babushkas* carried swaddled papooses on their backs; yet in little sheltered villages where the fishing fleets were going out, stored heat blazed off cement breakwaters. There, Mexican-looking boys in big hats mended nets, and women with heads tied up like Turks crouched on the ground in the shade of unJapanese buildings.

The houses were now of plain wood without paper *shoji*, almost Norwegian, with shingle roofs held on by stones and rich gardens of sunflowers and phlox and tiger lilies, orange and spotted and pink. Fat rosy brown children laughed by the roadside and gay little schoolboys ran through the leafy woods.

Some of the fishing ports had immense walls and iron doors to shut out the sea.

In one of these little towns we became entangled with a festival. The streets were clotted with men in *tenugui* and *happi* coats, chanting and beating on drums, girls and women in brilliant kimono, floats decorated with cherry blossom. It was like a country *romeria* in southern Spain. A little distraught policeman with bulging eyes and sweat streaming down from under a white helmet pranced distractedly backwards before us with arms outstretched, blowing his whistle, trying to prevent the curious wandering under our wheels. When I stood up the crowd were quite thunderstruck. Ignoring the procession they pressed close to the stationary bus, staring open-mouthed, lifting their children for a better view.

We were so much delayed that the driver had to go very fast to catch my train at Kuji. He drove me right to the station entrance where the conductor, jumping off with my bag, ran ahead to flag the train while I waved my ticket before the collector's startled eyes.

Along the darkening coast women spread seaweed to dry and a quiet surf broke upon grey sand. The blue shining afternoon sea had grown sombre and far out a row of lights shone from the fishing fleet. Briefly I saw high thatched roofs with dormer windows and flowers, grass, even little trees round ridge poles and TV antennae; then the rice-fields purpled, cottages merged into hills.

At Hachinohe it was night. The big gloomy station was noisy, confusing. I felt tired and forlorn, but Keiichi's note produced a guide to the nearest *ryokan*. Compared to Miyako it was slightly *déclassé*. Men in *yukata* sat about in the entrance watching TV and the maid at the desk seemed to think I would understand Japanese if she wrote it down. After much dumb-show I retired to the stuffiest Japanese room I had yet been in, with a good view across a small courtyard into the gentlemen's washing-place.

As I lay down to sleep the telephone rang. Far away, Keiichi's voice said, '*Ryokan* okay?'

'*Hai hai.*'

'Okay *lettra* ticket-man?'

'*Hai hai.* Thank you . . . thank you for everything. Tomorrow morning, five o'clock train. Towada Express.'

'*Hai.*' A sad sigh. 'Good night, Nassi-san. *Sayonara.*'

When Towada Express flung itself into Aomori station the passengers seemed to go mad. They scrambled off and ran down a Freudian platform towards a far-distant flight of steps. I was swept up and along with them, hoping they led me to the Hokkaido ferry, but at a sudden broadcast announcement they stopped, wheeled and charged the opposite way where I now saw another staircase. They were running, I realised, to queue up for seats.

'Excuse me,' said a little toothy man as we puffed along the platform and up the stairs. 'What do you think of the Japanese people?'

'Kind . . . very kind,' I panted. 'Very friendly to strangers.'

'Kind? Maybe,' he said. 'But dirty!'

'Dirty? The Japanese *dirty*?'

'*Hai.* They spit.' He looked ashamed and disgusted.

'The Japanese always smile,' I said to cheer him up. We were now forming into queues at the barrier. 'They don't show their worries. This is remarkable. In my country everybody looks worried, even when they're not.'

He seemed amused.

'*Hai hai*, they smile. Not happy, but they smile. Maybe country people more happy. Not in cities. But they smile . . . *hai*, they smile. This is Japanese custom.'

He waved me on to the head of the queue. As usual no one protested.

5

Rishiri Froat on the Sea

On PAPER, Hokkaido resembles a grotesque fish with high dorsal fin, an eye, a spike on its nose and a strong swimming tail. Hakodate, where the ferry from Aomori was to land us, is on the inner side of the tail-fin, four hours across the Tsugaru Straits.

When the signal was given the queues began to stream, scramble, stumble, lollop, lumber, lurch on board with their luggage – peasants and fishermen carrying boxes and cartons and bundles and bags and *furoshikis*; mothers carrying babies on their backs and *furoshikis* in their hands; city slickers with smart zippered bags and *furoshikis* tied round *presentos*; girl students with huge rucksacks and *furoshikis* containing *bentos*; boy students in little yellow or burgundy corduroy hats and mountaineers' boots, with tripods and rucksacks and hatchets and ice picks and ropes. All, except the boy students, had *furoshikis*; all, except the peasants and fishermen, had cameras. All the students had maps and timetables which they studied

58

continuously and would continue to study till their holiday finished, in trains, boats, buses, stations and youth hostels.

I had been advised to travel first class on the boat if I wanted a seat but second class European was so good and so empty I stayed there. Most of the oncoming horde went into the Japanese section...a great empty carpeted room where they could lie down on the floor to sleep, be sick, eat, gossip, read or write. Only a few Japanese students came in with me. Later, in other boats, I also travelled Japanese.

With a place on the carpet secured, the passengers put on their shoes again and swarmed to the kiosk for food, drink, sweets, petrified squid in plastic bags, coloured postcards and long unfolding sets of views which they addressed, stamped and dropped in a special mail box. There was an air of being abroad in exceedingly foreign parts, of adventure in posting a letter at sea. In many ways I recognised my own excitement the day I posted a letter from Troy.

No one looked back at Honshu, beautiful as she drew away, her mountains turning to clouds.

Hakodate is usually dismissed as dirty and uninteresting; but all ports have character and this is an old fishing town with a wide bay and a mountain behind. From Mount Hakodate there are fine views across the buildings to the sea.

There was also, for me, the discovery of *soba* – hot noodles – at the station. *Soba* is the *pasta* of Italy, the *pilaff* of Turkey, the bread of France...the food you can always turn to when tired, hungry, broke or discouraged. Unlike railway rice, which is usually cold, *soba* cheers and warms, no matter how bleak the wind or bitter the rain, how long the wait or draughty the station.

At first sight Hokkaido is not Japan. Wide, beautiful, colourful, it is Russia, Bulgaria, Thrace. There are orchards and gardens and hop-fields, poplars and haystacks; two-storied farms with red roofs and square windows, houses with chimneys,

59

barns with Scandinavian roofs and high concrete silos wearing red Prussian officers' helmets.

My companions found all this exciting, and when, climbing into the mountains, we saw the Saghalien firs, which do not grow in Japan's other islands, they jumped up to take photographs. Immaculate Christmas trees from Siberia, silvered, eternally snow-powdered, precise and lovely, each keeping itself to itself, in the forests their fresh tangy scent brings refreshment on the hottest day, and their formal shapes, among red-roofed farms and silos, turn the hillsides to nursery-toy farmyards.

All day we sweated up the fish's tail, round the edge of Uchima Bay, then inland through mountains and rice-fields and back to the sea at Otaru. Mountains were slowly offered, slowly withdrawn as we plodded past or over or round them. Evening came, the heat declined, boy students sang softly together with eyes half-closed. And at last, in the darkness, Sapporo.

Having longed all day for Sapporo to come and rescue me from the train, I now did not want to get out, to break my mood of travelling. There was an express called *Rishiri* for the north in an hour. It was fully booked, had no sleepers, no reserved seats. When you are acting foolishly you become very obstinate. I joined the queue of excited young students and waited doggedly, hungrily, wearily, got a seat, swallowed a sleeping pill and put my hat over my face. I take sleeping pills so rarely that they put me out like a light. I was asleep before the train started, but a charming girl woke me to ask if she could change places to sit with her friend. I moved without opening my eyes.

I next woke to find a fat man shaking me, complaining that I had his place. Drugged and docile, I let him move me to an aisle seat with nowhere to rest my head. I drifted off again and woke as my neighbour thrust me from her shoulder. Mumbling apologies, I went back to sleep but once more, for the fourth time, was recalled by an urgent woman jerking my arm.

60

Through the fumes I resented intrusion, returning conscious-ness, discomfort, the insistent hammer of the human voice. I dismissed the woman petulantly, pulled my hat down and re-turned to sleep. It was not till next morning I realised she had been offering me a better seat.

Dawn was terrible. In the cold stuffy carriage bodies lay in all sorts of attitudes. Men and girls were curled up, half-on, half-off the small hard seats, heads pressed down hopelessly against adamant arm rests. Babies were laid out in pairs. Several boys lay on newspapers spread in the centre aisle; a girl slept on an inflated rubber mattress between the seats, among stockinged feet. A man with two seats to himself had propped up one end with Sapporo beer cans and lay at a comfortable angle. Others had draped legs out over arm-rests, even thrust them up the wall at right-angles.

Drugged, chilled, hung-over, this fearful awakening endeared the Japanese to me as nothing else could. For all their clean-ness, control, courtesy, correctness they are at heart just as susceptible, human, indifferent to appearance as anyone else I have ever travelled with.

In a bleak wind we staggered from Wakkanai station to the bitter harbour, through unmade streets thick with black mud, oil, grease and slush. The blackness, the lusciousness of the mud is Wakkanai's chief distinction. There are also immense earth-movers and concrete-mixers and wrecking machines, ugly grey buildings and towers and weather balloons against a grey sky. It is horrible, this most northern Japanese town, and three American camps on the outskirts have not improved it.

Shivering, we clustered like refugees in the waiting room at the quay, where four tough-looking little pea-green boats waited. I peered through the sleet, looking for Siberia across the Soya Straits, and tried to cheer myself with a bowl of *soba*.

Only a few mountain climbers embarked with me on *Rishiri Maru*, for the island of Rishiri, off the top of Hokkaido. In the stuffy cabin I lay down on the carpet and straight away went

61

back to sleep, vaguely aware the man beside me, lover-close, was heaving earnestly.

The heaver woke me at Rishiri. Eyes shut, I felt my way into my shoes and joined the procession of Doré figures crawling up from the lower deck, sighing, groaning, dabbing at foreheads and eyes.

Across the bitter sea a large unfriendly island gloomed. Above rocky coasts, awash with chill waves, truncated mountain slopes descended from a blanket of mist. This was Rishiri, Fuji of the North, the most perfect mountain after Fuji-san.

It was raining heavily as we landed at the grim little town of Oniwaki. The students, heaving their packs, set off to walk to their wet healthy camping site. Alone, I stood shivering in the deserted street wondering what to do next.

A few women in *mompei*, with sub-editors' eyeshades and headscarves clattered up to the local store. Their faces were very round, very flat, like Eskimoes, but they seemed friendly. In two minutes, they demonstrated on my watch, a *basu* would come and take me to Oshidomari, on the other side of the island; meanwhile, why stand in the rain? Come on into the shop.

Inside was dark, but warmer. I dimly saw hardware, vegetables, dried fish, barrels, ball-points, sweets and cigarettes. Deceptive postcards showed bright-coloured local scenes: *Fair sight of Rishiri in winter* (with snow)... *View of Setting Sail* (departure of pea-green boat)... *Rishiri-Fuji froat on the sea* (a green cone rising from a purple sea against an azure sky).

The *basu* came. I was the only passenger.

Desolation, desolation all round the wintry coast. Seaweed spread on grey beaches, rough grey hovels against sodden green slopes, grey stones on grey shingle roofs; grey boats dragged up among grey rocks. A grey sea, pockmarked under needle-point rain; seagulls and great black menacing birds squalling and circling, and always the sense of something behind the shoulder, the brooding presence above in the mist, the invisible unloving god.

62

Flung from side to side as the bus lurched and floundered in and out of pot-holes, I glumly pictured the next few days on this gelid island. I knew only that it has a beautiful mountain, is inhabited by fisherfolk and, with Rebun, lies off the top of Hokkaido. Across the water is Saghalien, which belongs to Russia. In good weather it may have the charm of all fishing coasts; but, as in Brittany, lack of sun makes a difference. Its present bleakness, cold sombre colouring and relentless diagonal rain chilled me to the bone.

At Oshidomari the rain had lightened enough to show a curved bay behind a high protecting headland. Old houses, slips, tackle, nets huddled together below the hill; deep-sea fishing boats with bright flags were moored in a small crescent harbour.

I climbed down from the bus and said 'Dozo . . . ryokan?'

The flat-faced, short-legged conductress grinned and waved at a building a few yards ahead. I sloshed towards it.

With its silvery weathered boards it might have been on the Black Sea coast of Turkey or Bulgaria, yet in its simple solidity and proportions there was a Queen Anne–Georgian touch. It sat at the roadside, handsome, hospitable, with a wide central door in a dignified porch and carved decoration above, square-paned double windows beneath gently sloped blue-green roof. Not till you entered its double doors did you see the broad shining platform, the racks for shoes, the kneeling maids, the *bonsai* tree, the flower-arrangement in the *tokonoma*, and know you were still in Japan.

My room was small, square, clean, smelling of hay and tea. It looked out over the entrance porch to the fishing boats and high headland with the lighthouse and beyond to the sea. It was my greatest pleasure in Rishiri. From time to time, when the clouds lifted, I would dart out and take a bus or go for a walk; but inevitably the grey cloud would move in from the sea, the mist descend over the mountain, the bitter rain beat in my face. Sometimes I stuck it out, clambering over the rocks to photograph, with palsied fingers, drawn-up fishing boats, Eskimo women and babies; but usually I fled from slopes or streets, rocks or fishing-coves back to my room where, warm and dry in *yukata* and padded *tanzen*, wet hair spread on my shoulders, I could sit on the *tatami* at the window, drinking *o-cha* and eating bean-jelly cakes, watching the loading at the harbour, pitying saturated hikers and mountaineers squelching up the road to the youth hostel at the local shrine.

There is a shabby melancholy about this *Jinja*. Its grey *torii* and stone lanterns, phallic columns and shrine building with high Isé-type cross-beams all look dejected.

Apart from the fishing fleet's movements, the main interests of Oshidomari life are the arrivals and departures of the pea-green Wakkanai boats. Promptly on the dot they come in, promptly go out, moving briskly, steaming straight out from the quay as though they cannot get away quickly enough.

Though there are street signs and notices and occasional *bonsai* trees outside doors, Oshidomari does not look Japanese. The houses, of horizontal boards, are roofed with slates and small shingles or sheet-iron painted bright blue. Wooden doors, square-paned double windows with white frames replace paper *shoji*. Many doors and gables have a carved decoration like an elaborate trefoil. The whole character is northern, battened-down, built to protect, to withstand a bitter climate. In the streets women wear *mompei* or dark kimono, old men wrap up their heads in white cloths tied under the chin. Mothers carry their babies inside their coats. Many children wear white, red or black tights under their dresses or pants. They have rosy cheeks, not surprisingly in this raw wind. There are large, furry, not very agreeable dogs.

Among the grey rocks boats are drawn up, with reels for nets at the sides or nets on handles, as though for catching gigantic butterflies. The deep-sea fishing boats are big and powerful, built for northern tempests, and the smaller ones in the pebbled coves almost arc-shaped. There are high headlands and hardy yellow daisies and seagulls, a sort of Atlantic–Breton look, melancholy in this dismal weather and fine mist. The mountain comes and goes in the clouds. I must take its

64

beauty for granted; yet I cannot believe it approaches Fuji-san, for Fuji has more than beauty. There is her supernatural quality, her effect on man's spirit as she floats high in a blue sky, her white upturned unfolding fan ghostlike, ethereal, unattached to earth.

> ...a god that watches over Japan,
> Over Yamato, the Land of the Sunrise,
> ...her sacred treasure and her glory.

I had finished my dinner of *sashimi*, red roe, crayfish, fish soup and fish *tempura* and was waiting contentedly for the maid to come and spread my bed. Earlier, going to the bath, I had noticed a great deal of padding up and down stairs; now from down the passage I heard a rhythmical clapping, the sound of a flute or pipe.

In a large room men sat cross-legged in a semicircle. They wore blue-and-white *yukata* and each had a scarlet lacquer tray set with blue-and-white dishes. Among the trays were bottles of beer and *saké* and in the centre one of the maids knelt, very humble, with scarlet cheeks and head hanging down. I wondered if they had been teasing her, if she were embarrassed or if this were no more than the proper demeanour for serving at a stag-party.

At one end of the room a boy stood playing a flute. The others were clapping in unison, singing occasionally, radiating good cheer. Some were plump, elderly, jovial, baldish; others scholarly, with metal-rimmed glasses. A few of the younger men were very handsome, and there were amusing humorous faces with merry eyes.

They were all gaily drunk, flushed, laughing loudly, fraternising rather emotionally. They invited me pressingly to join them but though I accepted a small glass of beer I stayed at the doorway, sitting *à la japonaise*.

They had probably not drunk very much; Japanese men have very weak heads. It is said to be due to the lack of fat in the diet.

The maid escaped, looking hunted. Later, at nine o'clock, I found her doing the washing. She had risen at dawn, worked all day, carried dozens of trays up and down stairs, laid out and taken up beds, scrubbed floors and walls, washed dishes, washed and ironed sheets and *yukatas*, but remained cheerful, smiling and kind.

I asked for Japanese songs. A thin aesthetic man sang a strange and beautiful dirge, and the boy played a sad haunting air on his flute. Everybody looked slightly lachrymose; then a little bald man sprang up and did a grotesque comic dance among the trays.

'You American?'

'No. Australian.'

'*Australia!*' Grinning, they pointed down to the ground; the little bald dancer mimed a kangaroo; his friends rolled helplessly, flashing gold teeth and glasses.

There was something naïve and childish about their noisy excitement. Small-time businessmen out on their office excursions always seem rather touching. It is such an *occasion*, they have such pathetic pride in their cameras (which are going to produce such ghastly pictures), their new zipper bags, which they keep opening and shutting, the *presentos* tied in *furoshikis*, which they are taking home. They start off so formal and smart and so quickly slide into giggles and foolishness, undone by so little drink.

But what of these men's wives? Where were they? What were they doing? What sort of time were they having, left behind with the children? Looking patient and sad, like Mr N.'s wife? Would the master describe his adventures when he got home; or was it none of her business? Would the courtesy and gallantry shown to the foreign woman be turned off like a light, inside their own houses?

It was certainly turned off next morning, replaced by embarrassed faces, averted eyes. I wondered if they had hangovers, if they had lost face by dancing and singing before me; or if I had lost face in their eyes by watching them.

6

The Hokkaido Fish

FED UP with Rishiri's surliness I set off for Rebun, across the sea, in the pea-green *Rebun Maru*. As she gave her last warning hoot, 'Auld Lang Syne' oozed from the loudspeaker. This is a favourite departure song for boats and trains and is played in waltz time with Japanese words about the sadness of parting. Removed from its convivial New Year's Eve heartiness it becomes haunting and poignant and greatly appeals to the Japanese sensibility.

A hand touched my shoulder. The maid from the *ryokan* beckoned me to the rail, gave me two streamers, bowed and pattered down the gangplank. As the boat drew out the maids lined up and holding their streamers before them like miniature muffs, solemnly and efficiently dispensed them with mechanical perfection. One more chore for these poor little overworked girls.

Rishiri receding was no less chilling than seen at close quarters. The dismal coast, the huddled villages merged, then vanished into grey sea and sky.

Rebun seemed just as grim, but without the beautiful mountain froat on the sea. On the quay at Kabuka THE SHOP FOR SOUVENIR was full of monstrosities made of local shells and stones, shells in plastic bags, head-towels printed with Rishiri mountain and red plastic kewpie-faced octopi with inflated tentacles standing out all round like *tutus*. When the mist came down over the island's green trees and mild slopes, I decided not to stay. With a new load of old men and women with wrapped-up heads we put out through the beautiful fishing fleet to the iron-dark sea.

It grew colder; the wind increased. The passengers went below to be sick in comfort. I found a sheltered corner and warmed my back on a steam pipe. Dozens of little barrels packed on the foredeck had the frosty look of fish coffins. A couple of wild-eyed students were earnestly getting drunk on a tiny bottle of Nikko whisky.

'Russia,' said a boy, tapping my arm, pointing into the distance where, clear of island mists, the horizon showed a blue land mass.

'Rishiri?'

'Not Rishiri. Russia. Saghalien.'

We turned the headland and entered Wakkanai harbour.

The dorsal fin of the grotesque Hokkaido fish is green and empty, slightly rough, with scattered farms, round-topped silos and low fat haystacks. Yellow daisies, purplish-blue bellflowers grow in the fields and the forests are full of Saghalien firs. Few people were visible as we passed. Sometimes incurious figures appeared in the gardens of houses with Dutch-looking roofs, or on the flat road one saw an ancient man, a woman pulling a heavy cart of milk-cans while a man walked behind.

Near Asahigawa, in the centre of the island, the country is more domesticated, with rice, corn, hops, red- and blue-roofed barns, houses and silos. It is still vast and empty compared to Honshu. This emptiness fascinates the Japanese who go in herds to enjoy it.

Moving further west, through Kamikawa, Engaru and Kitami, the landscape grows richer and kinder. The mountains keep a decent distance and rice fields stretch out with their little flags and bright roofs, their rivers and trees. Here and there are wigwam shapes. These are poles stacked out in advance by the farmers, to be used as rice-drying hurdles.

Towards Bihoro and Abashiri, in the west, forests and flowery slopes give way to an exquisite broad green valley among serene hills. This is idyllic country, gentle, intimate, rich, reassuring.

As you travel across Hokkaido the haystacks change. The short fat shapes become higher, built up round a pole or even a tree-trunk; then they grow small, like puddings, then again wide and flat; then high once more, like letter-boxes or bell-tents with a frill on top. They stand, tall and thin, like little armies, or small and squat, like crouching children. Round Nayoro they have white plastic skirts or green plastic capes and even collections of individual sheaves wear little hats, and near Bihoro they are propped up on three poles, like Pushkin's house on hen's legs. You are conscious all the time that this is a land of neat, industrious people.

'Excuse me please, what is your purpose in coming to Asahigawa?' said the young man, who was leading me, at the ticket-collector's behest, to a *ryokan*. 'Only Japanese tourists come here; not Europeans.'

I was wondering myself. The grey chill of Rishiri was here replaced by intense heat. Asahigawa was all dust, glare and charging traffic. I felt fragile. I had not had a restful night at Wakkanai with its sluts, drunks, mud, dirt and American canned goods. In the rough ill-lit streets there are a few old ramshackle Hokkaido houses with carved decorations over the porch but all else is ugly and slummy. For the first time in Japan men had accosted and followed me, and during the night drunken shouts and brawls echoed round the railway square. At the cement *hoteru* a blowzy embittered woman had put me into a small stifling room which, looking straight down into the brilliantly-lit men's lavatory at the station, received its miasmas as well as the sound of departing and arriving trains.

'You are going to Chikabumi, maybe, to see Ainu people?'

'Not today. Tomorrow I go to Abashiri.'

'Ah! Abashiri! Very beautiful. Beautiful rake. You like water-ski? I go there my vacation to water-ski on the rake. In winter they cut up the ice on this rake.'

'Is is far to the *ryokan*?' I wiped my forehead. 'Perhaps a taxi?'

'Not far. No taxi. You like my city?'

'Very fine.' The streets were certainly wide.

'*Depato!*' He gestured proudly at a large building. 'Very business, Asahigawa. Here we make lice-wine. You like Japanese lice-wine?'

'You live here?'

'I live. I am student, Sapporo. I study economics. I hope maybe graduate university after one year. But jobs very hard. Many people. Japan very poor country.' He smiled as though giving good news.

All those clever industrious students, so eager to learn, to graduate, what happens to them? What would happen to this bright charming boy with his economics degree, among all the thousands of others?

'Maybe,' he said, confiding the solution. 'Maybe I go United States. So I practise my English.'

Reciprocal feet on the seat, I have found, is a way to Japanese favour. When I appear, stretched legs are lowered, hoofs snatched from the opposite seat with resigned shame and guilt; but if, having taken my place, I bow and say, '*Dozo...*' patting the space beside me, wide smiles replace injured feelings. The invitation is at once returned and we settle down in mutual comfort and esteem, feet nuzzling each others' thighs.

Though one gets fed up with second-class travel, first-class in Japan is a dreary affair. The carriages are clean and

70

cool, sometimes frigid, with air-conditioning; hot towels are given out and the seats are superb; but the price for all this is the well-heeled Americans, the stuffy Japanese businessmen you travel with. There is no fraternisation or swapping of food, no jolly little monkey-men, chirpy *obasans* or meek young mothers who let you play with their gorgeous over-stuffed babies. You don't take your shoes off and put your feet up on the seat, nor do your companions tuck their legs under them or sit in lotus position. It is all rather lonely; while *Hikari* (Light), the famous bullet-train the Japanese are so proud of, which goes at a hundred miles an hour and from which you can ring up and in which you are irreparably sealed, is positively spooky with its strange silent vibration, its strange silent passengers.

When I got into the train at Asahigawa there were a number of students and hikers. I have been told that well-brought-up girls are very chaste but have seen a great many student couples here in Hokkaido travelling alone and clearly in love. Japanese friends suggest that the parents do not know … it is easy enough to set out in a party and split up, or meet by arrangement. They say parents no longer have much authority and mothers are often intimidated by daughters with superior education. It all sounds very much like life in the west; yet when I talk to girl students I meet, the majority say they will make traditional marriages, with a go-between and a husband chosen by the family. Since distinguished go-betweens add prestige to both family and marriage, they are often used, even when the couple have already chosen each other.

In the green mountain pockets round Daisetsuzan National Park, the villages have an alpine touch – grey shingle roofs and piles of logs by the roadside, sparkling rivers and forests and slopes of blue, white and yellow flowers. The hikers left the train at Kamikawa for this great reserve, which has everything dear to the Japanese heart – volcanic ranges and snow-covered

71

peaks, forests and strange flowers, ravines and gorges, rivers and waterfalls, even hot springs.

Watching these hikers pile eagerly out to people the solitude, I wondered about the famed Japanese feeling for nature. I am sure it is genuine, but it often seems more like respect than love. They don't tangle with nature, they observe and photograph from approved points at desirable distances. Is it because they know too much? Or are just obeying the regulations? Yet in other ways they have a real sense of comradeship for all forms of life – wrapping straw round trees in winter, propping up the branches of ancient giants, putting little paper caps round the heads of chrysanthemums. On country stations shrubs and gardens are lovingly tended, there are flowers in ticket-offices, bus-drivers' cabins, even trucks sometimes have a vase with a flower. Yet they also despoil. 'We Japanese love nature,' they say, throwing their empty *bentos* and bottles around. Is this a modern development, or is it perhaps a native trait, more unselfconsciously realistic than a house-proud attitude? *Bentos* under a tree spoil the tree for us; they do the tree itself no harm.

I went on in an almost empty carriage to Engaru. Here, after a good deal of messing about, I took a local train to Shimo Yûbetsu, on the Sea of Okhotsk, where some of the Ainu live.

The Ainu inhabited Japan before the Japanese, but they live now in reservations. Anthropologists say they are a branch of a white race that came down from northern Asia through Saghalien. They were always rather primitive; when they were driven from the southern islands they left nothing but buried clay pots and a few place-names; but they were brave fighters. They withstood the Japanese invaders for hundreds of years, even defeated them in a great battle at Morioka, in the eighth century. Only gradually were they pushed back till all was lost but Ezo, the old name for Hokkaido, where they now live. The Japanese called them *Ezojin*, people of Ezo, when not referring to them as *emishu* (barbarians).

72

I had never seen Ainu before, nor had I seen the Sea of Okhotsk. Calm, silky, blue-grey, it spread out in the sun, 'the sea left behind', which is what the Ainu call it. As I looked at it I was overcome by a most fearful melancholy; the whole air seemed full of sadness. I took a car to the shores of Lake Saroma, not far from the town, which is not really a lake, for the sea comes in at one end of a long narrow spit. It was full of Number One oysters, the driver said. He seemed to sense I needed cheering for he chatted on kindly. The great lagoon (Number One in Hokkaido) offers tranquil water views and lovely forests; but in the afternoon sun it too seemed sad. My first Ainu further depressed me. A biggish shambling young man in trousers and an old striped shirt, with a beard, he was sitting aimlessly, drinking Coca-Cola. He may have been perfectly happy, may have just knocked off work for the day, but I saw him as symbolic of his people. I did not want to stay in Shimo Yûbetsu.

I went back to the station feeling Russian. The young man, who had European features and large dark eyes, had not glared at me indignantly, the prerogative of a proud conquered people, but affably smiled, inferring that he would willingly pose for my camera.

In helping foreigners the Japanese assume an air of eager enthusiasm that gives the impression they have waited their whole lives for just this minute.

I had been trying to steel myself to give up *ryokans* and stay at youth hostels. In this country everyone uses them, age is no barrier and they are the best place to meet all sorts of Japanese. Now, at Abashiri, unable to cope with the telephone, I appealed to the ticket-collector and at once, with familiar excitement, the staff were alerted, telephones bashed up and down (*Moshi-moshi*) and in two minutes a bed at a hostel secured.

Outside the station a petrified Ainu poses heroically on a pedestal, spear raised to impale a fish, a bear, perhaps even a

73

Japanese. Ainu monstrosities glower from shops and kiosks – carved souvenirs, rings, ornaments, brooches, key-rings, pendants, even hair-slides. Ainu designs are stamped on head-towels, Ainu appear on wrapping paper; horrible little bears with fish in their mouths are sold as Ainu art, coloured postcards depict Ainu posed in traditional embroidered garments. Screen-printed versions of these are for sale at high prices.

Abashiri is a big fishing port, with two lighthouses, one red and one white, at the harbour entrance. Streets are rough and unmade, but there is a good view from the Buddhist temple up on the hill. Deep-sea boats lie at anchor near the fish-markets. Along the coast are small pretty villages, wide lakes, low green fields and sand dunes. From one of these, among roses and bell-flowers, I watched the sun go down, the sky pale, the mist drift, the moon rise over the Sea of Okhotsk.

Entering the hostel – a cement barracks in a hot back street – I smelt the *benjos*. A juke-box thundered, electric lights glared. Urged to hurry if I wanted supper, I took my tray and from the serving hatch collected bowls of soup and rice, a plate of Spam, tinned potato salad and a cold fried egg.

Tea kettles stood about on laminex tables. I sat down, trying not to hear the juke-box, banishing thought of *ryokans*, kneeling maids, soft floor-lamps and exquisite dinners of sea-food. I would eat quickly and go to bed. So long as I didn't have to talk to anyone.

'Excuse me please, but you are American?'

'Excuse me please, may we speak English with you?'

'Excuse me please. What is your purpose in coming to Japan?'

'Excuse me please. What do you think of Japanese custom?'

When the earnest interrogation, the searching of phrase-books, the straining and shouting above the roar of the juke-box were over I went up to bed.

In a high-ceilinged cell eighteen iron beds were arranged in upper and lower tiers. The small window was closed; the

74

air smelt of must, mould, feet, dampish blankets and mattresses and stale human emanations. Clean though the Japanese are, the collected miasmas of eighteen sleeping bodies, night after night in a small hot unventilated room are inclined to add up.

A group of girls, twittering high on top berths, smiled, bowed and said 'Konnichi wa.' (How do you do?) They waved hospitably at an upper berth by the window.

I said 'Konnichi wa,' wondering if I had better not cut and run for the nearest inn; but it was only for one night. I would have a good bath and immediately fall asleep.

A raucous announcement gravelled out of the public-address system. O-furo was finished for the night; and not only o-furo, even water at the washing troughs in the hall. Nothing came from the taps, not enough to clean teeth. I returned to my eyrie, applied cleansing milk and cream, dry-cleaned my teeth and lay down, hat over eyes, to shut out the hard central light.

The problem was ventilation. The window was shut. With the door closed you stifled, yet each time it was opened a stench wafted in from the benjo next door. I fell into a sweating doze and woke, startled, at the rasping loudspeaker voice.

Immediately lights went out; officially night began. I cautiously worked my hand across the wall and with great effort pushed down the top of the window. A vagrant current of air oozed in, laden with essence de benjo.

In the morning I learnt that there is a beautiful hostel on the shores of the lake.

I seemed doomed to make mistakes in this area. At Bihoro, some miles out, I took what I thought was a local bus to Lake Akan, but when all were in, a uniformed girl with white gloves, smiling, relentlessly gracious, took up her stand by the driver and faced us with a tiny microphone in her palm. I looked at my fellow-passengers in consternation but they were waiting complacently. I was in for the day with a tour party and their guide who, like a disc-jockey, knew the unpardonable nature of silence. Information must pour from her lips without pause – facts, statistics, figures, heights, depths, acreage, details of flora and fauna, for Lake Akan is a national park and people must be told about it. When not talking she sang in a strange unmelodious little voice, with perfect rhythm and timing, of the lake's beauties. When the audience clapped she bowed and sang again.

As the morning went on with the ceaseless piping monologue, constant stops for mass photography, obedient in-and-out trooping at appointed spots to peer at sinister crater lakes, steam jets, baked earth, a sulphur mountain hissing and roaring like fire-hoses, forests, lakes, Famous Sights and Approved Views, I began to understand why western residents become so obsessed about the Japanese love of organisation, their unquestioning acceptance of discipline, their talent for submerging all individuality. Yet if I had not been directed out of the bus at Lake Kutcharo I should have missed the most beautiful moment in all Hokkaido.

From a slope I looked down on the lake, the eye of the great Hokkaido fish. In the background the passengers had set up tripods and were working fast and silently, photographing and posing, and a girl dressed as an Ainu sold soft drinks and souvenirs. Below, a Highland loch stretched into the distance. Though the sun was high, there was a sense of early morning. Soon perhaps the whole lake would sparkle; already heat glimmered in patches like submerged drifts of stars; but a light haze still hovered, in sheltered corners mists were still vapouring. Reflected headlands and islands were dark and unmoving, absorbed in nocturnal communion. Far away, softened mountain peaks were blue shadows against a chalky sky. No bird skimmed the surface, no boat trailed arrow ripples. A distant coil of smoke climbed the air.

On the hot green slope where I lay, a pale road wound down out of sight to the lake-side.

It was more than mere morning freshness. There was a presence out on the lake, aloof, powerful, impregnable, an ancient unwavering silence. The faint voices of passengers at the souvenir stalls, droning cicadas, a car slowly climbing the

76

winding road only intensified its strength. This positive, waiting, listening force was the lake's own long-preserved essence,
the weird virginity of timeless scenes upon which man can
make no lasting impression.

A few days later I left Kushiro, a large friendly fishing-port
in south-west Hokkaido, and went by a series of trains to
Shiraoi, an Ainu village on the coast south of Sapporo.

The only Ainu I had seen were the Coke-drinker at Shimo
Yûbetsu and a few seedy specimens selling souvenirs on the
shores of Kutcharo. They had beards and totem poles and
mangey bears on chains – killing bears is important in Ainu
culture – and looked rather like half-caste Australian aborigin-
als; but Shiraoi is said to be a 'representative village'.

This coastline is scruffy and grey and when we reached
Shiraoi I was prepared for a long hot walk into a primitive
landscape. Outside the station I was accosted by a gay little
man in a painted cart.

'Ainu village, Ainu village,' he called, flapping his reins,
jangling the bells round the scalloped awning, assuring me it
was too far to walk.

The sides of the cart were brightly decorated, the lugubrious
horse had an elaborate harness and we crunched very slowly
on fat rubber tyres. On one side of the hot road were poor
cottages; on the other, flat land stretched, presumably to the
sea. No breeze moved the torrid air. Quite soon notices, totem
poles, archways, parking lots, refreshment kiosks and lavatories announced the most representative of Ainu villages.

A long avenue of stalls led to a clearing, trodden bare, surrounded by Ainu houses. On the stalls were postcards, plastic
octopi, biscuits stamped with Ainu, wooden bears eating fish;
souvenirs made of shells and pine-cones, wooden bears eating
fish; head-scarves stamped with Ainu, wooden bears eating
fish; kimonos and musical boxes, purses woven in Ainu-type
designs, wooden bears, etc.; plants, *happi* coats screen-printed
in Ainu patterns, wooden bears ... good luck charms, soft

77

drinks, cakes and bears, bears, bears with or without fish, like Ceylon elephants going down from life-size to pea-size, and behind the stalls, strangely aggressive sales-girls, calling, persuading, almost demanding in a most unJapanese way.

The Ainu houses are softly coloured, roofed with thick overlapping layers of thatch, like tucks or terraced hillsides. The biggest resembles a Gilbertese *maneapa* in shape and proportions, though the sides are closed. Behind them are little log stockades and tiny thatched huts on Pushkin hen's legs. These contain live, miserable bears, mangey, atrociously smelly. Though thick fur and clumsy movements give a superficial impression of amiability, they have mean little faces with hard eyes and sharp bald noses.

Among the bear enclosures are thatched wigwams and wooden spears and animal skulls, mute trophies of the Ainu way of life.

There are no gardens, no grass, and what little grows further off is rough and sparse. Today the adjacent lake seemed grey and stagnant, with hot steaming mountains beyond and a stark public lavatory on the banks.

In the village the Ainu were off-duty. Fat elderly women in jumpers and skirts sat about moodily. They had short straight grey hair, broad pudgy faces and circular glasses with metal frames. Some had traces of blue round their mouths as though from eating blueberries, and wide embroidered head-bands, low on the forehead, tied at the back. They looked thoroughly bored. There were a few younger Eskimo-faced women but the rest were complete Russian *babushkas*.

Several plump white-bearded men in old cardigans smoked and dozed on a wooden seat outside the *maneapa*. With their pudgy faces, turned-up noses and beards they all looked like Tolstoy. There was nothing spectacular about their beards though these are an Ainu speciality. A sixteenth-century writer reported the beards were so huge, the moustaches so monstrous they had to hold them up with little forks as they drank.

It was cool and dark inside the grass-and-thatch *maneapa*.

A pleasant smell of wood-smoke rose from the open hearth in the floor. Furniture, Ainu coats, swords and pots hung from beams and were piled round the walls. A few Japanese sat on the floor being lectured about the olden days by a plump Tolstoy sage in an embroidered coat. From time to time he made spearing and lungeing gestures; also jokes, followed by expectant pauses – like the bus guides – during which the Japanese laughed obligingly.

Two *babushkas* glooming together at the door showed irritation when the Japanese attempted to photograph them out of office hours. Posing for pictures is part of their livelihood.

I could not tell the origin of the large handsome pots and stools, though black lacquer with red or gold suggested Japan, but the coats were easily recognisable as Ainu.

Ainu designs are bold and primitive yet complex. The colours are sombre – black, brown, dark blue, with white and occasional touches of red, yellow or green. There seem to be two main kinds of decoration. In one, the design is embroidered on the dark garment; in the other, contrasting material is *appliquéd* first and embroidered in a contrasting colour.

This *appliqué* and embroidery vaguely resembles *ti-vai-vai* – bed-spreads made in the Cook Islands and Tahiti. Though the Polynesian designs are based on local flowers and leaves and worked in strong colours, and most are straight *appliqué*, in some there is also embroidery.

The Ainu designs are made up of curling brackets and pothooks. They are rather repetitious and rigid, lacking the island colour and freedom and gaiety; but they are strong and dramatic and highly effective. The chain-stitch embroidery is intricate but I could not find out if it is done by hand or machine, or if the *appliqué* is cut from one piece, as in *ti-vai-vai*. It was impossible to examine the coats closely and any genuine work on sale was a ridiculous price. Cheaper, screen-printed replicas, though attractive, revealed nothing.

The first European to visit Ezo in the seventeenth century,

a Sicilian Jesuit named Jeronimo de Angelis, describes Ainu robes as like the dalmatics of deacons and sub-deacons. He noticed all the embroidery was in the form of a cross and when he asked why was told it meant they were a people of spirit, though they did not know why they had chosen the cross to show it. He reported that women hung glass beads round their necks and dyed their lips blue, which they still do; and 'both men and women wear drawers beneath their robes, but sometimes . . . in the hot weather they do not put them on.'

I was down at the lake when shouts, cries and whistle-blasts came from the parking-lot. Tourists were clambering from their buses with guides marshalling them into crocodiles, calling the roll; then their leaders raised their little flags and marched their charges off down the avenue.

By the time I got back to the village all the Ainu were in full costume, even the grudging old *babushkas*, and as the Japanese battalion halted, formed a circle and presented cameras, the performance began. Shuffling round in a ring with arms outstretched at their sides they chanted dolefully, stamping their rubber thongs, raising and lowering alternate arms in a graceless rocking motion, eyes on the ground, faces expressionless. From time to time someone made a chirruping sound, a whirring bird-noise. The Japanese shutters clicked.

When this mournful art-form was over – it lasted some time – the Ainu were ready to pose for pictures, with or without tourists. The women had put on splendid though grubby coats and head-bands, large metal earrings, large blue beads and painted blue walrus moustaches across their mouths, said to be originally a sign of their husband's ownership.

The Tolstoys wore embroidered coats over their cardigans, scimitar-curved swords and curious crowns made of straw, like two small sheaves joined front and back, with a wheaten tail behind.

Noticing that I was not taking pictures the chief Tolstoy approached and said with piqued vanity, 'Photograph?'

I shook my head. Incredulous, he beckoned to a Japanese, then took my arm and posed with me. The Japanese, of course, understood he was to take the picture on my camera. Tolstoy grew happier when I remembered that posing is a source of Ainu income. He sat up most professionally and summoned others over to take their turn. Though the women were bored the men were enjoying themselves.

But I had had enough. I had felt so dreadfully sorry for them; now I wanted to get away. I fought my way back down the avenue where excited stallholders were shouting and thrusting forward their wares. Some tried to detain me and make me buy wooden bears. You could not escape these horrible animals even outside the village. Walking back to the station I passed many cottages which were no less than bear factories, where the men carved and hammered while the women blackened the rough forms with what looked like boot-polish.

7

'Stretching Across to the Island of Sado . . .'

I WAS GLAD to have seen Hokkaido, though in a sense I did not feel I had been in Japan. I could understand how this very foreignness must appeal to the southern islanders, yet for all its beauty it had not greatly moved me.

And there was something else, hardly Hokkaido's fault, that came from moving too much, looking too long from train windows. Though I had been travelling, eating and sleeping with Japanese night and day and not seen one European, I felt frustrated. I wanted the scenery to stay still, to stop being pulled across my vision like an opening-out scroll; I wanted people to have same faces for more than a few hours, to feel, as I had at Ofunato, that I was living among the Japanese rather than watching them. Since Keiichi and Mrs Nonomurta had offered to arrange for me to stay on a farm if I went back to Iwate, I wondered why I was now going obstinately down the Japan Sea coast to the island of Sado, a popular tourist resort.

I had made this decision because of the beautiful name and because of the *haiku* by Bashô ...

A wild sea!
And stretching across to the island of Sado
The Galaxy!

but I was starting to wonder. The way people said, 'Ah! Sado!' made me uneasy; I had discovered there were good boat services, hotels, tours, excursions, a fine climate. The island is renowned for its camellia trees. There is local singing and dancing, the Sado *okesa*, and natural wonders and scenery and tombs of famous historical exiles ... an emperor, distinguished courtiers, the priest Nichiren, founder of the Nichiren Buddhist sect. It sounded a kind of Capri, beauty, history, eternal spring, souvenirs, postcards and tourists; also, since this was the best time of year, hotels and hostels booked out.

South of Akita the pines grow diagonally, away from the sea wind, tough, enduring, adaptable, graceful, disciplined, clean and orderly, like the Japanese people. Thatched roofs have a network of crosspieces along the ridge pole. Pinewoods lead to deserted beaches where women move slowly across the sand in horse-drawn carts with solid wheels. Rocks, islets with shrines, graves, grotesque trees, fishing villages with beautiful boats and nets and breakwaters piled with cement blocks like white seals; and inland, houses have carved gable-ends, smaller, more Chinese than in Hokkaido, and rice-fields are the colour of sunflowers. Riper than in the far north, the rice is shoulder-high to the working women whose wide sedge hats, rising and vanishing, mark them out from the motionless scarecrows that stand and lean, startling, humorous, eerie.

All over the countryside the battle goes on between man and the birds – clever Japanese wits against bright persistent raiders. In different districts they use different means of protecting rice – metallic streamers stretched criss-cross, twisted to catch the sun; little plastic flags, red and white, which give a crusader look to the almond-green fields; bells on wires, balloons,

83

coloured umbrellas, white gauzy nets, round cardboard faces strung on lines that bob and twist like trunkless ghosts; and scarecrows.

Japanese scarecrows belong less to the sphere of old-hat-and-coat-on-two-crossed-sticks than to that of ventriloquists' dolls, witches' dummies, sorcerers' manikins. They are not merely innocent objects for deluding birds, but waiting presences, in league with the unseen. When they stand motionless in the hot stillness they belong to the world of hidden eyes silently watching, the Something by whose permission you get safely out of the forest.

The gay ones pop out from the rice in headscarves, like women reapers; others are ghoulish under their wide hats, dead men propped up, faceless beneath the bandages. That some are merry does not lessen their power. It is no more than a good mood. Only a fool is deceived by the wide grin and rakish hat, the outstretched arms carrying lanterns painted with Hallowe'en pumpkin faces. Sometimes they reveal their true character – menacing, sinister, macabre – even in the full light of day. In the evening, by moonlight, they are watching ghosts, the children of *Sohodoro-na-kami*, god of scarecrows, protector of the fields.

Occasionally they swivel convincingly; more often they stand statue-still. This immobility is most disturbing of all; yet after a typhoon, lurching or lying face down in the flattened rice, they are pitiful. They seem to have lost their souls, as though *Sohodoro-na-kami* has flung them over in rage and abandoned them.

The Japanese are aware of their spooky quality:

> Something makes a sound!
> With no one near, a scarecrow
> Has fallen to the ground!

'You are vagabonding?' a girl student asked politely. 'You are going to Niigata-Tokyo?'

'To Sado.'

'To Sado! Ah! Sa-do!'

At Niigata docks, where you take the boat, kiosks sell sweets, cigarettes, dried fish, *saké*, Nikko whisky, Sado dolls, Sado hats, Sado-decorated cakes, Sado *sembei*, Sado *bentos* and Sado paper-carriers. The dolls, in blue and white Sado *yukata* and Sado grass hats with red ribbons, stand in the Sado dance, knees bent, arms and hands in a beautiful faintly Balinese pose. I added one to the *kokeshi* dolls, the *Tohoku* wood and straw horses, the *Tohoku* doll with straw boots and straw raincape, the rough beautiful *Tohoku* pots, which got broken, already distending my bag.

I sat gloomily watching the growing crowd, telling myself I was a fool, that Sado would be a mistake, that it would be dark when we landed and I had no idea where to go. The youth hostel book listed three baffling establishments, miles from anywhere. I was even thinking about night trains to Tokyo when a kindly student, to whom I had spoken, offered to guide me to his chosen hostel.

The boat was large, white, very handsome, very touristy, with deck bars and kiosks and broadcast music. There were streamers and 'Auld Lang Syne'; the passengers laughed, shouted, wept; but as soon as we steamed out into the calm mellow evening they settled down to eat, drink or be sea-sick, while the loud-speaker gave out the strange, shrill, bizarre, delightful Sado *okesa*.

Approaching an island in darkness is always the first time. One is always Ulysses when the black bulk against the stars shows lights along the shore and the sea sounds give way to sheltered stillness and voyaging becomes encounter; yet no excitement or pleasure can quite destroy the sadness of ending a journey, however short.

People woke up, groaned, rubbed eyes, groped for bags and *furoshikis*, formed into queues. Wedged in the crowd near the gangway I searched for my student. Had he forgotten me or was he jammed between bodies on another deck?

As the gangway went down the passengers cascaded over the landing stage and through the terminal at such a pace that to pause was to be trampled on. I saw lights, crowds, banners, archways, touts. WELCOME TO SADO! WELCOME TO XX HOTEL! *Hotel Lady? Hul-lo! Hi Baby! You want taxi? You want Japanese* hoteru?

Impossible to find my student. I swam with the tide into a dark lane, where, youth hostel book in hand, I seized a passing young man.

'*Dozo . . .*'

He peered at the address, said '*Hai, hai,*' took my bag and began to run. We hastened round corners, across muddy streets to a noisy terminus. He triumphantly waved me into a bus, pushed my bag in after me, bowed and made off.

But where would the bus take me? Where in God's name should I get out? It was crowded with drunks. One neighbour exhaled the sweetish smell of *saké* into my face; the other was in a hot dishevelled sleep, head lolling towards my shoulder. Stuck down at the back, far removed from conductor and driver, how was I to get information from these drunken yahoos?

The conductor had shouted '*Hai dozo . . .*', the bus was already churning when a gigantic rucksack crashed through the doorway. Close behind, a body crawled in and crouched panting under its yellow corduroy hat.

The men cheered and whistled as Yasou, my student, groped his way down the clotted aisle.

'*Ah so!*' He sounded as relieved as I. 'Excuse me please. Many people. Not find you.'

'*Hai dozo!*' said the driver again, very firmly, and we were off.

In two long rows, among the laughing, shouting drunks we lurched sideways, to and from each other, while those in the aisle swung round on the end of their upstretched arms. It seemed to go on for hours, over a rough dark country road; then we stopped suddenly. Everyone shouted. Yasou grasped his rucksack, beckoned to me with his head, and pushed down the aisle. As we descended the conductor called directions after us, waving vaguely towards the distance; then we were left on the road in the dark.

In my state of fatigue and hunger, with no sign of food or shelter, on a pitch-black night in the heart of the country with only a chance acquaintance, I should really have burst into tears; but a marvellous happiness came, a sense of something wonderful about to happen. As the lighted bus vanished over the hill I looked up and saw the stars stretching out over the island of Sado. Silence came down, the silence of night in the country, made up of little sounds. I sniffed. The air was soft and green-scented, as though unseen living plants grew all round.

'*E-to!*' said Yasou and sighed. He gestured down the road where a light glimmered.

'Hostel?'

No, not the hostel; a farm. But he would ask the way.

We clambered over boulders and through sticky mud. The road seemed to be under construction. Without a torch, we tottered and groped. Now I heard water running away in the darkness. Though here suggestive of hidden pit-falls this sound is always witchcraft, and I barely noticed Yasou's apologetic *Chotto matte* as he blundered away towards the light. Feet deep in mud I stood listening. The water ran on, unseen, pure sound; and as at Lake Kutcharo that hot cicada morning, all was one . . . water, night, stars, the scent of green life, my own grimy carcase.

Yasou came back. The hostel was over there . . . he pointed into absolute blackness . . . not very far. '*Anoné* . . .' He took up my bag. I put one hand on the handle, more for guidance than to help.

The water ran beside us as we walked, close, tantalising, invisible. It sang in the dark, uncaring, detached, busy about its own affairs. We slipped and slid; sharp stones like blue-metal tore at our shoes. A glow-worm light filtered through *shoji* on the left and, solid against the stars, the roof of a farmhouse, high, hipped and gabled, shaggy with thatch.

'Wait!' Yasou put down my bag and felt his way step by step. *Shoji* opened; a sliver of yellow light fell out upon sunflowers and phlox.

Not yet; further on.

More stones and rocks; the water still running; then another faint light, another high roof against stars. A dog ran out barking. Again a strip of light widening as *shoji* slid back. We were now in the heart of the countryside, in a black flat sea; yet I knew there were trees somewhere, still, silent forests, invisible like the water, but watching.

'The next one!' said Yasou humbly, as though it were all his fault. How could he know that I did not care how long it went on?

The water had left us; but now came another sound. I stood still. 'What is it?'

'*Uguisi.*'

It came again, somewhere out in the darkness, the first Japanese nightingale, like the first English cuckoo, never to sound quite the same again. On that spring morning I had sat down on the banks of the Windrush among cowslips and bluebells, but there was no sitting down on this summer night. Yasou was plunging ahead, towards a pin-point light so far it seemed to shine up from below the horizon.

Now our footsteps were deadened. Sharp rocks had given way to a soft padded track. I sensed moisture round me, sniffed it in the air.

'Where do you think we are? What is out there?'

'Lice,' said Yasou.

When we started our walk we had laughed at our predicament; now our voices were lowered, as though fearing to be overheard. *They* were listening out there, the *kami*, the gods in the unseen woods; and what of the silent watchers, leaning above the rice, blind bandaged faces, empty sleeves hiding skeleton arms?

I had forgotten that I was arriving unheralded at a youth hostel, possibly full of students. I knew without thought that all would be well.

'Ah! *Ssss!*'

Sensing perhaps that I walked in my sleep, Yasou touched

my arm. The light was now a yellow rectangle. We passed through a gateway and were presently leaving our shoes in a duck-boarded entrance. I sat on the raised floor while Yasou padded down the corridor seeking the host.

A large man with ruffled hair and *yukata* came from a side room. Though not yet nine o'clock there was a sense of midnight, of care not to wake sleepers. The two men conferred in low voices. Dreamily, I deduced from the shoe-rack that the hostel was empty.

'Tonight only?' said Yasou.

Startled, I addressed the host.

'No no. *Please!* Tonight, tomorrow night...after tomorrow...'

Sometimes in travelling you find that you have come home. Recognition through the senses is always complete and immediate and beyond resistance. Difficulties, commonsense, even dangers must not prevent the reunion. I was ready now to sweep aside any obstacles threatening my homecoming here in this still unseen but long known countryside. Perhaps the host knew it; perhaps there just were no obstacles; in any case I could stay.

We ate supper in an empty room with long tables and maps on the walls and afterwards washed up our blue-and-white bowls in a huge old kitchen. We spoke little. Yasou was stunned with fatigue and I with wonder. I thanked him for all his help; then we bowed and went to our rooms.

The hostel was an ancient *ryokan*. At one point in the unlit corridor I was aware that I was entering an older part of the house. Behind painted *fusuma* was a square room with *tatami*, and *shoji* closed for the night. I pulled a *futon* from the cupboard, made my bed, undressed and put out the light. Then I opened the *shoji*.

Darkness, the smell of flowers and water; a faint dripping and trickling, and beyond, a weighted-down stillness. A frog gaggled briefly and fell silent; then the nightingale called from the woods and again there was silence.

8

Lone House in the Midst of the Corn

WAKING EARLY I looked into a still-ghostly sky.

Beyond the *shoji*, within touch, flowering *crêpe*-myrtle brushed the low eaves. An irregular pond already reflected leaves and sky among red and yellow water-lilies, iris, a mossy stone islet. In this country garden, fresh and dewy after the night, flowers and fruit-trees grew together with camellias, azaleas, twisted pines and young bamboo.

I went out barefoot in *yukata*, with hair hanging down. Beyond the pool, maples were starting to bleed. Among the blue iris a great bird contemplated pale golden carp that seemed to swim in their sleep. Someone had made a little waterfall where the pond spilled over and trickled away through the flowers. The rough stone lantern might have come from the same loving hand, which no doubt had also trained the convolvulus – red, blue, purple, white – up their fragile frames.

I hurried to dress and go out. In the hall a large tortoise ruminated in a glass box. It regarded me with its tired blasé eyes, then lowered leathery lids and turned away with a tiny

90

contemptuous yawn; but reptilian hauteur could not spoil my mood. Waking, I had found myself in the heart of the country, in the midst of rice-fields. The inn was a ship afloat in an almond sea, where wooded peninsulas, headlands and islands showed dark against greenish-gold waves.

Seeing where we had walked last night I wondered that we had survived. In the road at the bus stop were deep pits and crevasses. On the path where we had stumbled, listening to running water, men and women now bashed and hewed at jagged rocks, mixing cement beside a deep canal. A couple of planks flung off-handedly across the canal, one barely touching the bank, led to the first house where Yasou had edged his way. That he had not plunged to his death was part of Sado's benevolent magic.

The thatched roofs I had seen outlined against the stars belonged to beautiful farmhouses with half-timbered black-and-white walls. On some roofs thick double-thatch skirts over ridge-poles were held down by a crosswork of bamboo poles; others had purple-grey tiles and ornate Chinese curves. Flowers grew round doorways and farmyards.

Flowers everywhere scent the air all over the island – in gardens, fields, by the roadside. A white starry creeper like jasmine, blossoming trees, high hedges of mauve and white wild hydrangeas, crêpe-myrtle, tree peonies, azaleas and all humble garden flowers, now at their height; and in spring are added camellias, wistaria, iris and fruit-blossom.

It is so rich, so beautiful, so unspoilt. Hotels in the main towns, Ryotsu and Aikawa, may be full of tourists but the peasants just go on with their lives; country buses carry schoolchildren, housewives, ancient men and obasans. The little conductresses, plump in their ankle socks, have no microphones or white gloves. 'Or-ryee!' they cry, hauling in the woman who has run up the hill; 'Or-ryee!' as the bus creeps through narrow streets, scraping walls and eaves. Grapes grow over doorways, figs and loquats hang over walls, rice-terraces cascade down from narrow valleys to open into broad rivers and on to the wide sea of gold shot with green. Fresh light feathers of bamboo break the dark cypress woods, and all over the landscape high green hurdles wait to dry the rice. In fields where it is already hung, neatly, like well-thatched roofs, stubble patches indent the supple sea; in others, sheaves lie piled in ordered rows, awaiting blue-and-white harvesting women in umbrella hats. And all day, every day the mountains change colour, deepening, fading, receding, retiring into their white veils and clouds.

I am the only guest at the inn, Yasou having gone to climb his mountain and hike his way round the coast. The host's babies crawl in the corridors, his children run in the garden. The tortoise ignores me. I eat alone in the big hall, looking out on the iris pool with the carp, and carry my blue-and-white dishes to the dark gleaming kitchen where the cook hovers, equipped and dressed for a surgical operation.

Outside the front door the family shrine shelters among *crêpe*-myrtle and Andalusian sunflowers. Alone on the ground floor – the family sleep upstairs – I lie each night with the *shoji* wide open, watching the stars, listening to the waterfall out in the garden, the song of the nightingale.

Each morning I go out at dawn. At five o'clock on a hot day the rice is lying down, all damp from the night; freshcut dewbeaded bamboo poles line the lanes. Birds are twittering, crickets trilling, men going to work in the fields. On the dark peninsulas trees are motionless, already heavy with heat. A lark flies up at my feet, a needlepoint shock of exquisite pleasure. The inn, anchored beside its island of bamboo and pines and flowering *crêpe*-myrtle might be the house in the cornfields:

> Far out in the meadows, above the young corn,
> The heavy elms wait, and restless and cold
> The uneasy wind rises; the roses are dun;
> Through the long twilight they pray for the dawn
> Round the lone house in the midst of the corn.

But the tender bowed locks are of rice, the woods are not innocent. A crow barks, the sound of the Shinto shrine; the wheel that creaks far away carries poles for the high drying-hurdles; the ghostly white flags drooping over the rice, the grotesque scarecrow, the cricket, the sad strange *hotorogisu*, the cuckoo, the bird of the outer world, are all part of an unchanged Japan.

From the *jinja* up on the hill, from the bamboo grove, from the path through the rice I watch the sun move down the narrow twisting valley, lighting on cedar and cypress and green and gold terraces. Against the sky the mountains relinquish their nocturnal shadows for day's blue haze and drifting white mists. The air, full of coming heat, is still moist from yesterday's rain. On a post an immense bird broods. Once or twice he stretches a wing as though opening a fan, then falls quiet again. I can hear the water in the canal, smell mud and flowers and a green bamboo scent. There are doves in the woods, the red trunks of pines. With mounting heat, the cicadas have started to sing and now the fields are peopled with sedge hats that disappear into the rice and rise up like divers as women work with their sickles, singing their curious mindless songs.

The archaic sound comes in snatches, as though they sing unconsciously. I do not know what they sing; perhaps ancient, traditional, perhaps Japanese pop. It does not matter; the sorcery is in the manner of singing, like the glad shouting unaware song of the Gilbertese up in the coconuts, gathering toddy.

In the late afternoon, in the evening they are still working, still singing. When I walk through the paths in the rice I am submerged; like the peasants and scarecrows, only my head shows. It is secret and warm and damp down in the greenish uncut reeds. To look out over the golden froth you must climb up the bank.

Swallows flash through the evening light; the strange cuckoo mourns from the forest, the cricket releases his ascending questioning trill.

It rains. The drops beat down on the supple rice with a soft hissing sound. I walk in this light fine rain along the canal, full of jumping fish, to the lake with oyster beds and thatched boat-houses among bulrushes. On the hill, up the long steep grassy stone steps, a cryptomeria avenue leads to a shrine... Buddhist or Shinto, or both? It has a handsome Shinto *torii* with tiles on top, Buddhist lions making positive and negative grimaces. On the gables fish stand on their heads. An old woman goes on weeding in the rain. I sit on a stone and look down on the rice-fields, the oyster lake, the thick wooded hills with thatched farms and cottages and across to the mountains. In spring this hill will be covered with flowers. I feel that I have never really seen bamboo till I came to Japan. It was not like this in any other country. Its almond plumes *do* bow down.

Up at the temple it is beautiful and peaceful, but I am chilled to the bone. I walk home with rats-tail hair and find the *ryokan* has been invaded. Trays of *o-cha* are being hurried along the corridors, there are voices, padding feet, the rattle of sliding doors, the cries of infants. It is only three o'clock but the maid comes and kneels, saying '*Dozo* ...' *O-furo* is ready.

Alone in the inn, I have taken *o-furo* in solitude, soaking and wallowing in the heart-shaped tank. Today there is barely room to get in. When I slide back the door from the changing-room, clouds of steam and noise blow in my face. On the tiled floor fat mothers, with wide-spread legs, soap babies; mothers kneel, soaping toddlers, mothers bounce up and down in the bath, nursing desperate excited infants. Plastic ducks and boats take up any spare space in the water. Every woman is shouting, every baby is yelling. Beyond the glass partition the men bellow at each other or at the women. The partition is only a gesture. They are all wandering in and out, up and down the corridor, young men and women, fat matrons and babies, ancient grandfathers with lean shanks and withered bottoms. No one wears a stitch. It is a Hogarth scene without cripples

94

or invalids. Cheerful, rowdy jokes, roars of laughter, clatters and bangs show they are having a jolly good time.

Across the hall naked and half-naked men and women dress and undress, feed babies and gossip. In the doorway the *o-furo* man grins benevolently by his huge furnace, happy to be the cause of such pleasure, such jovial good cheer.

I jump down from the pathway to stand with the harvesting women among the stubble. They work quickly and skilfully, bending to cut sheaves with sickles, straightening up to bind with strands snatched from a bundle tied to the back. Bending, straightening, snatching, binding, over and over; then lifting huge loads of sheaves under each arm, carrying them to the high green hurdles and hanging them to dry. They wear gloves and sleeve protectors, blue-and-white *mompei*. White *tenugui* are kept close to the face by the strings of their umbrella hats. These peasants are solid and sturdy with broad cheerful faces, many with gold teeth, many no doubt younger than they appear; but here and there slim young women stalk nobly through the stubble, upright and straight despite loaded arms. Motionless, waist-high in the rice, beneath an overcast sky, they are touched with the supernatural. Rigid torso, gloved hands, swathed face concealed under *tenugui* and hat rouse ghoulish thoughts of the lost soul imprisoned in every scarecrow.

After school the children come to help. There are heavy low clouds and a smell of imminent rain. Men, women, boys and girls pile green bamboo poles on small carts for rice-drying frames. The leaden sky presses down on the suspended stillness. Soft come the sounds of little trucks in the distance, tractors pulling loads of logs, voices calling, cicadas, twilight birds. Across the yellow sea beautiful half-timbered farmhouses shoulder into rich, high-peaked volcanic hills. Gently sloped grey tiled roofs blend into darker trees. The long low buildings might have grown out of the earth.

There should be castles on these hills; the landscape is

feudal, belongs to the past; but the people in the fields are of the present; they call and sing and laugh as they make their way home in the dusk. The light fades; from the high chimney behind the inn smoke rises as *o-furo* is heated. In farmhouse kitchens there is talking and laughing and noisy TV. Rice and *saké* and bawdy jokes make a cheerful row, a protection against the dark world outside.

When I ask about Ogi, across the island, the host makes urgent signs. The morning bus is just now leaving Ryotsu; I cannot possibly catch it, there isn't time to walk to the road. Host, wife, grandmother, cook, housemaid confer, talking excitedly. The host vanishes. His wife bustles me to the front door where he is now hooting his car horn. We plunge off through the rice, not the familiar path by the canal but up and round a moss-green wooded hill. Houses, gardens, farms catch at me but there is no time to stop. We enter a leafy lane and emerge at a curve in the road. Flowering trees droop over garden walls, bamboo throws green shadows on still-moist earth. The host explains where to catch the bus, where it will come from, which way it goes. He digs into his pocket and brings out a ball-point and envelope and writes, in spiky Roman letters, the name of this stop, the name of the junction where I must change, the destination I must ask for. He runs back and forth, enquiring in cottages, studying the timetable pinned on a tree. He makes lists of times on his envelope, with arrows, outward and homeward and curving round to show connections. Villagers gather and point and explain; then someone runs up and signals the bus is coming. It is flagged to a halt, the driver instructed about my requirements and I am put aboard in his care. At the last minute the host stops us to make sure I know where to get out coming home. I nod and wave to show I have memorised the landscape.

'Or-ryee,' sings the little conductress and away we go.

It is a country bus, short on springs but free of tourists. All the passengers wear working clothes, all are loaded with *furo-*

shikis, baskets, bundles, boxes; all seem cheerful, healthy and spry. White dust blows in the window, low-hanging flowering trees brush and patter against the roof. In narrow village streets people draw back into doorways to let us pass.

I must change at Shinmachi. Driver and conductress lead me to the bus office to help buy my ticket. They demonstrate on their watches that there is a fifteen minute wait. The ticket girl offers a seat.

We have left the rich inland harvest scene and now follow the coast from Shinmachi to Ogi. This is a different Sado, a world of grey sand, thatched boat-shelters, wide bays with misty mountains beyond. From high cliffs we look down upon coves with black rocks and fishing villages. The houses stand in compounds, sheltering from the sea wind behind high fences; then we are on the edge of the water, looking up at terraced hillsides. Under fruit trees and hedges are wayside graves, primitive Jizos with red caps and aprons, shrines and *toriis* entangled with vines. Odd rocks in the sea bear a minia-ture scarlet *torii* and some are looped round with a Shinto rope girdle, showing they are *kami*.

It grows more and more beautiful. Hills soar up in plush waves above patterned troughs and hollows. Long valleys swing like hammocks between forests and bamboo groves. Are the Japanese artists because of nature, or have they designed the landscape? Everything seems *right* ... the emerald patch always breaks the monotony of the dark hills, the piercing tropical green invades the northern blue-grey at just the right moment; yet there is nothing false or precious. Exquisite, a work of art, it is also a slice of life. The rich dark plants out-lining each rice patch are edible vegetables used to mark boundaries; the picturesque figures with veils and umbrella-hats are reaping the year's harvest; the mouse-coloured huts by the lake, the rafts where seagulls crowd, cultivate oysters; the scarecrows and flags and white gauzy shrouds hung over the drying rice protect from birds. Life and work go on, united with beauty.

97

In the bus four drunken youth begin to torment a school-girl. They wear jodhpurs and black cloth *tabi* – gaiters with cloven hoofs – and stink of *saké*. When Japanese men are drunk their eyes get larger and rounder and bulge out like frogs. The girl sits in scarlet misery, head bent, enduring their crude persecution. I long to help but do not know how till the nearest youth turns to me. I suddenly say to him, 'Oh, shut up!' as savagely as I can.

The boys are stunned. They stare unbelievingly, eyes fixed, and henceforth behave like mice.

I have no compunction about my rudeness. The youth has already enraged me by drinking a raw egg close to my ear.

Ogi, having only one boat a day from Niigata, lacks arches, touts and banners advertising hotels. A few shops near the quay sell postcards and Sado souvenirs and beautiful little barrels of some fishy substance. Dehydrated fishlets, quite transparent, like spirits, lie in laced rows in plastic packets; but the town is quiet, the narrow streets clean. I find people getting on with their jobs and lives – making baskets, carving and gilding family shrines, pushing little carts with barrels of human manure for the gardens, arranging their wares in the shops. In shaded houses toothless ancients in *yukata* lie on the *tatami*, yarning and smoking. In the street a gossiping grand-mother with bare withered bosoms bows cheerfully as I pass.

For a few yen I buy a square basket with four little feet, resisting beautiful articles which I could neither carry nor use. All objects for everyday life are simple, strongly made and cheap – barrels, baskets, pots and bowls. I think, 'they are still unspoilt here,' and round the corner find a factory making the worst kind of European furniture at exorbitant prices.

Close by, nets are spread to dry on the sea wall – some brown, some a wonderful rusty red. Offshore are fishing boats with great reels on the sterns and rows of strong lights for night-fishing. Far out, little boats are as motionless as the black rocky islets.

On the other side of the town a calm semicircular harbour lies below a feathery bamboo hill. Ancient men in kimono shuffle between houses and fishing boats and in the grounds of the rather beat-up shrine children are jumping and skipping round monuments, phalluses and stone lanterns.

The shrine, neglected and shabby, is full of the wildest *ko-ema* – votive paintings in brilliant colours, weird three-dimensional primitives, thick with paint and devotion, people in boats, houses in snow-storms, ships in full sail with every rib, every rope shown in detail. It is all I can do not to pinch one or two. Dusty, uncared for, covered with cobwebs, they must have hung there for years.

I have not seen Aikawa, the biggest town on the island; I have not seen Sado dancing, the tomb of Emperor Junkotu or Nichiren's house. I have not climbed Mount Kompira or taken the famous boat-trip 'Excursion to Kaifu' along the coast. I have seen nothing but peasants and rice-fields, flowers and fishing boats, heard only crickets and nightingales, Japanese cuckoos and harvesting songs. There is nothing else I could ask for, except to stay on and on.

9

Capital in the East

TOKYO was to be the place where I left my luggage and came back briefly for clean clothes between journeys, but taken in small doses I find it stimulating and amusing. People who live here detest it and expect me to do the same. It is certainly noisy, the traffic fearful, the heat appalling, the atmosphere so saturated there is no air to breathe; but there is enormous vitality, endless contrast and variety.

Its main surprise is its intimacy. Though the world's biggest city it is a series of villages, like Paris. Once in your village you only notice the others when you venture out.

The villagy touches are all round – small street-markets, old women in working trousers and head-rags, with pigeon toes, heaving enormous packs; little monkey-faced men in black knee-length gaiters with cloven hoofs; morning glory trained up walls, grasshoppers in cages, the sudden sound of a Japanese cricket, a ravishing touch of the country in the heart of the city.

The city smells of fish – a clean smell. In some parts it reminds me of Istanbul without the dirt, but in general seems not Asian at all in the sense of flies, filth, stenches, teeming disease-ridden hordes. There is no copra – the heavy exciting insidious background to all other smells in many Eastern cities and towns. It is true that the Japanese people don't smell, even in a crowd, but some of the canals in the slums have a stench that beats the very best of Turkey or India. Yet the people there, though desperately poor, do not look degraded or show resentment to strangers. They even bow if you say good morning.

Tokyo has been greatly rebuilt since the war. It is a new city spiritually as well as physically. Only rarely, in a secluded garden or temple, or after some hours in an antique or print shop is there any feeling of the old Tokugawa Edo, even of the Meiji Capital in the East. Yet for all its modern cosmopolitanism it could only be Japanese. Narrow streets, cafés, bars. Hairdressers working late. Huge flower arrangements like targets on easels outside new restaurants, sent as good wishes to the management. Shops selling nothing but water-worn stones for gardens. Hundreds of red telephones and people ringing up. Everyone reading; bookshops crowded with standing readers. Cinemas, theatres, fantastic *Kabuki-za* with *samurais* flouncing and posturing on a wider-than-wide-screen stage. Air-conditioned arcades full of Americans. *Clack-clack-clack, Pachinko* (pin-ball) parlours with zombie figures pulling handles and men waiting outside to buy the prizes of food or whatever is won. People wearing masks, for smog, or germs. Tarts, prissy little typists, youths like juvenile delinquents, pale worried little clerks...what is a typical Japanese face? Some of these could be part Spanish, Negro, Polynesian, African, Mexican, Italian, Malayan, Sicilian. Many of my friends in Australia or Europe could pass as Japanese. Japanese noses are flattish, hawked, hooked, turned up. There are receding chins, full or thin lips, long faces, broad faces, high and low cheek-bones,

101

pale, dark brown, ruddy skin. Most skins are good, many are exquisite, but there are spotty youngsters. Eyes are mainly narrow but some are rounded. Have these been opened by surgery? A Japanese friend tells me everyone is having their eyes widened, it is so cheap. Her husband would like hers done. You can also get face-lifts and bosoms fixed very reasonably. Local bosoms require boosting rather than hoisting. This last was popular till a housewife died of it not long ago, since when people have been more cautious. But abortions are still good and dirt-cheap.

I had not expected the music. It goes on all the time. Judging from their western favourites – sexy tangoes, guitars playing *Jeux Interdits* – the Japanese are romantic and sensual people. But there is also endless Bach, Mozart, Beethoven, broadcast or in cafés. Some of these cafés are specially dedicated to one composer. You may sit and drink very good coffee and have your favourites played by request.

My first Tokyo village was Kanda, a sort of Left Bank with a university, bookshops, students, coffee-shops, and a Russian cathedral. I loved this quarter; but Simon, who is English, insisted I make my headquarters at his apartment at Sendagaya, near Shinjuku. Simon is production manager at Tuttles, the publishers. He has lived for several years in Japan and speaks Japanese.

The main street of my new village is very narrow, lined on both sides with shops and their outdoor displays, parked vehicles, people walking, gossiping, using the red public telephones, so there is no room for shrinking back. It is a channel of high-speed vehicles that sweep down with all the unrestrained *élan* of one-way traffic. The only chances of getting across are when the lights at the corner give a brief breather and even then you have to move fast, for Japanese drivers are quick off the mark.

We have a *sushi* shop, a Chinese restaurant, a noodle shop,

102

a dry-cleaner where they go to no end of trouble for you when you have lost your ticket and can't speak the language; a post office where the staff, presented with complex cables or overseas parcels, smile helplessly and gracefully decline to accept them. There is a shop that sells *yukata* – cotton summer kimonos – cake shops, fruit shops, hardware shops, shops with open baskets of splendid-looking vegetables and tubs of dried fish and huge jars of all-coloured pickles.

Down the hill is a little shrine with enormous straw sandals hanging up. Near here is the *tatami* shop and the man who mends shoes and does leather repairs. There is always a wave of grassy tea-scent from the *tatami* shop where the matmaker can be seen cutting the thick fresh straw into oblongs. The shoe-mender is rather contemplative. Nothing is done in a hurry. If you ask for things back next day he just smiles compassionately.

There is a public bath-house and a number of small attractive restaurants with *bonsai* trees, pebbled entrances and *shoji*, or *noren*, like tea-towels, across the door. On hot nights these entrances are watered to keep down the dust. Inside you sit up at the bar and take the food from the glistening cook, or kneel *à la japonaise* at low tables on a raised shelf and are waited on. A *tempura* meal, which includes soup, rice and tea, costs about Y400 (nine shillings) and is charming to look at and tastes good. It consists mainly of fish or vegetables fried in batter, and is very delicate.

Many cheap restaurants have plastic food in the windows with a price tag, so foreigners need only point; but *sushi* is also easy to order. At a polished counter all kinds of raw fish are laid out under glass. You are given tea and a hot towel to wipe your hands, then sit up at the bar and point to the fish you want. The young man takes up some cold rice, which has been cooked in spiced vinegar, and with sure precise beautiful movements rolls it in his palms to a neat egg-shape on which he lays your chosen slivers of fish – raw tuna, squid, etc. This is put before you on the gleaming counter, which has just been

103

wiped over with a hot cloth, and you pick up the *sushi* in your fingers, dip it in your saucer of *shoyu* and eat it.

Inari-sushi look like Russian *piroshki*. The rice is wrapped in bean-curd and fried. Inari is the god of fertility and the rice harvest. His messenger is the fox. The Japanese say foxes are very fond of bean-curd. Other *sushi* are cut from a roll. Sheets of seaweed are laid on a small rattan mat, the rice is spread over the seaweed with a strip of pink or yellow or both – perhaps pickle or anchovy – down the middle; then the mat is rolled up and quickly removed, leaving a seaweed cylinder full of rice which is cut into sections, resembling some kind of flower, dark-green round the edges, white inside, with a pink or yellow centre.

I love to walk round the Sendagaya lanes in the evening, when stone lanterns glimmer in dark little gardens and people are practising Chopin and *Für Elise* on pianos and radios churn out tangoes and TV *samurai* thunder into the night. Many houses are hidden behind high walls; most have delicious entrances – a pebble path, a stone lantern at foot level, bamboo, shaped trees – no matter how small the space. One or two of the most charming, chaste and elegant little gardens are said to be *maisons de passe*, known as 'one night hotels'.

The Japanese talent for making something out of nothing, of doing the best with what they have, recalls Spaniards creating gardens with flower-pots in little dark courtyards.

If Tokyo wakes echoes of Paris, the Japanese remind me of the French in certain ways. They are so sensible about small daily comforts, they know how to look after the flesh, when not subjecting it to devastating trials of endurance, for toughening-up or religious discipline. Thug-like men, who would think it unmanly to offer a seat to a woman or carry a wife's parcels, fan themselves with the grace of a *geisha* in buses and trains. Everyone understands about hats and umbrellas, about hunger and lavatories and public telephones, about cold drinks

104

being cold, tea being hot and coffee being strong. There are blinds in buses or trains to screen out the sun; hot food appears on chilly platforms; at wayside halts fruit, beer and soft drinks are found cooling in mountain streams or little ponds.

Like the French, when they desert their own traditions, their native good taste, they excel in vulgarity. They have also a quick grasp of essentials – when they want to – a no-nonsense attitude towards sex and nudity; and, in some of the modern girls, a rakish off-beat chic.

Such girls are far removed from those older women, permanently bent into a right-angle from carrying babies or loads on their backs. Japanese women do just about everything – run farms, work in the fields and on roads, saw timber in mills, build houses, mix cement, load logs on goods trains, drive road graders and tractors, make walls and dig drains, carry incredible weights. You find them as housewives and mothers, students, actresses or *geishas*, exquisite in tea ceremony, climbing mountains, arranging flowers, shouting and clowning as *samurai* in Kobe's *Odori-ko*, as nuns with shaven heads.

You wonder if they are appreciated, seeing them treated like dirt. You have to get use to this, it is the custom of the country; but it is annoying when you, a woman, stand up in a Tokyo subway compartment of seated males to give your seat to a poor old lady or pregnant mother with baby in arms, and a young man hops into your place before she can sit down. Men cannot be shamed into offering seats; they are more likely to feel shame if they do stand up, though not some of the younger ones. This, of course, is not Old Japan.

Though the women must carry the parcels and loads, men do not mind carrying their children, whom they clearly adore. Often in evening in villages you see grandfathers nursing babies or airing them on their backs or held on the hip. Mothers who carry their babies on their backs are not supposed to pull the child's legs forward round their waists – it makes them bandy – but they still use the sling-seat, with ties crossed over the chest so their offspring are permanently splayed. The children are thus constantly in contact with their mothers, on bikes, trains, in the fields, washing, shopping, doing housework.

Women wear special coats with extra room for the baby, but if the mother leans back in sitting she squashes him. The baby usually wears an absurd hat. The little girls have pot hats with flowers and the little boys Breton sailors with a bow on top and streamers down the back. These are worn even by the tiniest infants with ludicrous effect. Often they slide down inside the mother's coat till only the hat is visible resting on her collar. They frequently lose consciousness and slump down with flaccid hands dangling and head lolling.

The babies themselves are ivory blobs with glittering black-treacle eyes like boot-buttons. Do these eyes shrink as the face grows, or narrow against the light? The haircut is usually prison crop, straight round. When, as sometimes, the baby is slightly bald with smudgy eyebrows, it is a ridiculous caricature of a *Kabuki* actor.

There are all shapes and sizes. My preference is the small lively Honshu kind that chuckles and goes cross-eyed with exertion trying to get at my ear-rings. There is a Mussolini type, and often you see frail little women staggering under the weight of babies like *sumo* wrestlers. Generally they are very good; but they are all rather sensitive. If, in a railway carriage, one starts to yell, others, previously contented, begin to look uneasy and depressed. Lower lips are pushed out and down and presently all are crying without knowing why.

Ayako, my new Japanese friend, whom I met through Simon, is not at all a conventional ivory doll. She does not giggle behind her hand or walk with tiny steps. She laughs openly and, taller than I, strides so I cannot keep up with her. She tirelessly answers questions, leads me round Tokyo and will not let me go out alone, even in Sendagaya, without one of her street plans, all arrows in two-coloured inks with local buildings marked for identification.

The apartment is very close to Meiji Shrine. I had not expected to like this memorial to the Emperor Meiji, it sounds too big and formal; yet it is beautiful – high tranquil avenues, the sounds of Shinto priests walking on gravel paths, the flash of sun-speckled white, starched wing-like robes and black-lacquer caps, *toriis* of silver-grey wood, green filigree shade and scents of moss, earth, leaves; and in the early morning, soft splinters of mist among the tree-trunks. Sunlight slants down through this forest as through submarine depths. The only trees more majestic and noble are at Isé Great Shrine.

If you know when to go, there are splendid sights at Meiji – processions of priests escorting the Emperor's Annual Messenger, *samurai* on horseback charging down to let fly arrows, men wrestling with staves, ancient *gagaku* music and *bugaku* dancing out in the sun, with fabulous costumes and masks and archaic instruments; or archery in the woods, by silent, withdrawn men in black kimonos with one shoulder bare and beautiful gigantic bows.

Outside, all the way up to the great entrance *torii*, are little stalls selling food and souvenirs and charms to the jolly crowds with their children and picnic boxes.

Not far from this serene forest and all its traditional pageantry are two wildly exciting modern buildings. In winter Tange's Olympic swimming-pool becomes a skating rink and under its astonishing suspended tent-roof small figures circle and glide on an immense pale blue oval. Next door the gymnasium's bronze roof swirls like a pleated skirt in the wind. The buildings are all vitality, adventure, airiness, fluid grace. The use of stone is enthralling – great chunks, as square paving-stones in courts and approaches, tiny 'bricks' in walls – absolute harmony and identification between the architect's concept and the materials.

On Saturday mornings Ueno Park is full of cheerful families carrying *bentos* and beer cans and *saké* bottles. They take off their shoes and lean against the stone lanterns, bow at the shrine, gape at the zoo, march through the picture galleries, row on the lake and ride round on the little monorail. Better still is Asakusa on Sunday, with its fearful plastic cherry-blossom or autumn leaf decorations and arcades and endless crowds. People gather round open-air demonstrations with rabbits and guinea-pigs; simple country men, old working women earnestly watch quacks expounding the virtues of mysterious plants and leaves. Dried snakes and lizards for mashing up into powders are sold with more dignity from glass jars in shops and seem very popular. These reptile recipes are said to cure many complaints, including rheumatics.

From the great gate of Asakusa Kannon Shrine to the main building is an avenue of little shops. Here are barkers, food, souvenirs, toys, knife shops, second-hand clothes, dress suits, lanterns, men making *sembei* (biscuits) in various shapes, displays of flowers and *bonsai*, and in the courtyard before the shrine a great bowl of smoking incense, and stalls selling *ko-ema* for Y20. They show horses, ships, demons, childless couples, milkless mothers, husbandless maidens, tidal waves, octopi, and are dashed off with the robust vitality of all Japanese folk art. I bought a rather sad lady in kimono kneeling patiently on a blue-bag blue background with vermilion curtains, hoping perhaps for a husband.

Inside the shrine marvellous wild paintings of, possibly, the Mongol invasion are hoisted so close to the ceiling you have to walk backwards, face up, to see them, if there is room to move.

All round are streets of nude and sex shows and blue films, with stills on display. We went into a seedy pornographic side-show, mistaking it for a striptease. Outside are crude paintings of a stripper, a rape, a Caesarean operation. On the left, a live monkey in a cage; on the right, a stuffed mouldy puma or dog; inside, a diseased-looking man in a rough shed with earth floor. For Y30 you may enjoy old morbid-anatomy models of anal fistulas, piles, diseased penises and vaginas. Most of the two last have been mauled, perhaps by excited clients. It is rather like *Yamai no Sôshi*, picture-scrolls showing diseases and deformities to warn bad Buddhists what they might get in the

108

next incarnation, but there are also pictures of tortures, rape, with two or more men holding down one girl, and more and more female anatomy. Some scenes are meaningless cheats; all are grimy, covered with dust. They are not appetising, but worse is the silence, the neglect, the sordid sleaziness, the diseased perverted mind that assembled them. Who patronises such shows? Surely only the most desperate and deprived. We were the sole customers and as we stood in the gloom something grabbed, tugging my skirt, snatching at my legs. This was the ultimate horror – a live mangey monkey in a cage, with evil lascivious *human* eyes. The proprietor didn't even raise his head when we scrambled out into the back yard.

A good place to eat at Asakusa is the *Dojo* restaurant where you sit on the floor at long tables and country wenches bring sizzling earthenware casseroles of *dojo*, sad-eyed slippery threads, half fish, half worm. It is noisy and crowded, men shout and drink and the girls get rather hot and bothered but it is much more fun than the long-drawn-out performance of being hand-fed by Shinjuku *geisha*.

Since Ayako took me to a *mingei* shop I am always on the look-out for *mingei* toys. In Tokyo and provincial cities many of the big department stores have a folk art section and there are smaller shops that sell nothing else.

There is a great folk art revival in Japan. Some of the best potters, weavers, designers belong to the movement, helping preserve or restore the beautiful old wares and designs and working themselves in the same tradition.

The toys come from different Prefectures all over the country – horses, tigers, sheep, cats, monkeys on horseback, priests with bobbing heads, dragons, blowfish, strange human figures, masks, kites. Some are witty, some wistful, some rather sad. Some make trenchant comments on life and the human race but without bitterness. I never saw harshness or cruelty in any *mingei* toys. They belong to a world of gentleness. Even fierce creatures are mild and rather comic – bulls look apologetic,

109

dragons are soulful, tigers, for all their moustaches and rows of teeth, are more like pussy-cats. They are innocent; full of childlike humour.

Though the Japanese commit suicide rather easily, jumping into volcanoes or over cliffs for love or failing in exams, a humorous *joie de vivre* is evident everywhere: in cheap plastic toys; absurd red octopi with inflated sticking-out legs; mascots that dangle in buses and cars; little rattling glowering Daruma (the first Zen Buddhist Master) dolls; cardboard faces that bob on lines across rice-fields, the gay yellow boat with a dragon's head that takes tourists to Miyajima Island. Even among the welter of pompous pretension at Nikko, genuine *mingei* creatures, flowers, mythical birds peer out in bright naïve colours, all gay and innocent and entirely Japanese, among the wedding-cake *chinoiserie* of this monstrous memorial.

Yet the Japanese are excessively proud of Nikko; they dote on Nara's *Daibutsu* – Great Buddha – sitting glumly there in the dark with his gilt *boddhisattvas* going up behind on a heavenly Ferris Wheel and bronze vases of lotus with spaghetti stalks, the forerunners of plastic flowers; and at Kurashiki, on the Inland Sea, they flock to the Ohara Museum, a neo-Greek building full of second-rate European paintings while next door the folk art museum, blazing with life, colour, strength, humour, is almost deserted.

It is hard to know if this comes from snobbery, the worship of names, of size, or from the lack of assurance that makes people admire the new, the foreign, the hideous.

Each time I came back to Tokyo there was something fresh to see – *Kabuki* or *Nôh* theatre, antique shops, museums, temples, department stores, local festivals, the streets and the people.

The nineteenth of September is the night of the August moon. Some Japanese invite friends in for moon viewing, to eat rice dumplings and recite poems; others do their viewing

110

in public gardens and parks, drink too much *saké* and rather make fools of themselves.

We went to Hyakken, the Garden of a Hundred Flowers, created in the early nineteenth century by a waiter who rose to riches and who loved flowers, poets and painters. The garden was carefully planned and cultivated with many unusual plants and trees and is specially famous for having the Seven Grasses of Autumn. There are also stones engraved with poems, including one by Bashô, the great *haiku* poet.

It was a murky night. At the entrance, crowds were queueing up in a bare dusty yard. There was no moon, but the women and children had on their best kimono. In the garden pale kimono'd figures carried candles in wicker thermos-shaped baskets and Japanese lanterns hung in trees. Stalls sold food and drink, people were eating and drinking in open-air restaurants. In a brightly-lit pavilion, ten young ladies in gorgeous kimono were down on the floor hammering out a metallic tune on *kotors*, large, long, stringed instruments, while others with elaborate hair postured and sang in high thin nasal voices. *Clang-clang-clang* went the *kotors*; *Ay-ay-ay* shrilled the singers and away in the shadows someone rather sadly sang a completely different song. The crowd pushed and heaved and swayed against each other in rapture.

Tall lamps reflected their lights in ponds; people wandered over curved bridges and lovers held hands on benches. In another pavilion a so-called tea ceremony was going on with customers queueing up to be served as in a cafeteria. Away from the lanterns it was very dark and you had to feel your way; then we were in a sweet fragrant tunnel of little purplish flowers trained over arches – the bush clover of Japanese poems, one of the Seven Flowers of Autumn.

We groped round in the dusk, peering at the rest of the Seven Grasses. There was a sudden 'Aah!' from the crowd and for an instant *Tsukumi-sama* appeared through a slit in the overcast sky. She was gone almost at once and the moon-viewers resumed their eating and drinking and hand-holding

111

and promenading. The *kotors* clanged on, drunks lurched through the shadows, babies wailed and small children had to be picked up and carried. No one seemed concerned about the moon. It was not at all in the mood of Chiyo's poem ... *Whatever we wear, We become beautiful, Moon-viewing!* It was vulgar and noisy and crowded, gay and silly and full of a sense of life, of being among warm-blooded humans.

10

'Walk on!'

THOUGH I knew that Kyoto is a great modern city, riddled with tourism, I was unreasonably taken aback by the up-to-date station, the loud-speakers bawling *Kyaw-taw! Kyaw-taw!*, the swarming cars, taxis, buses and street-cars outside. The heat was intense. The long trip from Tokyo had left me feeling quite unsuitable for the Zen temple where I was going to stay and where, presumably, cleanliness was important.

I did my best in the crowded cloakroom, juggling with *benjos* and bags, with nowhere to put things, but the minute I washed my hands they sweated again; as fast as I mopped my face it melted. They would have to take me as I was.

Chotokuin is a sub-temple in the compound of Shokokuji, one of the five chief temples of the Rinzai sect. It was founded in the fourteenth century and has been many times burnt and rebuilt. I had written to Chotokuin's Abbot Ogata, to ask if I could stay; now I had qualms. What would he be like? Thin, pale, worn, a sort of Suzuki? A soft faint voice, frail hands, an air of saintliness? How did you address him? Would life in a

113

Zen temple be beyond me? What did one talk about? Or did one creep round silently when not sitting in *zazen* (meditation)? I had no small talk about Zen. That it has nothing to do with words does not stop people discussing it.

Shokokuji seemed a long way from the station. Cars, trolley-buses, trams ran parallel or cut across us at right-angles. Kyoto is all squares and straight lines. It was Saturday afternoon and everyone was out. Department stores were open, tourist buses drew up snorting at traffic lights, Japanese families, carrying *presentos* for living or dead, went to visit friends or cemeteries. I wondered where was the ancient capital of the Land of Yamato, the Reed-bearing Plain.

The taxi driver, who might have just climbed down from a tree, kept stopping to gaze at the address on the Abbot's card. High clay walls topped with tiles flashed past, glimpses of temple roofs, beautiful trees.

'Imperial Palace,' the driver said hopefully as though it might refresh my memory; and at last, '*Sah!*'

We had reached Shokokuji but could not drive through the grounds to Chotokuin. We went back to the long street, Karasuma-dori, and turned into a lane beside a clay wall marked with widely spaced horizontal lines. I came to know this wall very well. Simple, calm, beautiful, dignified, all the best of Japan, it never failed to reassure me that another Kyoto existed away from the noisy streets.

Past little shops, round a corner, through two stone posts, then a gravel lane between high walls and we stopped at a black wooden gateway with tiles. At the side, through a smaller gate, I glimpsed deep green grass, a white flagged path. It was so simple, so lovely, so cool and so right I could not believe it was for me.

'*Hai hai*, Chotokuin,' said the driver, hanging out to interrogate two boys on bicycles.

One of the boys, with thick surprised hair and a round amused face said in English, 'I am Mr Ogata's son. This is my home.'

114

I followed him through the gates to the little green garden and up the stone path. The gate closed behind us on modern Kyoto.

Inside the walled garden, smelling of moss and trees, the only sounds were crickets and birds. The temple, saturated in afternoon peace, offered a human welcome. There was a touch of gaiety in the tiled Buddhist roof, like curling-up eyelashes, with protective dragon peering benevolently down; and black beams, white walls, homely proportions and sliding doors suggested comfort and friendliness. There was no sign of the chill austerity I had expected. Chotokuin looked what it was, a home as well as a temple.

The Japanese lady in the entrance managed simultaneously to bow low and rush forward to help. I slid out of my shoes and into the slippers she held, climbed to the platform and followed her down a corridor gleaming like silk, the soft glow that comes from years of washing with a cloth wrung out in warm water.

The lady was pretty, with a flowerlike skin. Her movements were calm and graceful, her expression all sweet serenity; yet a gleam in her eyes suggested she found life rather a joke at times; as though slightly astonished at the world's absurdity.

'Mrs Ogata,' she introduced herself. 'Please ... no English. Mr Ogata ... English oh very good.' She waved at her overall. 'Excuse please? Ve-ry busy. Clean house.'

Her voice was soft and warm, her Japanese woman's humility full of dignity.

Mr Ogata – the name was informed with respect – had taken a young American couple staying at Chotokuin to a lesson of tea and flowers.

She led me round a small inner courtyard and opened a *fusuma*. After the glare outside the first impression was of emptiness; then I saw *tatami* on the floor, a low Japanese red lacquer table, a *haniwa* head and horse and above them, a scroll with a fan in the same clay colour. Paintings on the door panels were soft and faded. There was a Kyoto doll in a glass

115

case, a simple flower arrangement and beyond a narrow glassed-in veranda, a green bamboo grove.

'And here...sleep...' Mrs Ogata waved me into a smaller room with *futon* spread on the floor and shutters that screened out the light.

A table and chair, 'for your writing,' looking out on the courtyard. In the western bathroom she seriously explained the bath heater.

'Ve-ry hard. Match light – ready. Now turn...' She patiently went through the drill; 'Sho-wa,' she demonstrated. 'Toilet...' a wave, a smiling bow. 'Sorry...no English.'

Surely the Abbot could not be too formidable with such an enchanting wife. Yet she spoke of him with immense respect. 'Mr Ogata come...Ask Mr Ogata...Mr Ogata explain...Mr Ogata knows all.'

She was back with a jug of cold lemon juice.

'Please come. Mr Ogata home. Mr Ogata will see you now.'

She seemed anxious I should not delay. Outside the study she turned to make sure I was there, gently scratched on the door and said, '*O Cho San?*'

A voice commanded in English, 'Yes yes. Come in.'

I entered, bemused that she addressed her husband as Honourable Mr Priest.

There was a strong beautiful flower arrangement, walls lined with books, chairs round a large table and O Cho San.

He said briskly, 'Come in. Please sit down.'

He was utterly unexpected. From below a large shaved head two deep-set eyes regarded me very acutely. In repose the face was formidable, almost surly; but he welcomed me politely, asked a few questions, nodding abstractedly at my answers. I felt I was applying, not too successfully, for a job beyond my capacities. I longed for the shaded room and the bed on the floor. When the interview finished I returned there and at once fell asleep.

It was dusk when I woke, streaming with sweat.

'Nancy! Nancy! Where are you?'

116

O Cho San was in the outer room, tapping his stick on the wall.

'Nancy! Nancy! What are you doing about dinner?'

I had forgotten about dinner. I was too hot and tired to eat.

'Well then,' he said. 'Let us have a talk.'

He was now a different person, as though recharged. He sat down at the table and said in a businesslike voice, 'So! What is your schedule for Kyoto?'

I never have schedules. When asked, in a voice of authority, to produce one I feel inadequate, guilty, as though I have not done my homework. All the things I wanted to see went from my head. I said vaguely, 'Gardens.'

'Ah, of course, Zen gardens. But which gardens? There are hundreds.'

I wiped my sticky forehead and said 'Which would you suggest?'

He began to list them, indicating I should write down the names. He radiated good will, he was bursting with eager vitality. His magnificent teeth gleamed, his eyes became two humorous creases. He was not formidable at all. I liked him. But how to keep up with him?

'I'm not what I was,' he said. 'Can't get about much. I had an illness. Before that I went out a great deal. Now I must use a stick and cannot walk far. It is very boring. Put down Zuiho-in, Koto-in, Daisen-in temples – they are all in Daitokuji Compound. Ryoanji, of course, the rock garden; and Katsura Detached Palace, that has a Zen garden – the most perfect example – and beautiful tea-houses. Now – to go to Katsura you must first get permission from the Imperial Palace offices ...'

I mopped and wrote.

'Tea ceremony and flower arrangement are very important in Zen, you know. Also the *Nôh* dance ... If you are interested in these I can arrange for lessons of tea and flowers. *Haiku* ... you know about *haiku*?'

I was up to my eyes in *haiku*; also *Nôh* theatre.

'So! *Nôh* and *haiku* are very important. In my library you will find many books in English about Zen, *haiku*, gardens and so on. Please help yourself to whatever you want...'

Chotokuin is a Zen study centre; not for training monks, but rather for friends of Zen. Many words have been written about this inexpressible subject, its history and influence on Japanese art and life, and most of them are in O Cho San's library. I cannot think of a more agreeable way to spend a hot Kyoto summer than reading them in the shadowy temple, going out to see Zen gardens and buildings, taking lessons in tea and flowers. A number of Europeans and Americans have done this. One stayed so long he died there and is buried in the temple cemetery.

Though Zen's ultimate aim is *satori*, the highest of all experience, its daily life is down-to-earth, practical, full of humour, vitality and *joie de vivre*. Monastery discipline is strict and austere but those who have completed training need not shut themselves off from the world. They marry like other Buddhist priests, become masters of temples or go back to normal life, working hard and accepting whatever comes.

'So!' said O Cho San, hearing I had studied yoga for ten years. 'Excellent! But Zen is more suited to the Japanese nature than yoga. In fact, Zen and the Japanese people were made for each other. That is why it still flourishes here while it is neglected in China, the country it came to us from.'

Zen is the Alexander of religious experience; it cuts straight through the knot of philosophy, theology, intellectual knowledge to reality, sometimes by startling unorthodox methods, rather as the Tantrics used obscene language to jolt over-intellectual Buddhists out of sterile complacency.

Exasperated westerners who complain Zen makes no sense may be closer to the truth than those who try too hard to understand. It is not meant to be understood, it has nothing to do with reason. *Satori*, enlightenment, can never be reached through thinking, only after reason and thought are out of the

118

way. Illumination must be personal experience; it cannot be communicated by words. A curtain is moved aside from the window and there is the view; you are nothing and everything, alone and part of the whole. You cannot lose, for you have nothing yet possess all. It does not make sense; it just is.

The Zen training for reaching *satori* is hard and severe. Body and mind must be disciplined, completely relieved of possessions and attachments to give maximum freedom. The body is taught through long hours of sitting in *zazen*, to become entirely unobtrusive; the intellect is teased and baffled by insoluble problems (*koans*) till it cracks and gives up. When a mind has been prepared by training and discipline, enlightenment could be brought about by some quite insignificant happening or sudden shock, and Zen masters, recognising a pupil is ready, knowing the uselessness of words, often seem to behave like lunatics, tweaking noses, hitting with sticks to startle into awareness.

Zen was brought to Japan in the thirteenth century by the monk Eisai, who had gone to China for study. The Japanese word *Zen* is the Chinese *Ch'an*, the Indian *Dhyana*, which we call meditation; and *zazen*, sitting in meditation, is an important part of Zen training. It is closer to yoga *dhyana* than western meditation, not surprisingly, since Zen descends from India; but in yoga, *dhyana* leads to *samadhi*, a trance-like state which may be prolonged, while *satori* is essentially a sudden blinding flash. Zen, which is not practised in India, has been described as Indian philosophy transmuted by Chinese temperament, Chinese character, Chinese Taoism. A fierce-eyed Indian monk, Boddhidarma, who appeared in China in the sixth century, was the first Zen patriarch. This is the Japanese Daruma, who glowers on paperweights, charms, on zipper-bag fasteners and round-bottomed dolls. The Japanese believe Daruma's legs wore away through sitting in meditation, but a Chinese legend says that he was seen after death walking back to India, carrying one of his shoes. The other was found in his grave. It seems very Japanese – and very much Zen –

that the founder of a major religion should end up as a humorous mascot.

Apart from the training for reaching *satori* Zen has few rules and regulations, no priestly hierarchy or elaborate ritual. The monasteries are training-schools rather than places of pilgrimage; those who live there work hard, gardening and cooking and cleaning, and often the least attractive jobs are done by the more senior monks. Moral discipline is enforced 'to guard against libertinism' and to help in achievement of inner freedom.

Outside the training-school the Zen man, like the *Karma* yogi, just gets on with life. When asked 'What is Zen?' a patriarch answered, 'Walk on!'

O Cho San is very good company, full of humour, enthusiasm, curiosity, interest in the world. He has travelled abroad, several times working and lecturing in America, and speaks good English. Though he is an authority on Zen – he has also published books in English – his scholarship does not weigh him down or spoil his pleasure in being alive. He is tolerant and can laugh at himself. He never minded being teased and seemed enchanted when the young Americans and I made cracks about 'dry aloofness', *sabi* and *wabi*, qualities he talked of constantly.

He has his own work, writing and studying, but is also obliged to teach at a Kyoto university. He longs to give this up and complete the book he is writing, but cannot afford to. The amount he needs is very small but apparently he cannot expect to get it from his own country.

He is very direct and asks questions in a straightforward, rather unJapanese way. He says this is because he comes from Kyushu, where the people are considered rather rough and rude by Honshu standards.

Mrs Ogata is also from Kyushu. Her directness takes the form of openly expressed warmth and compassion. Unobtrusive, gentle, restful, serene, she is the centre, the quiet hub of the house. When we invited her to come out with us she always smiled at such absurdity. She would trail O Cho San down the path to the taxi, fixing his *obi*, his kimono, delighted that he was going out, and welcome us back with her sweet smile. She rarely went out, except for shopping, and was always busy at home, looking after the house and family. The rooms on those hot days were kept cool and shining, with a sensitive flower arrangement in the *tokonomo*. She arranged flowers beautifully, cooked perfectly, knew without asking if you needed another blanket and looked after us all with an intuitive, down-to-earth awareness of human and physical comfort. She was teaching Japanese cooking to the young American wife and sometimes took her to the market for economical shopping. She never ate with O Cho San and me. One night she invited the Americans and myself into the family dining-room for *sukiyaki* but even then she only cooked and served the meal.

I think she would have been astonished to know that Nell, the young wife, and I both regarded her as an unattainable ideal of our own sex.

O Cho San attends the main temple of Shokokuji on certain days with other monks and masters, and also conducts services in his own temple. Chotokuin, which is about a hundred and fifty years old, is both temple and house. The prayer hall is across the little interior court from my room. The family live on the other side of the building, near the main entrance. At this time it included a son training for priesthood and a schoolboy. I saw the elder boy only at morning service.

The young Americans cooked for themselves. I had breakfast with O Cho San and other meals out. Round the building are green and grey gardens and a small burying ground. Outside my veranda stood a large cement *Tanuki*, mushroom hat on back, *saké* bottle in hand, stomach to the fore. I was intrigued to find this jovial animal in a Rinzai temple; also a Shinto fox shrine in the main temple compound. The fox is a

121

kami, the messenger of Inari, god of fertility and the rice harvest. He carried the first grain of rice on his tongue from Korea to Japan. I had found many little fox shrines in country districts, had even bought a small ancient pair of Inari's messengers in a Takayama antique shop, but had not expected to see them in the grounds of Shokokuji. O Cho San said it was a relic of *Ryobu-Shinto*, dual-aspect Shinto. When Buddhism came to Japan it absorbed many Shinto beliefs and deities into its teaching and for several centuries the mixture persisted. There are still many traces, many temple-shrines which are hard to identify as entirely of one or the other. Matsuo Shrine in Kyoto has a curious figure, said to be one of the earliest of these Shinto-Buddhist gods. Most Japanese are both Shinto and Buddhist and some of my friends are Christian as well. They have Shinto weddings and Buddhist funerals, Christian church services, *kamidana* or family altars for ancestors in their houses, picnics at Shinto shrines, pilgrimages to Buddhist temples.

Chotokuin is a green isle in the sea, its only sounds the crunch of *getas* on gravel, Buddhist services, crickets and birds, yet two minutes away is clattering, crowded Karasuma-dori.

Next door is the boys' training-college and most of its noises floated across our garden, specially in the early morning. At five thirty I woke to clappers and drums, gongs, bells and chanting. I grew to love them all, they were part of my Kyoto life; nor did I mind waking early. These cool hours were perfect for reading *haiku* or looking at garden books. I would take a cold shower and get dressed, then lie down again and read. My bed was stacked round with O Cho San's books, among them R. H. Blyth, whom I had just discovered.

Presently the first bell would ring in our courtyard, then after a pause, at the second bell, O Cho San would appear in the black robe and brown apron of the Rinzai sect. He would enter the prayer hall with his sons, the schoolboy and the young priest in training. The boys took their places on their father's right, the elder with gong, bell and fish-headed drum.

122

I knelt on the left with the young Americans, usually still rather sleepy, still in *yukata*. We sat back on our heels, hands on knees.

Coming into the shadowy garden-lit room the first time I was startled to see a tape-recorder and record-player by the lectern. Aesthetically it seemed wrong, like a projector or TV in church; yet from the sensible Zen point of view, why not? I got used to it.

With hands together O Cho San approached the altar and bowed; then, chanting with his sons, knelt at his lectern. The boys chanted fairly briskly, striking the gong, the little *ting* bell, the fish-head drum, but O Cho San wandered off slightly, blowing his nose, fiddling with tapes or records.

I never tired of the chanting. The more I heard, the greater its power. Primitive, disturbing, it is a *mantrum* that rouses all kinds of vibrations with its rhythms, unexpected changes of tempo and weird droning dying-away, like an old-fashioned gramophone running down.

After the *sutras* we read aloud the Threefold Refuge . . . 'I take refuge in the Buddha. I take refuge in the Dharma. I take refuge in the Sangha . . .'; then *Hakuin's Song of Practising Dhyana*, and the Four Great Vows:

> However innumerable beings are, I vow to save them:
> However inexhaustible the passions are, I vow to extinguish them;
> However immeasurable Dharmas are, I vow to master them;
> However incomparable the Buddha-truth is, I vow to attain it.

The line about innumerable beings was rather apt at this time. I was very taken up with Issa's *haiku* and was walking round ants, enduring flies and mosquitoes rather than kill them. I have never felt the same about flies since I read,

> See how he wrings his hands,
> His feet!

123

At the end of the readings O Cho San would put a record on his player and we would sit quietly. It was less meditation than just being receptive. The music, the instruments were strange and powerful, a husky breathless flute, *shakohachi*, like a human voice, wistful, solitary, ancient, searching; but the music was not quite human. It had no familiar or comfortable reassurances, only the essential and absolute loneliness of all living beings, the loneliness that is also universal belonging.

We sat, eyes closed, among the scents of summer, while the pipe wandered down paths and abandoned them and began in another direction, questioning, lamenting, weeping, aspiring. It searched without doubting, as Bach searches, but while Bach concludes in triumphant affirmation this Japanese music is all unfinished phrases, suggesting, evoking.

'I chose it because it is full of *sabi*,' said O Cho San. 'It has the mood,' and now I knew what he meant by this untranslatable word.

On one side of the large dusky prayer-hall, pushed-back *shoji* revealed the summer morning. Frail velvet wings opened and closed above flowers; bronze and blue sparks flashed out from sun-caught dragonflies; stones were still cool to touch, birds all eagerness. Cicadas, not yet assured of promised heat, made a few trial croaks and at intervals the cricket ascended his questioning scale.

After the music there was a taped reading from Suzuki on Zen; then O Cho San would blow his nose, put away the tapes, clear his throat and say with gusto, 'Well, what are the plans for today? Suppose we take a taxi and go to so-and-so garden? There's an amusing restaurant at the temple where we can get lunch.'

At first, like the tape recorder, it was rather startling; as though having finished his sermon the parson asks the congregation how they feel about a barbecue; but once again, why not? It was straightforward, without nonsense or false piety. It was typically Zen.

*

124

The young Ph.D's, Billy and Nell, lived separately, but sometimes we shared taxis to go to temples and gardens. O Cho San liked to come with us 'to explain'. This usually meant sitting on the temple veranda in case we wished to ask questions. We rarely did. We were not trying to learn about these gardens or understand them but just enjoying the tranquillity of stepping-stones across moss or grass, green shade, water, stone lanterns. At each temple O Cho San was received with respect by the girls selling tickets, chairs were brought out, sometimes tea. My memory of those hot Kyoto days is all of shafts of gold light through trees, the silhouette of a hanging iron lantern, dim cool temple rooms with black and white calligraphy, an exquisite simple flower arrangement in the *tokonoma*. Sometimes we were lucky and there were few tourists; at others, as at Daisen-in, there were swarms, with guides reeling off commentaries and heads turning obediently from left to right. Koto-in, Zuiho-in, Obai-in, all in Daitokuji temple compound, were peaceful; Ryoanji, when I went back alone, after heavy rain, briefly deserted.

The famous rock garden at Ryoanji is smaller than I had expected and physically somehow frailer; but its atoll austerity is not frail. It is the bare bones of truth. It is not *about* anything, not for comparing to mountains or oceans or Bach fugues, but to be felt with whatever you happen to bring to it. What these stones and sand do to you is direct, or they do nothing at all. For this reason you prefer the American woman declaring it meaningless, complaining that it has no flowers, to the earnest young Englishman who began looking reverent out in the entrance.

From a certain point on Ryoanji veranda you can see both the rock garden and an exquisite garden of moss behind the temple – wisdom (stone) and compassion (moss), O Cho San said. In the moss garden little streams run beneath trees, among azalea bushes and twisted roots; stepping-stones rise or are submerged in green velvet cushioned slopes, moist-smelling on this humid grey day.

125

The first time at Ryoanji we were changing our shoes in the entrance when a slim gay gentleman in *yukata* came from a side door and exclaimed in delighted surprise. It was the Abbot, O Cho San's old friend, and after the bows, protestations, assurances he led us into a modern air-conditioned drawing room where in deep armchairs we drank tea and ate bean-jelly cakes. All new, the Abbot explained with delight, just finished. Come! and he led us through the rest of the house – modern kitchen, new bedroom and bathroom with fragrant walls that give off sweet scents in the steam of the bath. The whole house has this faint herbal fragrance from its golden wood, like the walls at Katsura villa.

'So! So desuka!' said O Cho San again and again. He marvelled with wholehearted unenvious admiration at the modern stove, the western WC, a mechanised bed which rose at the touch of a button and folded itself into the wall. The Abbot displayed his new possessions with a guileless zest and eagerness that was less showing-off than confidential sharing. He was still enthralled with the new bed and the two shaven-headed elderly priests pressed the button, raised and lowered the bed, prodded and bounced on the spring mattress, laughing delightedly, urging us to try.

When we had seen the rock and moss gardens we drank green powdered tea with the Abbot and his handsome digni-fied wife in a cool modern dining-room; then the Abbot led us through the lower gardens to see his new tea-house. Again the same guileless enthusiasm, the lack of envy or pride, the sharing and receiving. This was a perfect example for us, said O Cho San, of all that a tea-house should be. Observe the simplicity of its materials, the natural tree-trunks for posts. This tea-house had *sabi*.

We observed and admired, knowing enough to realise that though deceptively rustic and primitive, it had cost a great deal to build. Tea-houses can cost more than dwelling-houses and there are specialists in the art who build nothing else.

Further down the garden, a tiny house, once inhabited by

an artist, stands by a small lake. Stepping-stones, an old boat half-submerged, stone lanterns glimpsed among bamboo and maples already flecked with scarlet, all contribute to *sabi*; specially the mouldering boat. Never used on so small a stretch of water, it is there to complete the picture.

At the temple rest house, overlooking the great lake, families were gathered round enormous earthenware pots. A delicious savoury smell rose as people dipped in and filled their bowls. When our lunch came, in an earthenware cauldron I longed to take home, it was an excellent kind of minestrone. Beancurd, cut in stars, circles, cylinders, dyed different colours, floated gaily among the vegetables. We demolished it all, then lay back, lolling on cushions, fanning ourselves, dozing and watching the birds on the lake.

Later there was a discussion about the Abbot's material comforts, which Nell felt were hardly in keeping with the poverty, austerity, discomfort expected of holy men. O Cho San mildly pointed out that Ryoanji is a very rich temple, the Abbot could afford luxuries without harming anyone; but Nell was not reassured. Many temples are poor. Why didn't the rich ones, like Ryoanji, help them instead of installing mechanical beds? Was it not selfish to spend so much on your own personal comfort when others were in need?

Chotokuin is not a rich temple; but O Cho San smiled benevolently and changed the subject.

Kyoto is close to Nara, the earlier capital, to the valleys and rivers and hills of Hasé and Yoshino and Muroji and all the beautiful Land of Yamato of the poets. Whenever I disappeared O Cho San would say, 'Where's Nancy? Not gone to look at *another* temple?' This was his joke. Apart from Zen temples and Katsura detached palace I went to very few. I went to Ishiyamadera, on Lake Biwa, because it is said that Lady Murasaki lived there while she wrote *Genji Monogatori*. It is also said that she did not, and I feel this might be true for I cannot imagine anyone writing anything, let alone *Genji*, in those two little Stygian boxes off the prayer-hall. The temple, despite its superb trees, pagoda and moon-viewing house seemed excessive, oppressive and faintly menacing – feelings that never came in the simple Zen buildings.

I loved Ginkokuji, the Silver Pavilion, for its purity and for taking me so by surprise. It is astonishing, passing the modest entrance, to be confronted with a lake of sand, leading the eye to a glistening white sand mountain, flat-topped and symmetrical, and on to red pine-trunks on the hillside, and the textures and greens of the forest, three-dimensional in rich afternoon light.

The pavilion itself, shabby, soft, black and white, with a phoenix on top, seemed full of *sabi*. I did not care if it was once meant to be covered with silver, or if its name comes from the sand lake, which is silver by moonlight; nor that it has a tea-house designed by the fifteenth-century tea-master Shuko for the Shogun Yoshimasu. Beyond the sand lake and mountain are bridges over reflecting water, mossy slopes, clumps of blue bell-flowers. On this mellow evening a party of boys and girls were leading others along these paths and bridges. Those who were led stopped frequently, bent down to touch, with ineffable tenderness, to put their cheeks against flowers, leaves, tree trunks, to finger textured wood and stone with a curious light on their faces, to stand silently inhaling scents. They were all quite blind; but entirely at one with this garden and, in being so, radiantly happy.

11

Tea and Flowers

THE YOUNG American academics were learning the Zen arts of tea ceremony and flower arrangement. I had regarded both these practices as slightly rarefied; but since they are part of Japanese life, and doing brings better understanding than watching, I joined the lessons.

I soon found they are no more precious than playing Bach, and like Bach, require years of training and discipline. In flower arrangement the outward form is, in a sense, the visible sign of the pupil's inner development, his advance towards the emptying out of ego, the recognition of reality; in *Cha-no-yu* (tea ceremony) the disciplined movements, the setting, the atmosphere are designed to create a harmonious mood conducive to union with all and everything.

This is not to say everyone practises tea and flowers for their true purpose any more than *Hatha* yoga is practised in the west for its spiritual objective. O Cho San jovially suggested that many young girls study *Cha-no-yu* because it is a chance to wear pretty kimonos, and since it teaches manners and grace is a good way to get a husband; though older women who already have husbands could afford to take it more seriously. But whatever the motive, only good can result from the practice.

Flower arrangement and tea ceremony both began as religious customs. Buddhist monks in India, filled with love and compassion towards all life, would pick up flowers broken by storms or dying of drought and try to restore them in miniature gardens or sand boxes before the temple altar. After Buddhism came to Japan in the fifth century these rather heavy collections of plants and branches developed form and delicacy under the Japanese genius. Because the Buddhist temples were the centres of art and learning, the first great flower masters were monks, but gradually the practice spread into everyday life, particularly through the tea cult. Sand boxes of large branches before temple altars became simple flower arrangements in the *tokonoma* of tea-rooms or private houses. The altar itself became the *tokonoma*, the alcove where the rarest scroll, the finest *objet d'art* is displayed, still the place of honour in a Japanese room.

Tea ceremony came from China. Legend says it began when one of Lao-tse's disciples offered him tea as a form of welcome, for though the Chinese had been drinking it for hundreds of years it was used mainly for medicinal purposes. They believed it repaired eyesight, restored strength and soothed rheumatism. It was one of the main ingredients in the elixir of life.

In the Zen monasteries of South China the monks took tea during meditation to prevent drowsiness, but they also drank it more ceremoniously, gathered round Boddhidarma's (Daruma's) image. This formal tea-drinking, at which everyone drank from the same bowl, developed into the Japanese tea ceremony.

Though imported tea was occasionally drunk in Japan by the rich and privileged, it was not grown there till the ninth century, when a monk brought seeds from China. Even then it did not really develop till the end of the twelfth century when Eisai, the monk who introduced Zen to Japan, planted tea in

130

several areas. As Zen spread in Japan, the cult of tea spread with it, becoming not only a monastic ritual but a secular practice. Now it is part of Japanese life, and whether realised or not by the man in the street, has influenced almost every aspect of living – architecture, gardens, flower arrangement, domestic interiors, ceramics, painting, the love of simplicity and of nature.

Our teacher, Miss Tamon, lives some distance from Choto-kuin so we went to her house by taxi. O Cho San came with us, to interpret, he said; but since the physical movements of tea ceremony were demonstrated wordlessly, I suspect he came because he enjoyed the outing. He would sit in the corner, sometimes with a book, sometimes not, while Miss Tamon took us patiently through the preliminaries.

First, if not wearing a belt, something must be tied round the waist to act as *obi*, into which the *fukusa*, or napkin is tucked. The *fukusa* is taken out, the fingers are placed in a certain way, holding and folding it into a triangle; open out, smooth with forefinger, fold, tuck into *obi* . . . again and again and again. She was endlessly patient, endlessly calm. It looked so simple yet we could not get it right; it seemed at first fiddling and pointless, but once started the small square of lined silk became the focus of one's whole attention.

From folding the napkin we slowly advanced to etiquette . . . to receiving as well as serving tea, entering the room, how a guest should behave, how to take, when to eat the little sweet cake, to set it on the square of white paper provided (which we should remember to take ourselves if going to tea cere-mony). Again, what seems artificial observed without under-standing, assumed value in the performance. Though at this stage I knew little about the background, I began to suspect that we were skirting round infinite possibilities. We were not just being taught a stylised way to make and serve tea but to create *wa, kei, sei, jaku* . . . harmony, respect, purity and tranquillity. And something strange came from it. Slapdash

131

and impatient, I began by feeling this discipline was good for me and ended by loving it for itself.

Miss Tamon teaches mainly in an upstairs room but as we made our snail advance she took us to her tea-house in the garden. Here we put into practice what we were shown upstairs – the proper quiet way to approach the tea-house along the path, dipping purifying water from the stone bowl at the entrance to rinse hands and mouth, placing the fan on the mat and leaving shoes outside, entering humbly on our knees through the low doorway; bowing to show respect for the hostess, appreciation of her consideration for us, for her taste by kneeling before the *tokonoma* to admire her flower arrangement, her choice of vase and scroll, and after the tea had been served and drunk – our teachers hovering, prompting with mime – handling, examining, enjoying the beautiful bowls, the lacquered caddy, the kettle and other utensils.

All these actions we try to make as graceful and natural as our teachers show them to be; but it is hard. We feel we are not co-ordinated, we feel big, awkward, clumsy. (The relief when a Japanese pupil makes a mistake, upsets the tea powder, spills the hot water!) At first we create less harmony and tranquillity for ourselves than anxiety, fear of failure; but as the rhythmic movements are practised again and again we begin to relax, to glimpse a far-distant possibility of one day improving.

'Through tea ceremony performed to perfection, it is possible to create the state desired in Zen, even when not interested in Zen itself,' says O Cho San. 'Miss Tamon does this through the perfection of her art, though not interested in Zen as such.'

The perfection of Miss Tamon's art depresses us, shames our barbaric clumsiness.

The second half of the lesson is flower arrangement. In the western convention I rather fancy myself at this. Here I find I know nothing; worse, what I do know is wrong and must be discarded.

Long low tables are set before us, secateurs, shallow bowls, tall vases, and for each, a bundle of flowers, leaves, branches. Some of these materials are conventionally beautiful; others are unusual; others again downright unlikely. I regard horse-tail grass with consternation, having only seen it in boarding house vases. I have a great deal to learn.

Miss Tamon, who speaks no English at all, quickly and skilfully creates an arrangement for each of us, touches various points at different levels, as though to show something, and leaves us to it.

What is one supposed to do? O Cho San is absorbed in a book. Billy and Nell, after carefully studying their arrangements, have dismantled them cautiously. They are pondering deeply, exchanging cryptic words. Assuming we are expected to do something original I take my arrangement to pieces and put it together again as differently as I can. It is quickly done; but as I watch the measured, deliberate movements of the others I think uneasily of the hare and the tortoise.

Miss Tamon returns, puts her head on one side and nods approvingly at the others' what-seems-to-me-slavish copies of her own creations. At mine she is taken aback, almost affronted, but recovering with a brave smile comments to O Cho San that I am rather ambitious.

My arrangement of course is chaotic by Japanese rules, without shape, form, depth, meaning...utterly pointless. I have not put in – not having heard of it – the 'principal of three'...heaven, earth and man. I have left no empty spaces for the beholder to fill, I have gone all out to complete rather than leave unfinished, I have stated rather than suggested, shouted rather than hinted. Miss Tamon quickly dismantles my work and repeats the original formula. I feel indignant, unjustly used. Very well; if they just want things regimented, without imagination...I faithfully copy Miss Tamon's arrangement and am rewarded with approving smiles.

But there is much more to it than copying.

It is very confusing. One day, trying hard, I get nowhere.

133

My work is taken apart without comment, which means it's no good. I feel frustrated, I have battled in vain with those hideous branches and artichoke shapes to reproduce Miss Tamon's example. Next day, feeling relaxed, sympathetic towards my materials, I docilely follow the line of the branches. It isn't much good but Miss Tamon is pleased. She says it has promise. The minute she says this I begin to understand. Why should flower arrangement differ from other arts? Try to impose yourself on your material and you get nowhere. Become receptive and life flows in, and out again through your hands into your work.

After the lesson we return to the entrance and while sliding down into our shoes manage to hand over casually, nonchalantly the special envelope containing the fee. It includes the flowers which we take home for practice. Miss Tamon receives it in the same manner, as an afterthought of no consequence. I have read that some flower masters never discussed fees. It was left to the pupil's discretion to pay according to his circumstances, at the end of the year.

The general impression among the ordinary Japanese is of an almost Polynesian offhandedness towards money. If they can spend at all, they seem to spend gaily; and in circles such as these, in Kyoto, one feels any mention of payment to be in very bad taste. Yet not only is money given as presents at funerals and other occasions, the amount is written outside on the envelope.

Here there is no touch of commerce in the atmosphere, all appear to be doing each other a gracious favour. Miss Tamon usually dispenses refreshments – cold drinks or prepared fruit, and one day, when we were going on to see a garden, *soba* on rattan mats in red lacquer boxes.

Under O Cho San's guidance we have seen a number of tea-rooms and tea-houses, but it is Miss Tamon who provides the real gem. O Cho San is full of excitement.

'Miss Tamon studied Urasenke style of tea ceremony. Now

she has arranged to take you to Urasenke, the headquarters of the school. This is a wonderful opportunity for you, not to be missed. You are extremely fortunate. Urasenke belongs to the descendants of Rikyu, the greatest tea master of all, founder of the tea ceremony. At Urasenke you will see historic relics of Rikyu himself and Sotan, his grandson, who founded this school. There are several tea-rooms in the building and you will be served tea by one of Rikyu's family. Now you will be able to see Rikyu's ideals carried out ... you remember I have told you Rikyu established the *sabi* or *wabi* style? For four hundred years his descendants have carried on his teaching. Now they have pupils all over the world.'

When he said Rikyu founded the tea ceremony he did not mean he invented it but that the form and etiquette still practised by different schools are all based on Rikyu's teaching. He instituted the separate tea-house building – plain, simple, inspired by a country farmhouse – instead of a room or screened-off part of the dwelling-house. Through his example the ceremony was purified and ennobled, even the utensils, the settings became simpler, more graceful. His influence was away from ostentation, luxury, privilege. In the tea-room all were equal; the Shogun, the Emperor entered on their knees through the low door. It was the place of peace and harmony; the *samurai* must leave his sword outside before coming in. Money, display, brash newness, elaborate furnishing had no place – it was all a little old, a little shabby, a little mellow. The ancient leaking bamboo vase, the rough Korean tea-bowl, the humble flower arrangement all helped create the feeling of *sabi* evoked by the sound of the water in the kettle, like the sighing of pines, the quietness, the tranquil absence of doing and getting.

All must be close to nature, or give this appearance. After Rikyu's grandson Sotan had tidied the garden and swept the path bare the old man shook the branch of a tree so autumn leaves would fall, saying 'This is how a garden should be swept.'

135

But Rikyu was not a simple peasant. He was the teacher and friend of the Shogun Hideyoshi, and a man of strong character. One day Hideyoshi sent word he was coming to see his Master's famous convolvulus garden but when he arrived found all the flowers had been cut down and there were only pebbles and sand. He stormed to the tea-house, but was abashed to realise that Rikyu had sacrificed the whole garden in his pupil's honour. Only the most perfect convolvulus flower remained, displayed alone in a rare Sung vase on the *tokonoma*.

Rikyu was not afraid of Hideyoshi and they often quarrelled. After one disagreement the Shogun was persuaded that his teacher meant to poison him at the next tea ceremony. Without stopping to investigate he commanded Rikyu, then over seventy, to commit *hari-kari*.

The tea master obeyed calmly. He invited close friends and disciples to a last tea ceremony and presented them with his equipment as souvenirs. Then he sent them away, removed his kimono, and in a white robe, took out his dagger. He addressed it in verse, hailing it as his liberator; then plunged it into his stomach and died smiling.

It is sometimes said he was not entirely innocent, that he may have been concerned with politics; yet he does not look a schemer. In his portrait he sits pale, calm, handsome, wearing dark robes and cap, in perfect tranquillity yet with a sadness in eyes and mouth.

A typhoon was flicking Kyoto, it was pouring with rain as we dashed, most untranquilly, through Urasenke's beautiful mossy thatched Helmet Gate. The exquisite gardens of trees, shrubs, hedges, stone lanterns and flagged paths were glimpsed as through tears. Discarding shoes, coats, umbrellas in the entrance, we were welcomed and led through the building by a charming young man speaking excellent English.

For a *Chajin* (tea devotee) this was a solemn occasion. Here was a stone basin used by Rikyu, the gong presented to him by Hideyoshi, the stone lantern loved by his grandson Sotan, a

136

roji or garden path of beautiful stones made by Sotan – was this the path where Rikyu scattered the leaves? – a ginko tree nearly four hundred years old, wearing a rope girdle to show that it is a *kami*.

By the Plum Well, where the purest water rises, bamboo and wooden utensils and buckets are piled. The house posts and beams might still be alive in the forest. The sound of the rain, broken by leaves, enclosed us in a vegetable world of thatched roofs, mossy stones, wooden pillars and ceilings, straw matting, bamboo water-pipes, trees, shrubs, ferns. All was subdued, restful, tranquil; nothing suggested heat or hot blood or anger or violence.

In a dark room, above a burning altar lamp, strange eyes look out from behind a grille – a lifesize wooden figure of Rikyu, enshrined, watching, eerie.

Though it was a busy morning at the school no voices were raised, no signs of hurry or urgency. As though we were the only ones in the world we were led from room to room, treasure to treasure, finally to rinse mouths and hands at Sotan's stone basin and be served tea.

This was in the modern tea-room designed by a woman of the Sen family. I was perversely disappointed. It seemed as much Western as Japanese – a black serving-table like an elegant executive's desk with vermilion silk cords, a long polished coffee table. Instead of *tatami*, honan matting. On the executive desk a turquoise jar, an elegant ceramic glazed water bucket. Handsome, in excellent taste; but where was the *sabi*? The simple poverty?

We had been slightly concerned lest our behaviour as guests disgrace Miss Tamon. Without doubt much anxiety was removed by not being served on the floor; yet to sit side by side on the bench recalled doctors' waiting-rooms, and the black polished desk looked exceedingly business-like.

All this changed when the door opened and a young woman entered. She was extraordinarily beautiful, with a skin of flawless moonlit porcelain. Tall and slim, with long slender neck,

137

exquisite hands and delicate features, she moved like a willow tree swaying. She wore a deep prune-purple kimono and in her *obi* a scarlet *fukusa*.

She was a work of art, a product of generations of fine breeding, training and moulding. She bore no relation at all to the Japanese out in the streets, rice-fields and villages.

She welcomed us in musical English without a trace of accent, then sat at the black desk, took the scarlet *fukusa* from her *obi* and began to make tea.

It was like watching a ballet – the fluid movements, the slow graceful tempo, the little white hands, the tranquil expression, the bend of the long neck, turquoise against black, scarlet against purple. It was pure timeless beauty into which you sank, forgetful of life outside, a beauty intensified by the dripping rain, the rustle of wet bamboo and the gentle sigh of the kettle.

I lived two lives in Kyoto ... Chotokuin life – tea ceremony, flower arrangement, Zen gardens, *Nôh* theatre, *haiku* – and the life of the crowds and department stores, arcades, Shinto shrines and little restaurants. The heat grew. I had never been so hot, but I loved this city, even the long dusty streets which at first had so disappointed me.

At night I explored the narrow lanes round Gion or winding back-alleys in pure areas, where the little dark hovels, entered by positive tunnels, are crammed with teenagers, bicycles, dogs, babies, shoes, grandparents and television. Whatever else is lacking there is always the wavering blue-grey screen, the magic escape from hard work and poverty. Relaxed weary bodies stretched on the floor, absorbed peaceful faces testify to its blessed power.

Out in the streets, people sat on chairs, like Greeks and Sicilians getting a breath of air. Sometimes they slept there. One night I saw a shopkeeper curled up outside his door in a disused bath.

No room, no room to live, once you leave the broad streets,

the calm temple gardens. People packed in like biscuits or fish in a tin; yet always the *bonsai* tree, the lovingly trained con- volvulus, or if nothing else, the flower in the vase, the pile of carefully picked stones.

Sometimes I found myself in parts so grim and sordid I wondered if I were in an *eta* quarter. The *eta* are Japan's un- touchables. Though laws have been passed and movements started to abolish discrimination, it still exists, the outcasts still live in *buraku*, or special districts.

The *eta* do the lowest, most degrading of work, unfit for good Buddhists, since good Buddhists do not take life. Though the Japanese were early divided into the base and the free, the distinction intensified after Buddhism came. The base-born took over the killing and skinning of animals. Butchers and tanners and those who worked with leather – even shoemakers – became *eta*, and in the past were herded together in ghettoes in the worst areas, on river banks or wherever the land was of no value. They could not marry outside their caste and if ever one managed to rise above his background he lived in fear of exposure.

Since 1871 the *eta* have been legally free to live anywhere, but they rarely do because of social discrimination. The other Japanese say they are not really human, that every *eta* has one dog's bone in his body. Sometimes they are even referred to by the word *yotsu* (four), or by four fingers held up to signify four legs. Many non-*eta* have tried to help these unfortunates but progress is very slow. It is incredible that such a situation could result from Buddhism, the religion of compassion and tolerance. It seems even more cruel, more barbaric than dis- crimination against colour or race.

Each part of my double life intensified the power of the other – the glaring streets and the cool green garden, the noisy shops and the peaceful cemetery where crickets run up their scales and deep bells sound from Shokokuji compound. Coming in sticky and hot I would take a shower and lie in my shaded room while outside the sun beat down; but I could not forget

139

the silent man in the Shijo arcade among the crowds and the bright little shops. In white, with military cap, neither sitting nor standing, propped on a box, metal legs crossed beside him, and in front, on the ground, a little box, terribly empty. The passers-by ignore him. Defeat is shameful; he should have died with his comrades; so he leans there, endlessly. Who will take him away? Will he struggle alone into those hideous robot limbs at the end of the day? Does anyone care?

Japanese tell me these military beggars choose the places where there are most foreign tourists, yet putting money in his box I feel resentment behind the impassive face. Have I offended by seeing him? He needs help; without work, with almost no pension he needs every yen he can get, but pride can be stronger than sense. I wonder if he realises that he may have killed one of my family; if this does not even it up in his eyes?

Most of these abandoned casualties, by their silent resentment, chill the instinct to give, so that one throws the money into the box ungraciously, guiltily, and makes off as fast as possible. I have been told they hate our pity, our witnessing their disgrace; I have also been told they couldn't care less, since they 'do very well' out of foreigners.

Some Europeans say that one can admire and respect the Japanese but that they are not lovable. At first I thought this might be true. An appearance of cool neat efficiency is not specially endearing; but quite soon I began to suspect that they are not at all cool underneath. I saw young men weeping at farewelling ancient mothers, middle-aged couples sitting together in tender harmony, young lovers exchanging most ardent glances and little old fathers in tears at the rails of island boats. The way people leap feet first into emergencies suggests they love drama, and though they are intelligent and highly intuitive, and even officials can quickly grasp essentials, they quite often get in a flap, and in some ways are terrible muddlers.

Perhaps 'not vulnerable' is more apt than 'not lovable'. The

Japanese do not have the exposed fawn-like look of Indonesians, Malays, Polynesians. A touch of Spanish steel comes from pride, the tradition of not showing feelings. They do not suggest the word 'miserable' in the sense of mean, degraded, defeated. These mutilated soldiers, even very old ragged derelicts, emanate stoicism rather than self-pity, and among the more fortunate there is always the feeling of resilience and virility. One does not picture them helplessly crushed. If they cannot adapt, or avenge, they commit suicide.

The simplicity of the Zen temples enhances the colour of the Shinto shrines – of Heian's audacious vermilion paint and snow-trees covered with paper twists; of Gion shrine in Maruyama Park, the noisy vulgarity of its stalls and shooting galleries, the *torii* and avenues of red wooden lanterns. When darkness comes down on Gion, the scarlet lamps in the park, all the white paper lanterns light up round the shrine; and below is the long glittering street and the Kama River with its willows and islets and lanterns in restaurants and tea-houses.

The most bizarre of all must be Inari shrine on a public holiday. Shinto priests dazzling in white, black caps brilliant against scarlet and gold, blue sky, soft thatched roofs, maiden *kagura*, drums and pipes, prayers, *saké*, pigeons to feed, stalls of food, souvenirs, steaming cakes in glass cases, spun-sugar fairy-floss, china foxes, candles, little fish for offerings, instant portraits, wooden rice-spoons painted with the fox, Inari's messenger.

Fox after fox after fox ... foxes of stone, china, metal, with cotton bibs round their necks, on their heads, round their tails. Foxes, stone lanterns and *toriis* ... never so many *toriis*, whole avenues going into the forest, up the hillside, closer and closer together till they almost form a roof, splitting off into two avenues – an excess that seems hilarious after the restraint of Zen.

Here and there among the foxes a white horse, living or carved, stands patiently in a roofed cage, an offering to the

141

shrine; and in the trees crows bark, the harsh eerie Shinto sound.

The crowds seem happy, clapping to call the god, throwing coins into the box, jangling the bell, offering their little piles of *sembei*, fish, rice, sugar, salt, candles and bean-curd, the fox's favourite. But are they all as carefree as they seem? What of that strange haunted Mexican-looking man in the big straw hat, going from altar to altar, furtively dodging the crowds? In a secluded grove I see the *sembei* and the fish and rice offerings swept from the altar into his collecting bag, into his mouth.

From this world of noise, life and colour I enter the *Nôh* theatre where masked sleep-walkers glide on the glassy stage and the stylised green pine is the only scenery. The sounds of clapping and jangling are replaced by the weird *Nôh* chant, the TOK of the hand-drum, cheerful humanity by wailing demons and ghosts. And again I go out when the play is over and find street-cars grinding and school-children marching in squads to view national treasures and *geishas* dancing in restaurants at Gion, and return at last to Chotokuin's peace and harmony, to the lamp and the books on the floor and the sounds of clappers and chanting from over the wall.

12

Garden of One Light

BEFORE I came to Japan I had heard of the Itto-en community at Yamashina, outside Kyoto. In this village over three hundred people are living their ideals of humility, non-possession, self-less service and belief in One Light, the essence of all true religion. Marie Byles, who stayed at Itto-en several times and wrote of it in her book *Paths to Inner Calm,* advised me to write to Ayako Isayama-san if I wanted to go there. Miss Isayama, who speaks very good English and usually looks after foreign visitors, replied that I should be welcome.

When I told O Cho San I was going to Itto-en he began to talk about Tenko Nishida, the founder of the community.

'Yes, yes, I know Tenko Nishida – his followers call him Tenko-san. He is a remarkable man. He was a very successful businessman, you know, but he gave it all away... gave up everything and lived homeless, in poverty. They call him our Saint Francis of Assisi. He was a student of Zen for many years. What are you going to do at Itto-en?'

143

'Whatever the others are doing. Live with them, work with them.'

'Oh yes, they all work. They believe that work is prayer. He looked extremely mischievous. 'You know, of course, don't you, that one of Itto-en's most famous forms of work is cleaning out people's lavatories in unsewered areas? Are you going to join them in that?'

I knew about it, had given it thought, was prepared for it if necessary. Emptying *benjos* is about the most distasteful of work to the clean Japanese. Tenko-san's followers do it as a form of humility, as a practical service to others and to show their belief that no work is too degrading. It is done in a highly religious spirit. The workers gather to pray before they go out from their village, with their buckets hung on their arms and their hands in prayer, and as they walk they sing their *Rokumen Gyoken* (prayer in action) hymn.

'Some people call it the W.C. religion,' O Cho San said, 'But of course they do other work...all sorts of work. Itto-en is now a very thriving community with farms and gardens and its own schools. They have some very wealthy supporters. Apart from those who live in the village at Yamashina there are thousands of Friends of Light all over the country.'

Several times passing Yamashina on the way to Lake Biwa I had looked out at the hills and wondered about Itto-en. The day I set out to go there a flood of water was falling out of a black sky. It was another typhoon. Without raincoat or warm clothes I was soon soaked and chilled. After a long wait at Yamashina station a taxi sloshed me through narrow streets, under a railway bridge and up a muddy slope. At the top, a bridge across a canal led to a monochrome village below a high wooded hill. The driver said, 'Kosenrin.'

'Itto-en?'

'Itto-en? Kosenrin.'

I did not know what he meant by Kosenrin but since the rain had stopped for an instant I got out and crossed the bridge. The worried driver shouted enquiries at two muffled-

144

up figures, then nodded encouragingly and drove off, satisfied I was safe.

The rain began again. I stood in my wet shoes regarding the charcoal roofs and wet green leaves of the village of Kosenrin – Itto-en, the Garden of One Light. There was a wall with gates, and beyond, a pebbled court, gravel paths, trees bowed with water. In the gate-house squares of yellow light looked homely. I entered.

Yes, yes, they knew about me. The ticket-collector had telephoned from the station. Isayama-san was coming.

A large yellow oiled paper umbrella skimmed down the path. Gravel crunched under little blue rubber boots. Ayako Isayama-san stood before me, looking concerned; tiny, compact, with oval face, high forehead, black hair pulled back from a centre parting. She bowed and spoke, showing very white teeth.

'Welcome to Itto-en.' She seized my bag. 'Come, come out of the wet.'

Rain drummed on the maize-coloured umbrella as we scuttled beneath high sodden trees to a square new building. In the entrance, shoes off, we mounted the polished floor. *Shoji* were slid back on a pleasant Japanese room looking out upon tossing leaves, a little graveyard splashed with wet yellow flowers.

'This is your room,' said Isayama-san. 'Now you must take off your wet things and I shall bring tea.'

Prepared for a dormitory, I was relieved. My head had begun to ache, I felt sick and exhausted. I was depressed at the thought of being ill. There was also the slight discomfort of *being* here rather than reading about it. Though I had known Itto-en people were possessionless, devoted to the service of others, confronted by Isayama-san in the flesh, her welcoming kindness, I felt abashed, like a sightseer.

Isayama-san spent the whole afternoon with me. She said that since it was Saturday afternoon she was not working and was at my disposal to answer any questions and tell me about

145

Itto-en. At first I felt slightly apprehensive, as though expecting at any moment to be found wanting. I wondered how I had had the nerve to come here among people so much better than myself; but as the afternoon went on this unease evaporated. I became so absorbed in her telling I forgot about self.

This little lioness, the size of a child, with tiny hands, emanates a strong, steady unwavering power. I cannot imagine her dithering or giving up in defeat. She would work on and on for what she believed without reward or success. This can be sensed, quite apart from what one learns of her story.

'I had a good home, good parents, a good education, but I was not satisfied. Something was missing in my life; I was searching for something, spiritually. Then, while I was still at university, I read Tenko-san's book *The Life of Penitence*, in which he describes how he came to his life of service. I knew at once that this was what I had been looking for.'

She wanted to go at once and work with Tenko-san but her parents said she must finish her education and get married.

'But I could not think about anything else. After I graduated I went to see Tenko-san and asked if I could join him but he would not take me without my parents' consent. I was still very young; I also had very poor health. So he sent me away. I was very unhappy.'

There was a cousin who wished to marry her. They were good friends, but she felt marriage was not for her. She must serve humanity, she must join Tenko-san. The cousin was sad, her parents upset, so she left her home in Tokyo and went to Kobe to live there a life of service in her own way. She thought if she did this perhaps Tenko-san would realise she was in earnest and let her join the community.

'I lived with a very old lady, very poor, looking after her day and night. I also taught kindergarten. In this way I lived for two years, working very hard, without payment, eating very little because I had no money. At the end of two years I became very ill,' she said casually. 'My parents were worried

146

and very unhappy. They asked me to go home to Tokyo, but I could not. This life of service was what I wanted. And then, at last, Tenko-san heard what I had been doing and realised that I was serious.'

When she talked of her happiness at Itto-en, her voice rose and grew stronger, she almost burbled with joy.

'I have been here for fourteen years, and I grow happier every day. I do not want anything else in my life but this. I want only to stay here, to live here, to *die* here!'

I asked her to tell me about Tenko-san; how he came to give up everything and embrace poverty.

'But he had to, you see, to be free. Tenko-san could have stayed a rich man for the rest of his life. When he was young he was chosen to lead a group of settlers up to Hokkaido to reclaim and develop land. The project was very successful; but he found it was all built on exploiting and cheating. The whole world seemed full of dishonesty and oppression, yet he felt that there must be some way for man to live in peace and harmony, if only he could find it. He decided to devote his life to the search for this way.'

At the thought of Tenko-san her eyes shone.

'Tenko-san is a wonderful man. He lived for years as a penniless wanderer, meditating, fasting, praying, but he did not find any answer. Then one day in 1905 he went to a little temple at Nagahama, near Kyoto, to ask for a sign from God, whether or not he should go on.'

'He fasted for three days and nights in this little temple. On the third day he heard a baby cry in a house nearby. When the mother came to feed it the crying stopped. This was the answer Tenko-san had been looking for. So simple. It is a law of nature that a woman provides for the child she bears and the child trusts and depends on the mother who gave it life. Tenko-san says if we are born of God, God is responsible for our existence. He will feed, clothe and house us if we trust and depend on him. If we live this way we can exist without cheating or harming our fellow-men.'

147

'But you work here! The Itto-en people don't just sit about waiting for God to feed them?'

'No, no! We must all work; but it is not for rewards. We call it giving service. It is to show gratitude to Light, because Light looks after us and provides for us. Tenko-san believes there is only one Light, the Light that is not two...not God or Buddha or Confucious but the essence of all.'

After realisation came to Tenko-san he began to work without payment for whoever would let him, doing anything, everything, sweeping shrines, streets, parks, cleaning hospitals, emptying garbage tins, emptying *benjos*. He was penniless, homeless, in rags. People laughed at him, they said he was insane, a fraud, because he asked only to give service; others realised he was genuine, their hearts were touched and they offered him kindness, food, shelter. So he survived; and because he believed it the only way to exist without the conflict and greed that comes from possession, he continued to live homeless and penniless. Gradually people were drawn to him, they saw the truth behind his example and began to follow him.

'Tenko-san believes in example and action, not just in talking about it,' Isayama-san said simply.

Towards evening the rain lessened and a mist crept down from the hills, half obliterating the village...grey mist, grey roofs, houses, gravestones.

Isayama-san excused herself and presently came back with covered dishes of rice, fish, vegetables, grapes. She said, 'We will have breakfast and lunch in the communal dining-hall but supper we will have each night in your room.'

She ate lightly but eagerly. Before eating she joined her hands and prayed, repeating the gesture, with bowed head, before taking and after finishing any food. Though she made this prayer-movement (*gassho*) instinctively there was also a feeling that each time was the first.

As we finished a temple bell sounded. Soon I heard *getas*

148

outside on the path. People were going to the evening service. Isayama-san asked if I would like to join them.

The *Reido*, the Hall of the Spirit, is a little way up the hill. When we entered, men, women and children were filing in quietly. They bowed with palms together, then sat back on their heels on *tatami*-covered platforms like wide shallow steps on each side of the hall. At one end of this hall is a portrait of Tenko-san, at the other, like a round grey-green picture, a window upon a bamboo grave. There are wooden tablets inscribed with Zen calligraphy and three altars – to the essence of Christianity, to the essence of Buddhism, and in the centre, to Light. Above is Itto-en's symbol, the Buddhist swastika with arms bent round to form a circle and a cross superimposed. Below burns a lantern never allowed to go out, made from fragments of ancient temple and shrine lamps from all over the country.

The hall was in deep twilight. The service, with clappers and chanting, faintly familiar, but more fervent than our devotions at Chotokuin.

I felt strangely confused and light-headed, as though with a temperature; but I was determined to keep this to myself and after the service went with Isayama-san to the public bath, which is open several nights a week.

We were rather late and most of the crowd had gone. We slithered about in the suds, washing each other's backs. After this we were Nancy-san and Ayako-san. There is a special closeness between those who have shared a bed, a war or a Japanese bath.

Back at the house Ayako said, 'You are tired. You should go to bed. I must go now to Tenko-san.'

I looked surprised, for it was well after nine; but she said, 'Tenko-san is not so strong now. He is very old; so I go each night to give him strength. When I first came to Itto-en I was very weak and delicate. An old lady in the community, who was a healer, made me better. She gave me strength and taught me how to pass it on to others. There are different

149

methods but for Tenko-san I use my palms... I place my palms over his vital organs and concentrate on giving him strength.'

I asked if she did not find it exhausting, every night, after a working day that started at four a.m.

'Oh yes, it is very tiring; but someone else gives me strength, you see. There are a number of healers in the village; we help each other, so no one becomes really exhausted.'

'Where do they get their strength from? Someone must start the circuit.'

'Oh yes,' she said, 'That is true. The strength comes from God.'

I got into bed and fell asleep but soon woke, feeling feverish. The typhoon rattled the windows, rain battered the glass. When I slept I had nightmares. I thought I heard a bell tolling; then clappers that seemed to go past our building.

I put on the light and began to read Tenko-san's autobiography, which Ayako had lent me. It was all very strange, the fever, the typhoon outside and the thought that I was here and would soon meet this man who is called the modern St Francis of Assisi, the Tolstoy, the Gandhi of Japan. He must be a giant of strength to have given up everything for poverty, humility and selfless service.

About midnight, above the sound of the wind, I heard the clappers again, very slow, very close, then fading away. It was vaguely reassuring, a reminder that someone else was awake on this rather frightening night.

In the morning I felt weak but somewhat better. Since it was Sunday there was no early service and the families, who normally eat in the dining-hall, were cooking and eating at home.

The building where I was staying is new, simple and comfortable. Ayako and her room-mate, Nobo-san, sleep on the left of the guest-room, and on the other side is a pleasant

150

European sitting-room and a kitchen. Downstairs are *benjos* and a washroom, and a knitting-school where girls sit all day at machines making intricate garments.

Next door a printing press produces Itto-en's own publications. Down at the gate-house is the post office; up the hill the school, museum, library and *Reido*.

All is set in a beautiful garden made by Tenko-san and his followers. Little lanes lead up the hill between the houses and apartments where the community live, ending in bamboo and forest and the hills of Yamashina.

Normally Ayako takes most of her meals in the dining-hall but for visitors and at week-ends she cooks at the apartment, collecting supplies from the main kitchen. Today she had invited her senior English class to meet me at lunch, so after breakfast we took a large basin each and went to shop for supplies.

In the big kitchen next to the meal-hall men were dealing out from piles of vegetables, fruit, bread, eggs, pickles, and dried or tinned foods. All the customers carried basins or baskets, all were absorbed in their choosing but without fuss or hurry. Everyone smiled. No prices were asked, no money paid over. You took what you wanted, it was free, it belonged to all.

Ayako reached out and helped herself, piling the food in our basins. We were going to make vegetable *tempura*, with hot rice and soup from the village kitchen.

At home we cut up the vegetables, dipped them in batter, fried them in hot oil and lifted them out with chopsticks to drain on paper. We put two low tables together and sat round them on cushions, with bowls of golden *tempura* down the centre.

When the visitors came they were shy, smiling, eager, yet embarrassed and nervous about trying their English. Lunch began with a prayer and before each fresh helping of food people put their hands together in the *gassho*, quite unconsciously, as though it were second nature.

As we started a pixy-like little man hurried in and squeezed

151

down between two of the students. His hair was shaved almost to the bone and he seemed to be quite without teeth. Though his skin was ivory, facial bones and features had a northern look. His eyes were extraordinary, hazel-brown, radiantly glowing.

He was very spritely, talking and laughing, champing heartily with his gums; yet without interrupting his gay chatter his palms flew together before each helping, and he dropped his head briefly but very reverently. Ayako introduced him as Mr Somekawa, who heated the public *o-furo*. She said he would be having his meals with us while his wife was away.

Though some of the shy students were clearly dying to practise their English they giggled each time I spoke to them, but presently one of the boys began addressing me cautiously. He had been away from the community for some time, he explained, at the farm of Harry Thompsen, the Danish missionary who wrote of Itto-en in his book *New Religions of Japan*. This had been a wonderful opportunity to improve his English and learn many things. Mr Thompsen was a very fine man.

The others also started speaking, carefully and well but with embarrassed titters. The only one without shyness was the pixy man. He said, 'Hul-lo!' 'Good-bay!' 'Sank you!' and when I uttered a few words of Japanese joined his fists above his head and cried '*Banzai*, Nassi-san.'

The boy beside me confessed he would like to be an engineer, but when I suggested it was a good way to travel, looked bashful and said, 'I sink I stay here.'

'But wouldn't you like to see the world?' I asked innocently.

Embarrassed, he did not answer. Ayako explained: 'The Elders will decide his future. He will do the work they feel is most needed for the community.'

When Somekawa-san had finished eating he bent his head over his empty bowl, then got up. He bowed, smiled, and spoke to Ayako. She looked concerned.

'Somekawa-san says you are ill, Nancy-san. Are you ill?'

152

'Of course not.'

'Yes, yes, he says you are not well. He knows, he can tell. He is a healer.'

'But I'm all right.'

I felt the healer's eyes on me. They were glowing with a strangely affectionate softness and a quite dazzling radiance.

'If you like he will give you treatment after supper tonight, to make you better.'

I asked what kind of treatment.

'His own kind. Not like anyone else's; but it will make you better. He knows you are sick.'

I said no more. Though I had been talking and laughing I felt terrible. The fever had come back, with nausea, and my head throbbed. It was wonderful to give in.

That evening Somekawa-san began the treatment. He was now quite changed, had withdrawn into himself; yet at the same time seemed emptied out, his own personality thrust aside, as though become entirely receptive. I felt he no longer saw me as a person.

All his movements were quick and light, his thin dry little body charged with energy. He moved the table aside and signed I was to lie face down on the *futon* Ayako had spread. He rested his hand on my shoulder-blade and spoke. Ayako translated.

'It is your liver. Your liver had an illness. It recovered but now it is tired.'

I was startled. How did he know I had had hepatitis? With his hand on my back he began muttering.

'Your liver is tired because it is not used to Japanese food.'

'But I like Japanese food!' I said indignantly.

'Maybe you like it but your liver is not yet used to it. Soon it will be; but now it is tired. It has also had a chill. Maybe in the typhoon. You should rest.'

That was all I wanted to do. Keeping his hand on my shoulder, Somekawa-san muttered on.

'You are really healthy and strong; but now you are very tired. Too much travelling, too much chill. You must rest. Then you will recover.'

He began to prod, thump, slap my back, still talking to himself. His method was certainly brisk. The sudden digs were like electric shocks. He seemed to be working up and down the spine, perhaps on the central nervous system, for a slow flood of well-being, warmth and relaxation was moving through my whole body. It was not imagination; I was too apathetic, sick and indolent for wishful thinking.

From time to time he rested his hand on me and paused, as though listening; then he would say '*Korei! Korei wa! Korei wa!*' and follow up with a stab or thump. I asked what *Korei wa* meant.

'It means "this". "This one".'

When he had worked his way up and down spine and legs, neck and shoulder-blades I turned over and he prodded, smoothed, chopped and thumped at shoulders, ribs, solar plexus and knees. I kept my eyes shut, not knowing or caring how he worked. From the first charged contact I had complete faith in the treatment. The malaise was lifting, though my head still throbbed, I still felt feverish.

Now there was an impression of shadows passing swiftly before my closed eyes. Every nerve in my brain was suddenly alive, electric charges were coursing through my skull. The healer, mumbling to himself, had not touched my head. When, with an effort, I opened my eyes, I saw he was making passes with stiffened fingers stretched towards my face as though literally bombarding me with electric vibrations. My eyes closed again – I could not keep them open – and suddenly there came an extraordinary feeling of lightness moving up to the top of the brain, culminating in an almost bursting sensation. It was like the yoga description of *Opening of The Thousand-petalled Lotus Towards Infinity*.

The relief was dramatic. Oppression, lethargy, fever, nausea, all were gone. I felt liberated, invigorated, light as air, intensely

154

peaceful and happy. I lay still, infatuated with the *ease* in my head.

'*Hup!*' said Somekawa-san suddenly, brushing me down violently from head to foot as though sweeping away a pile of rubbish.

I opened my eyes. He was looking at me enquiringly.

'He says how do you feel?' said Ayako.

'Better; much better. Wonderful!'

He grinned and shook my hand and laughed, throwing back his head.

'He will come tomorrow. Every day you are here he will give you a treatment.'

'*Sayonara*,' said the healer. He put his palms together and was gone.

That night I slept peacefully, without nightmares or fever.*

---

*Like the Gilbertese, most Japanese have an instinctive talent for healing massage. In trains you see them pounding or kneading their own or each other's muscles and maids in *ryokans* often massage your shoulders if you look tired.

13

The Light that is not Two

It was dark and wet when I got up at five on Monday morning, stumbled sleepily down to the washroom and out to join Ayako. A church bell was ringing as we walked up the narrow street in the warm wet dusk. In through a door, hushed, almost secretly, slipping off rain-boots, we joined the silent queue, up the stairs, along passages so dark we must grope our way. Through my socks I felt the slippery shine of stair-treads I could not see, the smooth polished boards of the corridors along which I followed, like a somnambulist, past sombre doors and dimly-seen rooms and from time to time grey-green circular plaques, strangely alive, strangely three-dimensional. At one point a disinfectant smell suggested *benjos*; in an alcove, large coloured thread-balls in a glass case; a great drum; then Ayako turned into a doorway and bowed low and we were in the prayer-hall.

We waited, sitting back on our heels, as the others entered, pale sleep-walkers, with eyes half closed, hands pushed into kimono sleeves; and now I heard a distant chanting, droning, continuous, muffled, that seemed to come from below. It was eerie, vaguely remembered, known from a dream, slurred and low-pitched, intensifying rather than breaking the *Reido's* enclosed silence, as the sound of bees heightens the stillness of hot summer afternoons.

In this meek, waiting hush, suddenly, stunning the unprepared senses, the great drum outside the door stirred—*slow—deep—measured*—vibrations swelling out from a centre, out and round, very solemn and stern and compelling, each prolonged circling-out sound accorded full value, time to penetrate into human consciousness and awaken the deepest response, to reach its ultimate destination in the waves of silence before the next blow on the stretched skin.

Then the strokes became closer together, each beginning before the last had finished, so new vibrations and old fell on each other and mingled and mounted, creating a tension that grew in excitement. At first it was short and rhythmical like a shunting train, then urgent and louder and stronger and faster and shorter and shorter, furious, stertorous, like a wild grunting animal, and walls shook and there was a sense of violence let loose and whirling and threatening and shattering and utter destruction. Then abruptly silence again.

The Elders filed in, ghostly, hands folded. With clappers and little drums the service began.

Aum! A—um! Aaa—um! Arms raised, intoning. *Aum!* Arms up, across, out, down . . . *Aum!* Arms forward, up, out, down . . . palms up, forward . . . palms together, to the chest in prayer, then down to touch the floor. Facing the altar, twice turned the other way, twice again to the altar . . . *Aum* . . . the strange cry, like a wild bird, the sacred syllable, Mother of all Sounds.*

Each worshipper stood, eyes closed, absorbed in a private communion so deep there was no sense of human presence, all faces wearing the sightless indifference of serious illness or

---

* The movements are reminiscent of *Surya Namaskar*, Greeting to the Rising Sun, in Hatha Yoga.

closeness to death, the wiped-out expression of utter with-drawal.

It was strange, yet not out of place, to hear a harmonium. The plaintive reedy sigh, the sustained blurry note, like the droning of *sutras,* the not quite accurate stumbling fingers were in keeping with the innocent, sexless, slightly off-key singing. Then chanting began like a ticking clock, the rhythm changing to that of several clocks not quite synchronised. It was Tenko-san's testament, *One Fact of Life.*

The final chant was quiet and slow. Clappers sounded. Still chanting, the Elders led the way out of the hall and, chanting, hands in prayer, we followed through the dim corridors, past the drum, the coloured thread-balls, the disinfectant smell, the round grey-green plaques now seen as windows framing glistening trunks and leaves, on and on, two notes in a minor key, monotonous, hypnotic, haunting, without end or beginning. As we moved the sound drooped, became vague, almost died, revived and came strongly again; one note; then up to the second, repeated five times... on and on through the long dim corridors, the now twilit room where figures in white overalls stood, hands in prayer, on, down, still chanting. I walked in a strange confused dream. Was I drugged and in hospital, on my way to the theatre at dawn? Was I asleep? Was I dead perhaps, in a shadowless half-lit world?

At the foot of the last staircase I found the dining-hall entrance, where earlier we had left our rain-boots. We had come back to our starting point. Still chanting we took our bowls and chopsticks tied up in napkins from the pigeonholes on the wall, paused in the doorway to bow, and entered the hall. The chanting continued till we were seated at long low tables set with large pots of rice, soup, pickles, tea-kettles. Then clappers sounded; another *sutra* began.

This was much faster and brisker. Ayako chanted eagerly, hands together high before her face, her little body almost shaking with intensity. Still chanting, we served food to each

158

other, then palms flew together again as the chant went on. After that we ate in silence, passing and offering, making the *gassho* before and after each helping. When tea had been drunk, soup- and rice-pots were taken to the kitchen, then we washed our chopsticks and bowls in cold water, wiped them, tied them up in our cotton napkins with the chopsticks thrust through the knot. At the doorway we turned and bowed our thanks, put our bowls in their pigeon-holes, slipped into shoes and quietly left the building.

Every day Somekawa comes to give me treatment. I sit or stand obediently while he chops down on my shoulders, smacks at knees and ankles, dabs at my ribs. A deep *rapport* has quickly developed. We are old friends. His pixy-like humour and extraordinary intuition overcome any shortage of language. I call him O-furo-san, since he is in charge of the bath, but his real work is healing. He treats about fifteen cases each day, often walking many kilometres to patients outside the village. He is over seventy, thin as a rake, yet never seems tired or despondent. The radiant eyes that illumine his wrinkled face send out charges of vital happiness. He lives by spirit; he is all spirit, his spare little body no more than a means of moving about on this earth; but it is a gay spirit, all cheerfulness, humour and kindliness.

'*Korei wa! Korei wa!*' I say, meeting him in the village. '*Hup!*'

He grins with delight and cries '*Banzai! Banzai,* Nassi-san!' But when he works there is no joking. Sometimes I watch him healing others, always with his eyes tightly shut, as though listening, always his own personality emptied out. Thumps, bangs, kneading along the spine, sharp dabs with stiffened fingers on top of the head, passes across forehead and eyes; and in each case, I see on the faces the peace I have experienced.

When he puts his hand on an affected part it is as though he receives a communication. At first his hands seemed to have

159

their own life; then I realised that they are directed, instruments of a universal power. He has become a channel. 'Becoming a channel' applies to many forms of spiritual healing, including yoga healing techniques; but O-furo-san's method is individual. As he works he mutters unceasingly to himself, diagnosing the condition, or – between blows – commenting with surprise or interest ('*So-so-so!*') At times he seems to be praying.

'Soon,' Ayako translated to me one day. 'He says soon. Your subconscious mind is growing clearer all the time.' (*Bang-bang-bang.*) 'Soon you will experience heaven and earth without difficulty.'

'Where do you get your knowledge?' I asked him.

'It comes from God.'

'But he understands the body,' I said to Ayako. 'He knows anatomy. He must have studied.'

'No. O-furo-san has had no education at all. He was the son of a very poor man who made boxes for packing fish. He joined Tenko-san nearly forty years ago and has worked with him ever since.'

'But how did he become a healer?'

'He is a very spiritual man. For ten years he used to get up every morning at two or three o'clock and go to a small temple where he practised *Nembutsu* (repeating the name of Amida Buddha). Then he chanted *dharani* in the Shingon sect, and finally his small ego was broken into no-self. He got spiritual insight. He found he had power to heal. He is a spiritual healer. He has been doing this service for fifteen years. He works very hard, very violently, but feels scarcely any fatigue.'

When I asked O-furo-san where he got his strength and power he said again, 'From God,' speaking lovingly, as of a generous intimate friend. He always speaks of God – Heaven – Light – in this way, rather gratefully and tenderly; and when he makes the *gassho* at meals you know he is really offering thanks, really regards the food as a gift.

His appetite varies. Sometimes he eats nothing; at others he

160

champs down several bowls of rice, then finishes up what I have left.

'How much rice do you eat, O-furo-san?'

'Sometimes nothing.'

'But you should eat. You need food to give you strength for your work.'

'My strength doesn't come from food. It comes from heaven and earth.'

There is more than a touch of monastic life at Itto-en . . . the eating bowls wrapped in a napkin, taken out for the meal in the communal hall; the long low tables, the chanting, the simple food, the silent eating. At Itto-en the monastery diet of rice, pickles and tea is supplemented by barley with rice, by soup and vegetables cooked in fish stock for flavour and strength. Like many Zen communities, Itto-en is self-sufficient; it grows and prepares its own food, prints its own paper, has its own educational facilities. It is democratic – the master works as hard as the members. All are busy, all cheerful. There is no waste of time or materials; life is simplified to the utmost and private possessions reduced to the minimum, less for austerity than to give maximum spiritual freedom.

Zen has a saying, 'A day of no working is a day of no eating.' At Itto-en everyone pulls their weight; there are no passengers.

I was not to clean *benjos* after all; the time for this service had just passed. But since I wanted to do some kind of work I was to help sweep the gardens each morning and give English lessons.

Sweeping never came to an end. Every morning a fresh harvest of leaves lay on the gravel paths. Immediately after breakfast the soft *ssh*-ing sound of the sweepers and rakers began. It was peaceful and pleasant. Villagers crunched past on their way to and from their work, smiling and bowing and making the *gassho*. By the end of my session, when we stopped for *o-cha*, I felt their good will had brushed off on me, I was warmed by accumulated beams from their luminous eyes. This beneficence penetrated the lethargy and depression of the days when I felt ill. Aching, feverish, I would pause by the pond where coloured fish weaved through maple trees and through my form leaning on a garden broom, till sensing my presence they slid away.

Though always wet – three typhoons drenched us while I was there – the gardens are exquisite ... ponds, streams, water-falls, bridges, stone lanterns and gravel paths, and everywhere trees, trees, trees, avenues of cherry and maple and ginko. Here and there are small lawns, arbours for meditation; a Buddhist bell; the church bell. Before a little shrine to the dead the stone figures of Tenko-san and his wife, Sogetsu-san, make their way across the lawn, going out to give service. They wear *mompei* and carry bowls and seem to be living. Something of Tenko-san's spirit must have entered the sculptor, Seibo Kitamura; the work is so moving, so simple, so true and the faces have all the sweetness, strength and humility of the real Tenko-san.*

When Ayako called to take me to see Tenko-san I felt nerv-ous and shy. I knew I must thank him for letting me stay at Itto-en but what did one say to a spiritual giant, the founder of a new religion, one whose life and teaching are based on selflessness? I had never encountered a saint. Would there be profound discussions, far above my head, penetrating questions into my purpose, my contribution to the community's work; would I find a rarified spirit or, as some visitors had hinted, an empty shell, a man already losing touch with life?

It was raining again. With our blue rubber boots, our yellow oiled paper umbrellas we walked through the wet garden, over stone bridges and little streams, along a winding path to a house among trees. At the entrance a sweet-faced woman greeted us, a baby boy scrambled out curiously.

'Tenko-san's grandson. Tenko-san's daughter-in-law,' said Ayako, bowing and smiling.

She went in. I hesitated, but she turned back and beckoned,

* Tenko-san died some months after this book was finished.

and entering I forgot my diffidence. A pair of eyes were twinkling at me, kindly, full of wry humour. Tenko-san sat at a low table near the window with his face in the light; relaxed, leaning against a back-rest, a handsome old gentleman with a well-shaped head. At first glance, in his dark kimono, he could be any well-loved, well-cared-for grandfather. The humorous eyes immediately take attention from the rest of the face; then you see the quality that is never caught in photographs...a calm sadness and resignation, patience and sweetness, strength and humility. The face is gentle, yet I could believe, as Ayako had said, that it could be very stern. There is a slight resemblance to the portrait of Zen Master Ikkyu, in Suzuki's *Zen and Japanese Culture*, but it is finer, smoother, calmer. It is a man's face, a noble face and its essence is absolute peace.

It must be this combination that has made him so loved. Great goodness and spiritual strength inspire admiration and respect, but it is the humorous eyes, the kindly turn to the lips that bring love.

What did this spiritual giant ask me? He asked if they had given me enough breakfast; if I could eat Japanese food. If I hadn't had enough, if I didn't like the food I was to tell Ayako and she would fix it. Where had I been in Japan? Was I not afraid of travelling alone? Where did I live in Australia...my home...my family? How did I manage, not knowing the language?

My answers, translated by Ayako, seemed to divert him. I showed how I talk with hands, shoulders, face. When he laughed he lifted his shoulders and pursed his lips with a sort of inner amusement.

'He says he knows you,' Ayako said. 'He says he has known you before.'

I knew him too, as I knew O-furo-san, though I had not seen either before. It was the old friendship you sometimes find in the most unexpected people, in the strangest parts of the world.

Tea came, and cakes. We sipped, smiled, talked. I looked at

163

Tenko-san's hand holding one of mine – now soft and transparent, with brown marks, light and dry as a leaf – and
thought of the work it had done; I looked at the beautiful face
smiling down at the little grandson and thought of the colossal
inner strength by which this man had lived.

'Give her a chocolate,' said Tenko-san, and when Ayako had
brought out the box, 'Take another. Go on ... take some more.'

We sat, eating chocolates, looking at photographs. For all
the grey drizzle outside the room was full of light and homely
laughter. Little wind-chimes rang above our heads; the baby
grandson tottered and rolled. He and Tenko-san seemed to
share a humorous bond of understanding, catching each other's
eye, chuckling at private jokes.

'When you go home,' Ayako translated, 'take a photograph
of your father—' (the same age as Tenko-san) '—and send it.
He wishes to hear all about your father ... and he would like
to send your father his picture and his respects.'

As we left, Tenko-san's eyes twinkled. To Ayako he said,
'See she gets enough to eat, she looks thin!' and to me, 'Come
again. Come and see me again.'

After I left Itto-en people asked me about Tenko-san, and I
remembered that he is considered the greatest religious personality in Japan. 'He is a world figure ...' 'He was elected to the
Diet and was a member for six years ...' 'He tried to introduce
a Bill of Repentance for the Nation after the war ...' 'People
come from all over the world to see him ...'

It is true; but it seems to count less than that a great man,
at the end of his life, could be so tranquil, innocent and
humble, with such kind, merry eyes.

Whenever Ayako is not teaching or healing or doing things
for others, she comes to find me and we go for walks round the
village, along the canal, to the mushroom farm, the vegetable
gardens, the Folk Art Museum and the library. We have been
to visit a potter down the lane towards Yamashina, to take tea

164

with an artist, Tetsuya Seki, and his wife Hisaka, who live on the hill above Itto-en in a house quite buried in trees. Tetsuya-san designs and prints materials for special kimono, for weddings and ceremonies.

When we pass villagers on our walks Ayako and they put their hands together in the *gassho* gesture and bow. I have learned to do the same. People also smile at each other with quiet affection. They wear rather drab working clothes and their faces are often plain, worn, tired, but their eyes are like soft-glowing lamps. I have never seen so many luminous eyes. Here you see only the essence; the shell doesn't count.

Ayako has been explaining to me about Tenko-san and Itto-en. In the community there is now a new generation growing up. A number of the original members have intermarried and the children are being brought up to the Itto-en way of life, educated at the Itto-en schools. Ayako says the young people are very much in demand with employers outside the community because they are honest, hard-working, selfless and peaceable. They never quarrel.

When I asked if Itto-en people never disagree she said, 'Of course they do. We are not sheep, we have differences of opinion. But it never develops into a row, because someone always gives in. You can't have a one-sided quarrel. If one says "Forgive me, I'm wrong," usually the other also apologises. Nothing is ever gained by quarrelling. Even if you win, you lose in another sense. Tenko-san says this in *One Cup of Water*. If there are two men dying of thirst and only enough water for one, and both snatch at the cup, it will be spilt, no one will get any; but if one gives way, then a miracle may happen. The winner's heart may be softened and they may share. Some people think this is impossible; but it is the way we try to live.'

I said it was very uncommon but not unknown in the west. I mentioned Sir Philip Sidney.

'Ah so! Yes. Tenko-san does not claim to be inventing something new but only trying to show that it can work. He tries to

165

show the truth through example. But he does not call Itto-en a "new religion" as some people say; he calls it a way of life. He believes that "in having nothing lies inexhaustible wealth"; yet "though he holds no idea of acquiring possession, he enjoys production". These are sayings from his writing, *One Fact of Life* which we recite at our service.'

'Does no one really own anything here? Do you really live from day to day?'

'We do not own anything because everything belongs to everyone. In a way, of course, we make plans for tomorrow, for the work we must do; but in our hearts we are living from day to day. We accept whatever comes and do what needs to be done. We are taught to serve with no thought of remuneration. Things will be provided when they are needed.'

In the community there are no private incomes or salaries. Those who work at jobs outside the village turn in their pay to the common fund. Everyone has five hundred yen (ten shillings sterling) a month pocket-money '... for little things ... for stamps, to buy cakes and fruit for presents. For many years it was only three yen. Then it became a hundred, then three hundred, as the yen value changed.' Ayako says, 'Why should we need money when everything is provided ... food, housing, clothes? If I need rain-boots or a new coat I get them from the community, I don't have to buy. We have everything we could ever need, and this beautiful garden to live in.'

In the beginning Tenko-san and his followers were literally homeless: they slept on the roadside, in shrines or temples; but about forty years ago a very rich man made over twenty-five acres of land at Yamashina and the village was built. The village is called Kosenrin. The name comes from three Chinese characters meaning 'light' 'spring' and 'wood', but people often call the place Itto-en.

'Itto-en, which means the Garden of One Light, is our ideal, our spiritual aim.

'Tenko-san teaches we must never regard it as ours, as our property, or as permanent. It is a night's lodging ... a shelter

166

provided by Light. It all belongs to Light, to no one yet to
everyone.'

'Until he became so frail, every year, on New Year's Eve,
Tenko-san would leave the village and go back to his *roto*
(homeless) life. If the community wished him back they must
go and find him and ask him to return. They usually found him
cleaning a shrine, on the morning of New Year's Day; but
since he is not so strong he goes to a friend's house in Kyoto
and waits there.'

But the village is only a centre. All over Japan thousands of
people try to follow Itto-en ideals. They are Friends of Light
and include businessmen, doctors, scholars, lawyers, working
people of all kinds.

'Many are very distinguished. Many do things to help us.
For instance, here our children can be educated from kindergarten to university. In the community we have kindergarten
and primary school-teachers but our high school and university
teachers are Kyoto people who do this work without payment,
as their service to Light.

'Businessmen help too. Many firms send their employees
here for a short training in Itto-en ideals. We have this training
course for a few days every month. The young people come
here and live and work with us, they go out and render service
with the members of the community, emptying the toilets. We
call this *Rokuman Gyogan*. It means prayer in action.'

One day Ayako took me to the building where the *Swa Raj*,
Itto-en's two theatrical troupes, live when they are home. It
was empty. The players are rarely there. They travel all over
the country performing dramas and plays that incorporate
Itto-en teachings, particularly in reform schools and prisons.

Another afternoon she slid back my *shoji* and said, 'I am
going to walk up the hill. Would you like to come with me?'

Since she had a *furoshiki* containing plates and food I asked
who lived there.

'No one. There is a shrine there to departed spirits. I try to
go every day to make an offering.'

'Is it Buddhist or Shinto?'

She smiled. 'Perhaps it is both. There is only one Light.'

Beyond the school and the houses a small path and steps wind up through bushes and trees. We slithered on wet clay, wet shrubs brushing our shoulders; but the rain had ceased and when we reached the top rich shafts of light were shining out upon mountains and plain.

There is a little red shrine among the trees, Shinto in colour but containing the figure of Vimalakirti, the Buddhist philosopher. Ayako lit candles, burnt incense and prayed. From her *furoshiki* she took two china dishes and on them arranged piles of magnificent apples. She was very serious, very absorbed, very serene. It was less a dutiful rite than preparing a meal for beloved friends.

Below was a tranquil scene. Hills and fields glistened, the roofs of Yamashina were dark against the green of rice. In a pale washed sky a new moon floated. Reprieved from the rain, birds whispered. In the lacy bamboo a cricket ran up his trills, up ... up ... up.

After Tenko-san had been living his homeless life of service for some years a Kyoto businessman offered him a tiny house. It was the size of three mats – six feet by nine – and here he and his wife slept when not out on the roads. This little hut is now at Kosenrin. It is used by newly married couples in the community who stay there until they have a baby and need more space.

Ayako took me to see it, among the bamboos, then to the slightly bigger house in which Tenko-san and about twenty of his followers slept and prayed before the days of the community.

As we stood in the one simple room of this little house – now used by Itto-en bachelors – a door at the back opened and a man came forward, smiling. Behind, in a kitchen, a smiling woman was busy with cooking pots.

Ayako introduced us.

168

'This is Mr Panino, one of our Elders. He was one of Tenko-san's earliest followers.'

Panino-san wore dark blue working clothes. He was straight and slim with a face of extraordinary beauty. There was great tenderness in the tranquil smile, great happiness in the glowing eyes. Pale, no longer young, touched with transparency, the fine features were illuminated from within.

Peace came with him. He seemed to move in a calm benevolence. I wanted to float, to soak in his serenity.

Ayako related my story. '*Ah, so desuka,*' he said at intervals. '*So desuka.*'

He asked me about language. I said I had enough to get round with and sometimes I found it best that way. People's hearts come through more clearly when they can't talk too much.

'*So-so.*' We all agreed about that and he laughed when I commented on what the Japanese can do with the syllable '*So!*' But mainly I just stood while the others talked, absorbing as much as I could of his peace and serenity.

'Panino-san is a Shinshu priest. He first read of Tenko-san in the paper when he was only sixteen, and wanted to join him. Later he was in charge of a very large temple,' Ayako said as we walked away. 'He gave it over to his sister and joined Tenko-san fifty years ago. He is the humblest person in the community.'

Because Tenko-san teaches there is only one Light, the essence of all true religion, there is complete personal religious freedom at Itto-en, and as well as the Shinshu priest there is a Baptist minister among the Elders. In the morning a church bell rings for service, in the evening a temple bell. In his teachings and writings Tenko-san uses the New Testament as well as Buddhist *sutras*.

'In our services we have the Lord's Prayer and the sermon on the mount,' Ayako says. 'And we celebrate Christ's birthday as well as the Buddha's.'

*

169

Yesterday Ayako took me to see the Elders in meditation. Each morning in the dark *Reido* my skin roughens at the far-away chant buried under the ground. When I asked where it came from Ayako said, 'It is the Elders. They meditate before the morning service.'

Following her down the dark stairs my scalp prickled, there was the half fearful anticipation of going down into a crypt, catacomb, vault, any place shut off from the sun, where the air smells enclosed and of musty reminders of death and decay, though here overlaid with the sweetness of incense.

At a doorway beneath the *Reido* we stopped. In a square dim-lit windowless room, on a deep shelf or platform, three motionless figures, three pale carved images sat in meditation, eyes closed – sculptures hidden for centuries in Tibetan caves. I felt awe and a little chill and a strange fear that the waxen immobile faces were no longer living and dust was gathering on the dark robes. Such utter withdrawal was eerie. Only the shells were here, left behind, as empty as those discarded at death.

A little bell rang. There was a kind of terror and shock – as though an idol had spoken, a corpse moved – when the figures began chanting a *sutra*, eyes still closed, low, droning, sustained, as in sleep.

Ayako touched my arm. We moved away and up the long corridors where the great drum was pounding out through the dusk.

Every evening the temple bell sounds about nine o'clock. I thought it was a curfew but Ayako tells me that in the days before Kosenrin a bell rang at night to call the little community together, to pray for safe lodgings for those on the road. It is still rung to remind them of those days, and for prayers for members working away from the village.

The clappers I hear at nine, and again about midnight, are those of the nightwatchman telling us that all is well.

14

Warmed from a Sunset

ONE DAY, walking down to Yamashina, I passed a striking young girl. She was tallish and slim with creamy skin and thick short hair, cut with a fringe. There was a touch of worldly chic, almost of wildness about her, most unusual at Itto-en.

She looked at me searchingly as she passed, then turned back and spoke rapidly, excitedly in Japanese. She kept touching my shoulder, repeating the same words, almost urgently.

At last I said in Japanese that I didn't understand. She let me go and went on up to the village.

Often out walking with Ayako I noticed this girl hovering, and one day as we came back to the apartment she shot out from the knitting-school downstairs and wished us good afternoon. She hung about looking hopeful and followed us into the hall. There was something pathetic about her, like a puppy that tries to get indoors without being noticed.

Next day she appeared again at the front door so quickly I

guessed she must have been waiting. I was puzzled. She seemed so out of place, so different, almost defiant. At breakfast she would stare at me across the table, earnestly. She seemed weighed down with some kind of muffled despair. She popped out from corners as I passed and haunted the front door so often I asked Ayako who she was.

'She is a girl who has come here to live, to learn knitting. Her name is Yoriko. We often have young people for training. She goes to the knitting-school. Her parents think it is good for her to be with Tenko-san.'

She seemed reluctant to say more; but remembering the girl's intense stare, her dog-like following, her blind determination about something I did not understand, I said, 'Why does she follow me?'

'She wants you to teach her English.'

'Is that all? Why didn't you tell me?'

'She must not be a bother to you.'

'But I don't mind. Tell her it's all right.'

Ayako looked relieved.

'But you must send her away if she stays too long and becomes a nuisance.'

That night the girl appeared with an exercise book and a red-covered text book. She sat down at my table, opened her book and said carefully, in a deep voice with an American accent, 'Excuse me please. I . . . lurrn . . . English.'

'Where are you learning? Who is teaching you?'

'I teach myself. I lurrn ladio. I lead this book. I listen ladio, lead book.'

If she had taken the trouble to teach herself from the wireless she deserved to be helped. She began laboriously reading aloud from her text book. Her doggedness, her desire to learn were touching and I knew I should never be able to send her away after half-hour sessions.

Each evening she came with her books and we struggled with pronunciation.

'A-lound the corner.'

172

'A-round the corner.'
'A-lound the corner.'
'A-rrround . . . rrrr.'
'A-lllound . . . lllll.'
Eyes fixed on my face she tried faithfully to copy but it never came right.
'A red pencil.'
'A led pencil.'
'No no . . . a red pencil. A rrred lllead pencil.'
'A lled llead pencil.'
There was something maddening about her, yet I could not ignore her mournful insistence. Her voice was strangely deep and husky for a Japanese girl.
'Nancy-san,' she would sigh. 'Excuse me, I'm sorry Nancy-san'; and again, 'A-lound the corner.'
She was always saying 'I'm sorry' as though accustomed to being at fault.
Gradually communication improved. She was intelligent, she just needed practice. She told me, looking surly, that she stayed with an *obasan* in the village and did not like Itto-en. When I said 'What about Tenko-san?' her face lightened with affection. She said, 'Tenko-san very good, very good man. Isayama-san very good. I like Tenko-san. I like Isayama-san. Very kind.'
Her home was on the Inland Sea, near Hiroshima.
'You know Hiroshima? NO MORE HIROSHIMA. You heard about that? No more Hiroshima! No more war! You will go to Hiroshima?'
'Yes. Next month.'
Her face lightened again.
'Ah! When you come Hiroshima come my home. My parents say "Well-come Nancy-san." Come my home. My home Shingon temple. My father Shingon priest. My sister Yoshiko very good girl, speaking good English. My family say "Well-come, Nancy-san".'
As time went on she became more confiding.

173

'My father send me here because Tenko-san good man. I Bad Girl.' She looked thunderous. 'Everyone say Bad Girl!'

'Nonsense! Why?'

'Because *I ... go ... my ... way!*'

'But you're a good girl, Hiroshima-san.'

'Good girl Tenko-san, Isayama-san, Nancy-san. Other people ... Bad Girl. Bad girl at home. Send me Osaka. Bad girl Osaka. Send me Tenko-san. Tenko-san very good man. Bad Girl! I Go My Way! Now I learn English. Come Nancy-san's country. See the world like Nancy-san. United States Paris I come.'

'Doing what?'

'*Dessin.* Make *dessin.*' She began sketching clothes. 'Make *dessin* ... go Paris, USA, California my uncle. Say "Well-come Yoriko!" First, I learn English.'

She had it all worked out. With her looks, talent, determination and intelligence she would probably bring it off.

'Tonight I go Kyoto. Joypol Sartoro. You come?'

'Who?'

'Joypol Sartoro. Sartoro! *Francais!*' She waved a book of Sartre.

'Do you understand it?'

'*Hai.* Read in Japanese. Joypol Sartoro, tonight speak Kyoto.'

If she wasn't going to hear Jean-Paul Sartoro she was off to the Heian Shrine gardens or to visit a *maiko* friend in Gion, who was learning to be a *geisha.* She sighed enviously.

'My friend learn Japanese dance and singing. I play guitar. I sing folk songs. You know—?' She sang in her deep sexy voice:

> Where are all the flowers gone?
> Long time passing ...
> Where have all the flowers gone?
> Long long ago ...

'Don't you sing Japanese songs?'

'No. I sing American folk song. My boyfriend likes. My boyfriend sailor-boy. Gone away. Gone to sea!'

174

'American?'

'*Not* American!! Japanese boy.'

Well, at least that was something.

By now we were friends. She came for lessons, dropped in and sat meekly silent while others talked. She had strength, an explosive quality that awaited direction, that might flare into anything; yet she was oddly innocent, oddly devout. One night as she sat trying to draw me, struggling with Ls and Rs, the temple bell tolled outside. She immediately put down her pencil, folded her hands and bowed her head.

'Finish work,' she said. 'It is time to play.'

Across the fields from Kosenrin is the rag-pickers' village where the pigs are kept. Tramps, wanderers, the homeless and penniless may stay here free, with two meals as well as a bed, in return for helping with the pigs. In the days of unemployment there were often as many as twenty-five homeless a day but now, with more prosperity in the country, hardly anyone comes.

Though there are no tramps the pigs are still there, squealing and snorting and smelling atrocious. I met Mr and Mrs Susuki, who look after the village, and had tea with them in their office. They are both middle-aged, short, plain and humbly dressed, but their faces are full of kindness, they glow steadily, quietly, with the same peace and still happiness as Panino-san, the Shinshu priest.

They invited me to join them in meditation, which they have at their house every morning at half-past four and to which Ayako often goes.

During the night the rain returned and when I woke at four it was dark. I dressed quickly, with eyes shut, and soon Ayako tapped on the *shoji*. We crept out from the warm building, the silent sleeping vibrations of Nobo-san in the next room, into a stone-coloured twilight. It was not cold and the wind had died. It was strangely beautiful, the ashen light, the sound of running gutters and insects enjoying the soft insistent rain, the

175

darkened houses and narrow streets. High up, a window of yellow light suggested warmth and the comfort of sleep, in utter contrast to this drenched unawakened world where we walked, hushed, as though sharing a secret with the runnels and weighted-down leaves and hedges and drumming sounds on paper umbrellas, the grey-green scents of freshness, the night's harvest of rain.

The light burning outside the Susukis' house looked weak and left-on-all-night, against the strengthening sky. Inside, the building held a silence that neither waited, expected, demanded, resisted nor welcomed. It was the silence of *absence*. The air was warm, informed with breath and sleep and the smell of incense. Upstairs in the dim room we took *zabutons* from a low shelf under the window. I became aware of, rather than saw, two motionless figures in the dark corners.

A small lamp glowed on an altar; behind, a circular window framed three-dimensional grey columns.

The quality of absence I had felt flowed from this room. The two figures were present only in body, as the Elders had been that other morning; yet there was no chill, no rejection. The little trickles and gurgles outside, the gutters, the gentle hiss of rain, the happy creak of insects sealed us in together, emphasising our warm isolation. I felt wrapped round, not imprisoned but embraced.

In the dusk, the living tree-trunks in the window, so close, glistening, alive, were strangely disturbing, as though a god were watching. These circles of wet green trunks in different parts of Itto-en might be the essence of trees, a distillation of every forest that ever grew; a reminder that beyond the warm dusky room, shut in from the rain, there is a primeval world of which we are only a fractional part.

Long afterwards one of the figures moved silently, bowed to the altar, head to *tatami*, put away its *zabuton* and left the room.

Presently the temple bell began to boom. It reverberated through the dark room. It ceased. There was only the soft sound of water again.

176

Ainu house

Ainu coats

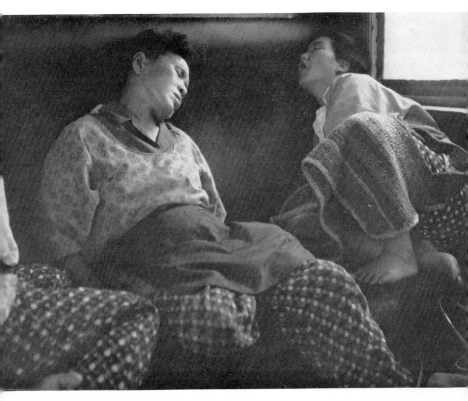

Second-class travel

Women of Sado

Kyoto Zen Temple gardener

At Chotokuin:
O Cho San and Mrs Ogata

At Itto-en: O-furo-san

At Itto-en: Tenko-san

Ayako Isayama-san, of
Tenko-san and Ayako-san
go out to give service

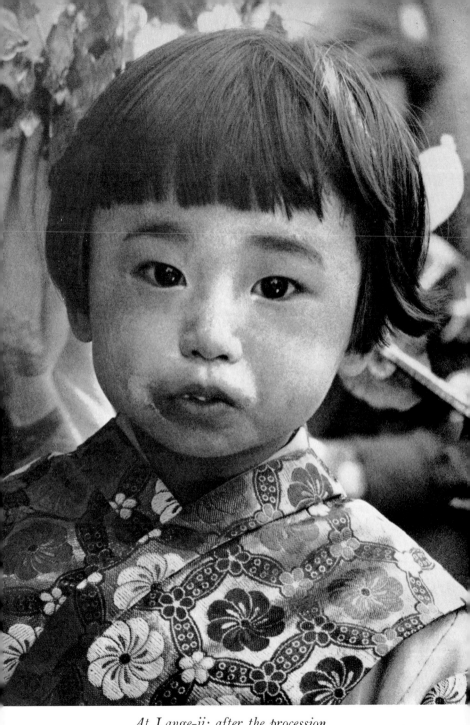

At Lange-ji: after the procession

Seto Naikai: Hakata

House on Innoshima

Harvest time: in Shikoku

At Takachiho, in Kyushu

In the mountains of Takachiho

Then the church bell rang, chiming, innocent. We bowed to the altar, put away our cushions and padded downstairs. Outside, morning struggled through an overcast sky. *Getas* sounded on cobblestones. Pale women with sleep-touched eyes, drowsy children came from doorways to start the day.

At Itto-en the children do not have separate birthdays or receive presents. All those born in the same month celebrate their birthday together by cooking and serving lunch at the school to their mothers and teachers.

This month the birthday fell on the day of the autumn equinox, *Higan*, when the dead are believed to be very close. There was to be a service after the children's lunch-party.

In the morning I went to help clean O-furo-san's house. Though it seemed to me spotless we swept, dusted, washed and polished floors, walls, stairs till he was satisfied. The upstairs rooms were attractive, plain and bare with *tatami* and beautiful old iron-bound polished chests set one upon the other. On one, at a little shrine, O-furo-san had set out small cups of tea and little cakes as offerings to the dead.

Since the day was a holiday the children spent the morning preparing lunch, round a huge tub of cooked rice, making *Inari-sushi*, rather like making mud-pies. In the classroom, desks were put together to make long tables, each place set with chopsticks, a tea-cup, fruit, cakes and a large plate of *sushi* and vegetables. After the meal the mothers wrapped up and took away what they had not eaten. The children waited on us, smiling and bowing as though we were giving them a great treat.

After lunch we gathered on the lawn below the stone figures of Tenko-san and Sogetsu-san. Today the shrine doors were open, for inside are the ashes of Itto-en's dead. We stood under our umbrellas while rain drizzled down and the Elders led us in prayer. Presently the umbrellas moved on up the hill towards the little shrine at the top. At the foot of the winding path we stopped to pray where two bamboo vases of flowers were hung on a post. A year before, a group of young men working here were caught in a landslide. Two were buried alive.

'We heard the earth rushing down,' Ayako said. 'But when we got here it was too late. The boys were smothered.'

The umbrellas went on up the narrow path, rubber boots slipping and splashing on sodden clay steps. The little red shrine was open. Candles and fruit were set there and incense burning. More incense was lit; then prayers, one hand holding the umbrella, the other making half-*gassho* against the handle. It was solemn and reverent yet very matter of fact. There was a sense of affectionate friendliness for the dead, still real and close though no longer visible. No one seemed to mind my being there or gave any sign of regarding me as an intruder.

I have forgotten I am in Japan, in a foreign country, that my skin and features are not the same as those round me. Differences do not exist. There are only people and we are all brothers and sisters.

By the pool below the little shrine with Tenko-san's statue is a summer-house for resting or meditating. When I went there last evening at dusk I did not at first see the middle-aged woman sitting back on her heels, hands folded, her whole form expressing resignation. I knew from Ayako that she had just lost a son and wondered if I should withdraw; but as I hesitated she took the cushion she sat on and silently handed it to me with a bow.

I bowed, signing I could not accept, but graciously she insisted. She did not speak but her gestures, head movements, whole inclining body expressed quiet welcome. I felt wrapped round by loving kindness, as when I find Ayako has put my shoes ready for me after church or washed my muddy thongs.

We sat in the summer-house by the pond while it grew dark. The rain stopped; clouds moved from above the black

178

trees, stars shone back from the water. In the pond a lantern reflected a long spindle of light. Little frogs began to mutter.

It is strange to live among people who have no possessions, yet who seem perfectly happy. It is also strange to mix with those who have received enlightenment. Though they laugh, talk, joke quite normally you sense a still centre, a quiet core. They are alive and a part of life yet detached; warm and human yet withdrawn. Their peace and serenity brush off on you. You leave them touched by their glow, warmed as from watching a sunset.

When Tenko-san's name is mentioned here people get a particular look in their eyes, rather as O-furo-san does when he speaks of God. They adore their leader, yet appear more protective than reverent towards him.

Ayako's hands seem as though they want all the time to be flying together in prayer. I do not think she is conscious of this, it is as though they have a life and will of their own, to give praise and show gratitude for her happiness. I have never seen anyone hold their hands in prayer with such extraordinary fervour, such ardent *joyful* wholeheartedness. She prays and chants in the same way, as though *this* is the moment she has waited for impatiently all day, all her life; and in the *sutras* her voice is the clearest, strongest, most tireless, the voice of a leader, not in the sense of physical domination but as one who shows the way, goes first, cannot wait in her eagerness. Her frail little body is a channel of immense spiritual strength.

I often think of the work those hands do during a day... starting at half-past four, praying, teaching, cooking, helping, ending late at night by passing strength to Tenko-san. Today I watched her working on O-furo-san. She 'swept' him from head to foot with astonishing power in her tiny hands; then massaged different muscles, closing her fingers round them, seeming to grip, almost rub them.

My own life here is punctuated by her constant acts of

179

kindness. Coming out of the *Reido* or from meals I find my kicked-off thongs set ready for me to put on, my forgotten chopsticks returned to my pigeon-hole outside the dining-hall. Rubber boots, oiled paper umbrellas are always put out for me at the entrance. Instinctively she anticipates wishes and needs. I am anxious to fit in and give no trouble, ready to eat what the others eat, but she often suggests meals at home so we may have toast instead of rice, fish instead of root vegetables, and fruit appears just when I long for it most. She always smiles, never seems annoyed, never in a hurry.

Sometimes I feel such a fraud, literally unworthy to be among these people at all. This comes on from time to time when I am alone but rarely when I am with them because, oblivious of any differences, they do nothing to evoke it. I know I should never be good enough to live in this community, that I would not pass Tenko-san's tests, with my worldliness, selfishness, love of freedom, yet among the others I forget my shortcomings because no one sits in judgement.

During the day I sweep up leaves, give English lessons, help at odd jobs, walk to Yamashina or along the canal and talk to the people. Squalls and tempests keep tearing across the village as typhoons follow each other. The green hills vanish, trees bend down with water, roads turn to mud; then the rain lifts, mists descend, steam rises from the ground.

My lessons consist of helping pronunciation and trying to encourage shy pupils to speak. They know quite a lot of English but have no chance to practise. When they do speak it is earnestly, with American touches learnt from their text books:

'Have you a dog?'

'Yes, I do have a dog.'

The teenagers are charming but most enchanting are the babies who giggle and hopefully call out the wrong names when you hold up a picture card.

Sometimes I join in morning physical exercises up at the school. These take place in the open to recorded instructions and music. Adults and children bend, stretch, jump and twist together.

I have also helped in the daily school cleaning. Each morning four boys and four girls, sometimes with teachers, sweep and scrub the entire school ... corridors, classrooms, washrooms and *benjos*, from floor to ceiling. It is all done quickly, cheerfully, efficiently and with great vigour. The children are brought up to service and selflessness.

Every day we have visitors at the guest apartment; people are always dropping in for a cup of *o-cha*. One day when I felt an *unexpressed* longing for honey, Akira Nakata, in charge of trainees, appeared at the door with a large jar of delicious honey from his own hives, tasting of flowers. Yoshio Harakawa comes and talks about Kyushu. He has given me records of old songs from Takachiho, which he says I must visit; Hisako Seki, the artist's wife from up the hill, brought me a *furoshiki*, designed and printed by her husband, and every day there is Hiroshima-san with her English book, O-furo-san with his treatments.

Bang-bang-bang-bang. 'Hup!' '*Korei!*' Prod-prod-prod. Eyes closed, the ceaseless mutter, the dabbing hands, electrical charges shooting through my head, the cloud dispersing, the weight lifting. O-furo-san, working on me, driving out the malaise, the lethargy, the depression.

I had felt so much better after the first treatments but a couple of days later seemed to relapse.

Lunch here is often boiled pumpkin or turnip and rice but one day there was a green vegetable which I mistook for spinach. I helped myself lavishly and though the flavour was rather like vicious wild garlic, ate it all.

An hour or so later I woke from siesta dripping with sweat, shivering with fever, head splitting, face flaming. From lips to stomach my alimentary canal seemed scraped with ground glass; linings felt inflamed, membranes seared. I lay on my *futon* longing to die, too confused to get up.

181

'You are sick,' said Ayako. 'We will get O-furo-san.'

He came and crouched, silent, palm flat below my ribs, head bent as though listening. He muttered, '*Korei, korei*,' then suddenly, '*Nida!*'

'Ah!' said Ayako. 'Did you eat a green vegetable today at lunch?'

'Yes. It was rather strong.'

'It is a good vegetable. We call it *nida*. We take it to keep our insides regular. How much did you eat?'

'A plateful.'

She held up her hands.

'Oh NO! But we take only a tiny bit. Too strong! Too strong for you. Too strong even for us if we eat too much.'

O-furo-san said nothing, keeping his dry little palm on my stomach. I began to feel a comforting glow but my head still ached. I longed for him to work on it but did not like to ask, since he had dropped his other work to come; but as though he knew, he began making his dabs at my skull, his lightning passes before my closed eyes. Again the heavy pain dwindled and shrank and dispersed.

'Now you will sleep,' Ayako translated. 'You will be well in the morning.'

And in the morning I was.

When I said I wished to do something for O-furo-san Ayako mentioned he wanted part of his garden weeded.

The morning I appeared for work O-furo-san said '*Ha!*', smiled, bowed politely and handed me a little weeding-tool. He indicated a pathway beside the canal which to my eye, though apparently not to a Japanese, seemed very tidy. We must root out everything so he could plant azaleas.

I squatted down and started to dig but suddenly, saying '*Chotto matte*', he scuttled away. He came back with working gloves and insisted I put them on.

A light drizzle began as we chipped and dug. He suggested I stop but when I said No he grinned, raised his clenched fist and said '*Banzai!*' We went on. Mist came down from the hills, the ground grew sodden, women came out to take in washing. Somewhere nearby, the canal or a drain or a cesspool smelt rather strong. Little stones cut into my knees where I knelt and my hair was in wet straggles, but I was completely happy.

One day I took the camera to work.

'O-furo-san!' I said suddenly. He looked up, grinning, as I took the picture. But the photographs show just a cheerful little old Japanese man. The lens caught only his face; his spirit eluded me.

I have been to say good-bye to Tenko-san. Last time I went he seemed very tired, rather absent, and sat silently as though patiently waiting, but today he was gay. He reminded me about the photograph of my father and told me not to forget to take his good wishes. He even remembers my father's age.

I do not know what I felt when I said good-bye. I do not expect I shall ever see him again, yet this does not matter at all, though I have grown so terribly fond of him. Whatever it is that I feel does not depend upon meeting again.

Everyone came to see me off. I embraced O-furo-san, both with tears in our eyes. To my surprise Ayako and Hiroshima-san came in the taxi with me to Yamashina. It was pouring again. Ayako seemed astonished when I kissed her at the ticket barrier. Hiroshima-san came on the platform to carry my bag. When I came here I knew no one. Now I feel I am leaving a family.

15

A Saint in Samadhi

WHEN Ayako Isayama heard I was going to Koya-san, the sacred mountain south of Osaka, she immediately wrote to a friend living there, a Shingon nun she had known at university.

This mountain-top, with its monastery and fifty-two temples, is the headquarters of Shingon Buddhism. The settlement was established by Kobo Daishi, an extraordinary ninth century priest, who not only founded the Shingon sect but was famous as scholar, writer and teacher, artist, calligrapher, educator and man of action, loved and respected by emperors and common men. Of all his feats the founding of the monastic community on this remote mountain peak is the most astonishing, increasingly marvellous as you make your way there.

How did he reach it, in the first place? Legend says he was shown the way by a huntsman (a god in disguise) and his dog; but even with gods to help, fighting a way through the forests, up the titanic mountain sides, is still a fantastic achievement.

184

These days you go by car or bus, or from Mamba station in Osaka, in a small corridor train with blue plush seats and neither *benjo* nor food-vendors. Beyond Osaka suburbs the single line runs through a narrow valley by a winding stream, through cultivated and forested hills to the mountains. It is an enchanting train – very intimate, very much a local. Leaves and fruit brush the windows; pale yellow pears, orange persimmons hang within reach. You can hear the faint tinkle of bird-frightening bells in orchards. The dark-leaved plants, outlining the banked-up rice-fields, are splashed with spidery coral lilies, called *manjushage*, flowers associated with cemeteries, I am told. I do not know if they grow here by accident, if they are to ward off birds, or the Japanese being what they are, to give colour and contrast in this almond and spinach-green landscape.

At Koyashita, where the climb into the mountains begins, we take on a new driver with a voice like a *Nôh* chanter. The little train struggles and strains in and out of short tunnels, up the sides of the mountain. Now we are leaving the valley of red lilies and yellow rice, the slopes of matted convolvulus vines and saucer-shaped terraces, ascending through villages whose grey roofs glisten with rain, and volcanic forests of cypress and bamboo, cedar and red-trunked pine. As we climb and wind, climb and wind I look down through streaming windows over saturated green leaves to the olive-grey river and across to high cultivated hills. Though mountainous, it is not alpine. There is the softness, the vines which blanket the jagged peaks, the hint of poetic melancholy I have found in other Japanese mountains, even the Alps, at this time of year. I wonder if snow would bring the diamond clarity of Europe's Alps or if this country's mountains are always mysterious, always withholding?

We continue to climb; we enter tunnels; the rain seeps down. Ahead, soft threads of mist garland the trees. The *Nôh* chanter begins to intone: *KAWya-san! KAWya-san!* The train glides into a station and stops.

185

I got out with a handful of country people in sweaters and coats. The air was cold. On the right a flight of steps led up to a cable-car. I could see nothing but a high mountain with its top hidden in mist. Suddenly, Koya-san became immensely exciting, as mysterious, as strange as a peak in Tibet.

The cable-car had seats upholstered in thick mustard velvet, set in ascending rows. The *obasans* and workmen took their places calmly, as though in a bus. Simmering, I sat at the wide rear-window from which I could look down as we rose.

A voice said, '*Hai dozo* ...' The door shut, the car began to move. There was no grinding or swooping or rushing; only a quiet vibration, a gliding. The earth fell away, not as in a plane, nor as in any other cable-car, funicular, ropeway, chair-lift or flying-fox of my experience. We did not swing out and over; we *ascended*, straight up, vertically, like angels in a film. There was a sense of *Up*, above the station-roof, through the house-tops, up, up, towards the trees on the mountain-side, through the trees, past the trees; among, then past their twisted trunks, through their wet leaves and out above them into the mist. Through swirling veils we looked down on the tops of the mountain forests, speckled with red, out and down to the slopes below and across to the opposite peaks. Surely we could not go higher! We approached the peaks, we were *among* the peaks, level with them on the skyline. It grew colder; the air bit the ankles; the ears popped; incoming breath stung; and still we ascended, straight up, up, up. The rain dripped. Now, far below, a sheer drop into a sea of mist, of dimly-perceived trees. We were out of the world, hanging above a great chasm. A chill mist wreathed the windows as though we had floated through clouds.

The cable-car stopped. The doors opened, we scrambled out and up the steps to the ticket barrier. Without a flicker of excitement the locals moved off to a waiting bus.

Outside the station, misty rain persisted. Shivering, I sought a place to change into warm clothes and found only an all-purpose *benjo* with gents' specials round the walls. My dress

186

was off when the first male client entered and faced into the white-tiled recess. Three others used the facilities as I changed but so naturally that I did not feel *de trop*. They bowed on leaving, hands still doing up flies.

When I came out, the bus to the town had gone. A taxi drove me for miles round the side of the mountain, winding and curving through fine rain, with magnificent pines and cypresses above and below.

Ayako's Shingon nun works at the girls' high school. As we passed through the little town I saw temple walls, the deep green of cryptomeria, beautiful roofs, a vermilion pagoda, a scarlet bridge and a lake. Deep-toned Buddhist bells were tolling. There were scents of damp earth and trees, of ancient buildings and incense and burning leaves. A pearly light hung over Koya-san. Smoke rose straight up on the quiet air. The mountain's breath was suspended.

At the school the driver put out my bags and tapped smartly on the wall. A young man appeared, said '*Ah! Miyake! Chotto matte, kudesai,*' and was gone. The taxi-driver exposed his gold teeth reassuringly, bowed and drove off.

The young man returned with a blushing, giggling school-girl who bowed and helped me off with my coat, either para-lysed with shyness or knowing no English. She could not understand me, nor could the other girls who now appeared. Each time I spoke they went into paroxysms, hand before mouth, like the chorus of *The Mikado*; but so merrily that I laughed with them. They led me to a large room with a desk and patted a sofa. I sat down. We all smiled. I said 'Miyake-san?' They said she was coming. When I asked if they spoke English they went into convulsions again.

After they had retired several people looked in, smiled, asked me to *Chotto matte*, bowed and went away. It was a businesslike room with a telephone, ashtrays and cigarettes on the desk. I wondered if Shingon nuns smoked; I began to form a picture of Sister Miyake – stout, strong-faced, spectacled – and hoped she would not object to my red stretchy pants.

187

Then the door burst open and a girl came in at a rush. Tiny, pale, with delicate features and perfect teeth she danced lightly towards me, gesturing with little white hands, chattering beautiful English.

'I am so *sor-ry* to keep you waiting! I was at a meeting! Did the girls look after you? I could not get away! You must be *starving!*'

So gay, so youthful and full of vitality, I did not notice that her hair, cut like a boy's, was speckled with grey. She wore a white robe and a wooden rosary round her neck. She talked quickly, in her eagerness almost impatient with words.

'So! So! So! Ah! Ah! Ah! So!' Staccato bursts, flashing teeth, sparkling eyes, little hands flying.

'I must leave you again for a minute... Excuse me. I am terribly sorry. I'll be back. You would like some lunch? Good good... I will send. Wait. I'll be back.'

The door opened gently. Sister Miyake introduced the dignified gentleman gliding in.

'Our headmaster. This is his study. I will not be long.'

The headmaster bowed gravely and sat down as though he had no other work but to entertain stray foreign women. Though he said very shyly that he did not speak English he gradually began to talk.

'Australia, Ah so!' Then, to my astonishment, with a note of slight reproof, 'Dawn Fraser. Olympic Games.'

I remembered there had been an Incident: Australians had behaved badly. It was mortifying to hear it here years later, from this scholarly creature.

We talked in his limited English, my still more limited Japanese about English and Japanese literature. When I spoke of my interest in *haiku*, my love of Bashô, his face lightened and he grew so enthusiastic I hoped he might forget about Dawn Fraser.

'So!'

Sister Miyake skimmed in, scarcely touching the floor, followed by a girl with sweet rolls and bottles of coffee.

188

On the sofa, when the headmaster had gone, the little nun fanned herself.

'Today is a crisis! I have been down at the printers, checking proofs. We are working against time. I have undertaken to produce a booklet on Koya-san and it is late, late, *late*! If it doesn't go off today it will not be out when it is needed!'

She smiled as though it were rather amusing to be so harassed; but did not hide her relief when I assured her I did not need looking after.

'Splendid! Marvellous! Then I can see you when I've finished at four o'clock.'

She munched, drank from her bottle, smiled, nodded. '*So-so-so-so!*' '*So-so-so-Mah!*' When she spoke of Koya-san she became radiant.

'I adore every minute here. When I have to go to Toyko, even Osaka for a few hours, I cannot wait to get back.'

After lunch she put a black kimono over her white robes and little white half-goloshes over the front of her *geta*. We took a taxi to Henjosen temple, which is also the youth hostel. Apart from the little triangular sign outside there is nothing to show this . . . no bicycles, rows of shoes, no institutional touch. The courtyard is well cared-for, the interior as calm and restful as Chotokuin. There is a small office, a long washing-room and many well-kept *benjos*. Koya-san is not a sacred mountain of flea-ridden monasteries with inedible food. Hundreds of pilgrims come every year and stay in the beautiful temples, some of which have exquisite wall-paintings and provide excellent service. Officially there are no charges, but, Sister Miyake said, guests are expected to make a donation.

The hostel was empty. The priest was out but an assistant took my bag and said formalities could wait. Sister Miyake led me down the road to the Treasure House.

'Now! Most of Koya-san's best paintings, most valuable works of art are in this museum. Because of fire, you see. The temples are always burning down. Safer to keep our treasures under one roof.'

189

'But if the museum burns down you will lose them all at once.'

'So! But we are very careful that the Treasure House *doesn't* burn down! We take very special precautions, always watching. There is even no electricity. Too many fires...we lost our lovely pagoda...now we have a concrete one...No, it's better under one roof. Imagine trying to save things in dozens of temples all at once! So! Enjoy yourself. See you at four!'

She pattered away, jangling her rosary beads, swinging her black umbrella.

In a deep soft twilight I wandered among Bosch-like scenes ...black gods surrounded by flames, scarlet and gold *boddhisattvas* with lotus feet, magnificent *mandalas* woven or painted in blue, red, terracotta, ochre. Buddha entered Nirvana while all living creatures wept round him; Buddha ascended to paradise attended by trailing clouds and *boddhisattvas*. In this dim frustrating cavern, where poor lighting is aggravated by reflections on protective glass, there is absolute peace and no sense of time. The calm smooth impassive faces, the rounded majestic forms seem very Chinese, very remote, imperturbable, almost abstractions, so passive, so idealised. You would never expect to meet them out in the world; but in the more typically Japanese paintings the people are real, there is life and vitality, even humour. Two exquisite horizontal scrolls in fresh vivid colours showing incidents from the life of St Kobo (including his meeting with the huntsman and dog) have an immediacy, an informality, a powerful simplicity that kept me glued to their long glass cases while pilgrims shuffled past and attendants gave me faintly uneasy glances. Here were living people and dogs, horses, *samurais*; even the coloured-faced gods looked alive.

A guide led a handful of pilgrims through the shadows. His voice was subdued, almost a whisper. Rosaries rattled, coins clinked before the saint whose aid was besought. Here and there a figure in white, with mushroom hat, remained crouched on the floor praying, while the others moved on.

The St Kobo scrolls, Sister Miyake told me, have been locked up for hundreds of years and were only recently brought out for display. Protected so long from the light, the colours are stunningly fresh; and the paintings, so carefully hidden, have retained all their original force. The Japanese believe that constant exposure to the public gaze robs works of art of their inner power.

Grey walls, dark trees; deep Buddhist bells, vibrating solemnly; clappers and gongs; drums beating insistently, rhythmically, hypnotically; incense drifting, the sound of *getas* on gravel or stones, the flash of saffron robes, of smooth-shaven heads. At sunrise, lights still burning in the great square, I wander by the lake with the scarlet bridge and Shinto shrine. A deep bell booms at long intervals. The sun shines out between crypto-merias, catching the scarlet pagoda, the green-mossed roofs of the holy *Meido*, the ancient *Fudo-do*. A priest crosses the square in white with a mustard-gold cloak, a rich subtle luxuri-ous colour, far removed from the crude saffron of cotton robes. Though such shocks of beauty come constantly in Japan, it is always the first time.

In clear sunny weather, under pale typhoon-washed autumn skies, the mountain is dazzling, exciting, stimulating; but more beautiful still when the mists rise, the grey sky descends almost within reach, fine Irish rain powders skin and hair and the air smells of cypress and wood-smoke, of damp earth and water. Monochrome colouring, the hint of swift-falling dusk and majestic melancholy are most fitting, for the sacred mountain is a great tomb, where dead from all over the country are brought to lie near St Kobo, in graves or as ashes. But though the saint is here, in his mausoleum, his followers do not believe he is dead. For over eleven hundred years he has been sitting in *samadhi*, awaiting the arrival of Maitreya, the Buddha of the future, when he will wake to greet mankind's final saviour.

Beyond the little mountain town, past the beautiful temples, over a wooden bridge, the walk to St Kobo begins. For a mile and a half, graves, monuments crowd together on mossy slopes, in leafy glades, and through them the pale path leads, up and down shallow steps and over small bridges, on and on, through the dead, beneath an avenue of noble, magnificent cryptomerias, so high, so dark that there is no sky. I am the only living human. Shall I ever come to the end of this path? Shall I walk for ever through these pale trunks, these groves of tombstones, stupas, pagodas, chortens, *boddhisattvas*, Jizos, stone phalluses, totems and lanterns? It is not very late but the constant twilight is deepening. It grows dark. Rain begins, I hear it on leaves and ferns, but nothing penetrates the sombre shapes above my head.

Grey and green, grey and green ... grey stone, grey trunks, grey path, grey rain; green grass, green moss, green leaves all shining and dripping. The sound of water, the smell of damp rotting leaves. The only colour, the only message from life the leaf-sprays in beer-bottles on graves, the scarlet caps and aprons on Jizos, even on shapeless stones. Are these primitive Jizos or *koshin* – stones that protect?

I have been walking for ages. My rubber boots make soft flopping sounds. From time to time I leave the path and plough up a hillside to look at a grave, stirring up mushroom smells as I go. Some of the *boddhisattvas* look utterly bored and fed-up, out there in the rain, others seem quite worn out, leaning their cheeks resignedly on their hands. The Jizos are better company. The plump jovial ones with aprons tied on like bibs might be just sitting down to a meal. Others seem to peer or leer; others again have no faces at all, all smooth and worn away.

It is like the poem by the thirteenth century priest Jakuren:

> The drops of pattering rain
> Are not dry on the cypress leaves
> Before trailing mists swirl
> On an autumn evening.

One cannot ask loneliness
How or where it starts
On the cypress-mountain.
Autumn evening.

I think about *sabi*. I do not feel it in this necropolis; too
majestic, too immense, too tangible; yet despite all the thousands of dead it is not macabre or forbidding, like Turkish
Ottoman mausoleums. There is only peace and benevolence –
the atmosphere of all St Kobo's shrines, no matter where; as
though his own presence pervades them.

Now there are shrine buildings, a bridge and wide steps. A
smell of incense; white paper twists tied on trees, wooden inscribed tablets set like a picket-fence in a little waterfall,
dozens of *boddhisattvas* in a row and among the graves a man
pouring a cup of hot tea for a Jizo ('Oh yes, the dead like hot
tea', says Sister Miyake. 'They also like cakes and sweets.') At
the top of the steps, a great hall with thousands of brass lanterns gleaming, for the dead who want to be close to St Kobo,
and through an open side door a dazzling glimpse – deep red
carpet laid over *tatami*, gleaming wood floor, black-and-white
shoji, the glimmer of brass lamps, rich saffron robes flung over
a black lacquer kimono stand; a pile of scarlet *zabuton*.

Behind the great hall, St Kobo's little thatched mausoleum
stands in a sea of stones with stone lanterns and the bronze
vases and bronze lotus I so dislike. Incense burns before an
octagonal building wherein lie the ashes of thousands of
fortunate faithful. Before St Kobo's tomb, immense perfumed
cauldrons smoke endlessly and faces are turned towards him,
humbly, hopefully, wistfully, tragically, imploringly.

'*So! So-so-so-so! Mah!*' said Sister Miyake as we squelched
through the mud and I told her about my stay at Itto-en. We
paused and sat on a damp stone. She had taken me into Konko-
buji, the Temple of the Diamond Mountain, the headquarters
of the Koya-san Shingon sect; we had looked at the new

concrete pagoda which she does not like; the little *Fudo-do*, the oldest building in Koya-san, with each of its four sides different; the *Meido*, with exquisite mossy roof of cypress bark and its portrait of St Kobo, so sacred that it is never shown. We had crossed the scarlet bridge over the lake and looked at the Shinto shrine. She had explained many things, answered many questions about Koya-san, St Kobo, the Shingon sect. She was so gay, so alert, so alive I forgot she was a nun on a sacred Japanese mountain. Quick tongue and clever brain, fine pale features and mischievous eyes reminded me of a Chilean friend with whom I giggle and chatter in much the same way; yet her background is full of tragedy.

'Till about fifty years ago women were not allowed at Koya-san, not even to come on the mountain. It is still hard to become a nun here.'

'How did you manage it?'

'My family were very good Buddhists, very devout. I had always thought I would like to be a nun. When I was twelve my mother died and I was very unhappy. I wanted to give up the world, but my father would not permit it. He felt I should finish my education and get married. So I stayed at school; then I went to the university and studied Chinese literature. That was in Tokyo. My home was in Kanda – not far from the Russian Nikolai church. But now Koya-san is my home. Here I have my house, my work, my religion. What else do I need? *Anoné*... If we sit on this cold stone too long we will be sorry.'

We wandered on into the mist.

'But how *did* you become a nun?'

'Well... when I left university I got married. I had a baby. Then the war came. It was a bad time. Suddenly, in the space of one year, I lost everything – my husband, my ten-months-old baby, my father, my brother. I had one brother left. The following year I lost him too. I was quite alone.

'I did not want to go on living. I decided to withdraw from the world, to be a nun. I tried to enter Koya-san but they would not have me. They feared it was only because I was so

194

unhappy, that I might change my mind afterwards. They advised me not to rush into it while I was in such an emotional state. They sent me away. I was very unhappy; but I was still determined.

'I had to do something to keep myself occupied, so I went to the Women's Christian College in Tokyo and studied English and English literature. This is where I met Ayako Isayama-san. But I never gave up the idea of coming here. I studied and studied and prepared myself and after ten years I came back to Koya-san and sought entrance. This time I was allowed to stay. They realised I was serious.'

I thought of Ayako's determination to join Tenko-san.

Sister Miyake began to smile and clap her little hands which had been rubbing her rosary beads.

'I underwent the most rigid training. It was so strenuous I became quite ill.'

'What did you have to do?'

She laughed as at delicious memories. 'Oh ... meditating all night; pouring cold water over myself at midnight ... that sort of thing. My health broke down. But I persisted. Finally I finished my training and was accepted. My health is good now because I'm so happy.'

'What do you do all the time?'

She laughed very merrily.

'Work, of course. I work very hard, teaching English at the high school. Seven years I've been doing it. I will stay here till I die. I've never been so happy in my whole life.'

Across the road among trees and lawns is a small dove-grey temple with three white *shoji*, like a soft little Georgian house with white shutters. I hung about it, fascinated, not liking to trespass but longing to see inside. One morning its bell began tolling at five o'clock and going out into the chilly dawn I saw priests and monks in white hurrying up the road. They were entering the temple ground in double-file, white shapes against grey roofs and green mossy lawns, mossy roofs and walls. In the garden a monk in black pushed the bell with a great wooden battering ram, timing it at spaced intervals, peering round to see who was coming. He looked immensely old, rather crude and arboreal against the shaven white-robed monks.

I slid through the gates to the green dewy garden, enchanted to get in at last. The monks had gone inside the temple, rows of black and white *getas* were lined across the entrance and I could see white figures moving, kneeling beyond the open *shoji*. Now several dignitaries in green robes with black caps appeared on the little veranda and knelt at the doorway. Believing my presence known I had made no attempt to hide and realised too late that I should not be there. The old bellringer, looking appalled, gestured sternly for me to leave. I bowed and withdrew, disappointed; yet if I had stayed hidden I doubt if the monks' devotions would have suffered.

In youth hostels you have to look after yourself. You go to the kitchen to eat or collect your food, take back your tray and wash up your dishes. You make your own bed and put it away in the morning. You often sweep and tidy before you leave; but at Henjosen I was treated more like a privileged guest then a hosteller, perhaps because the priest's son was Sister Miyake's pupil.

Though a party of female pilgrims arrived, I was not expected to sleep with them. They took over one of the big rooms, while I had a smaller one at the back with a view of the garden, where I could hear the life of Koya-san. At night, beneath piled covers, I woke to the bells, solemn, reminding, echoing but never sinister, never threatening, not even admonishing. I would think of the *Duomo* in Florence, of St Paul's, under the dome, the sound sinking down, down, down, as though through water. It is easy to understand the belief that these deep-toned bells bring comfort to the dead.

✻

Sister Miyake came to dinner bringing bean-jelly cakes and a soft white-and-purple *furoshiki*. We sat at the low table drinking *o-cha* and eating the cakes till *o-furo* was ready. With darkness the mountain-top grew very cold and I shivered on my long trek to the bath.

Our supper was excellent.

'Are you a vegetarian?'

'Yes. If you don't want that I'll eat it.' She reached out and took the turnip and taro I had left. 'I love them, but yams are my favourite food. So easy to cook and eat. I am so busy, you see. No time. And I love yams. I more or less live on them.'

It became colder. We wrapped ourselves in bed-covers. Sister Miyake clicked and rubbed her rosary beads and talked of her life, her work, Koya-san, St Kobo, Shingon Buddhism. The priest and his family went to bed, the pilgrims turned in. The temple grew silent. The cold dark-green stillness of midnight in the mountains stole up the streets and pressed against the closed *shoji*. Bundled up in our bedclothes we talked on, about yoga, Tantrism, mysticism, Shingon ritual, *mantras*, *mandalas* and *mudras* in Shingon and yoga, while the great bells sounded outside.

When I left, Koya-san was radiant. The air nipped the skin, exhilarating, exciting as I stood by the road in the clear light, eating *sembei*. On Sister Miyake's advice I was taking a local bus down the mountain to Hashimoto, too early for the temple breakfast.

I was the sole passenger. This was very different to the ascension through the mist. Beyond the *Daimon*, Koya-san's great entrance gate, we launched out at once upon an ocean of petrified waves, obliquely lit with sun-shafts, dyed with turning leaves. All was sharp, brilliant as we swung above the earth. Rounding corners we seemed to fly out into space, above mountain-peaks outlined in gold that receded into the farthest distance. Far beneath us, deep narrow crevasses smoked with rising mist. We swooped low above a vast soft choppy sea, we

197

raced on the top of the heights, on the very crest of the spurs with visibility to the end of the world. I was quite drunk with excitement. Even inside the rattling bus, dazzled by stabbing shafts of light, there was a sense of absolute freedom; liberation. I wanted to shout, to jump out, to spring into this limitless beauty. This was the way to die.

But now it was changing; no less beautiful but no longer superlative, elemental, pure spirit. As high up as possible the rice terraces start, the hand of man tames the landscape. Looking down to the valleys it was now an aerial photograph. I was a passenger after all, not an eagle.

The bus filled with workmen and schoolchildren, brown, ruddy, smiling. Country women in *mompei* and head-scarves waved from the roadside. People were climbing incredible heights, harvesting isolated rice patches. The river curved far below, trees appeared softer under convolvulus vines. Bamboo and green leafy trees replaced pines and cypress and cryptomeria. Soon came tiled or thatched black-and-white houses, in steps up the hillside, red lilies in almond-yellow terraces, sinister scarecrows leaning about in the rice.

It was beautiful still, but I was on earth again.

16

Tonosho

COMING DOWN from Tokyo, with clean clothes and a bag so far innocent of folk toys or pottery, I looked at the Inland Sea on my map and gloated. I had been away from the water too long; now I was going to drift from island to island, in brilliant sunshine, across a blue silky sea, day after day. The question was, where to start.

Seto Naikai, the Inland Sea, which is a national park, stretches from Kobe to Beppu, on Kyushu, and as the train left Kobe I looked eagerly for the Aegean scenery I expected. A thick stuffy haze covered Kobe and the coast. I consulted my map. There was a large island, Shodashima, fairly close to Hinase, a small town on the sea, which might be a fishing port.

I left the train at Hinase. It was indeed a fishing port – it smelt entirely of fish – and was wrapped in a turgid cloud. The grey sea was greasy and seemed to sweat; there was no air to breathe. In my queer little *ryokan* I lay sleepless, fighting mosquitoes, embalmed in *essence de benjo*, feeling Hinase a bad mistake.

The men at the railway, the *ryokan* host had assured me there were boats to Shodashima; that it was a beautiful island where olives grew. But when I went to the quay in the morning, something seemed to be wrong.

Though the boat was there, exceedingly small, no one was going aboard; in fact people were coming off, looking dejected, moving resignedly to the station. As I approached a frantic little man rushed up waving his arms. No *funé*, no boat, he shouted in Japanese, and when I gestured at the boat, said vehemently it was not going. He kept repeating 'Shodashima? Shodashima? Shodashima?' and I kept replying '*Hai hai hai*' but we did not get much further. He grew quite frenzied when I attempted to cross the gangplank. A youth appeared on deck and waved me back. The boat wasn't going; there was a fog. I must take the *densha* along the coast to Okayama where presumably there was a bigger boat and no fog.

I had just sat down and pulled out my book when I felt a tug at my arm. It was the little man from the quay, eyes blazing, teeth bared. He was making desperate gestures towards the road, saying '*Basu! Basu!*'

I didn't want to take the bus. I had resigned myself to the train. I said '*Densha!*' He said, '*Basu!*' I said '*Densha!*' He said '*Basu!*' The waiting passengers began to join in. A bus was coming instantly, if I hurried we could catch it. It would reach Okayama long before the *densha*, take us right to the *funé* for Tonosho, on Shodashima.

But I didn't want to go to Tonosho; I wanted to go to Obi, on the other side of the island. Never mind, they shouted. Get the boat to Tonosho, then a bus to Obi – Tonosho, Tonosho, *funé* ... *basu* ... Obi ... Tonosho ... *basu*. Officials fetched out railway timetables and looked up trains, pored over maps, wrote lists and drew diagrams; and all the time my friend, whom I now thought of as Tonosho, was dragging me to the bus stop.

I tried to resist, but something told me that against all better judgment we were to be travelling companions. I have frequently been befriended by such little men and the result is

200

always confusion, discomfort, delay or disaster. Tonosho had every mark of the supreme saboteur inspired by a burning desire to help. He had large yellow teeth spread out like a handful of cards, small demented black eyes, a dark bristly chin, long dirty claw nails and movements which gave an impression of arms too long – prancing, as though ready at any moment to spring high out of danger, back to his native tree.

He wore a desperate little cloth hat rammed down askew, carried a big plastic carry-all, several fishing rods of different kinds and a large bundle of boxes done up in a *furoshiki*. A man's zippered handbag hung from one wrist. His speech was intense, eager, slightly hoarse. As he talked he made urgent dabs... *Korei* ... *koko* ... *ima*. It was clear he knew all about me.

When I said I would take the train he was greatly upset. But he was going to look after me! Get me safely to Shodashima! He was going there to visit friends and relations, he would take me with him, his friends would be honoured ... and if I wanted to get to Obi he would see that I got there. He would get me a *basu* from Tonosho ... He would do everything ... everything ...

I had picked up my bag and was bowing good-bye when the bus swirled up. Workmen and schoolchildren peered out. People half stood for a better view. Tonosho scrambled to the door and thrust his little black face up towards the driver. There was a flood of excited Japanese and much gesticulation. The conductress, in bobby-socks, stated her opinion. Suggestions were given, advice offered, people looked at their watches and made calculations. The driver leaned over his little metal fence and assured me, with smiles and bows, that he would get me to Okayama in no time. The passengers looked anxious, as though much was at stake.

I was definitely under pressure. I clambered in over Tonosho's fishing rods, wondering who had said the Japanese were calm and inscrutable.

201

'*Or-ryee!*' yodelled the little conductress, jangling the bell.

Grinning triumphantly, Tonosho dragged me, with his *furoshiki* and fishing-rods, down the crowded aisle, and with a hectoring nod extracted a stunned schoolboy from the best window-seat.

The boat was to leave Okayama at nine-thirty. At eight-forty the *densha* overtook and passed us at such a rate it was clear its passengers would catch the boat, which we would not, for the *basu* was meandering round the coast in a most dilatory manner.

We were still on the outskirts of Okayama at nine-fifteen. Tonosho caught my eye and looked quickly away.

The bus stopped in a wide dusty street and people spilled out. As I descended Tonosho sprang forward and seized my arm, plastic bag, *furoshiki* and fishing-rods clutched to his chest, dragged me across to where a bus stood trembling as though to take off. He moved sideways, like a prancing crab, saying '*Funé-funé-funé.* Shodashima-Shodashima-Shodashima.' He became quite ruthless, shouting to hurry up, quick, quick, quick, almost thrusting me, hot and furious, before the moving wheels. The driver stopped, opened the doors and waited politely as we flung ourselves up the steps.

I wedged myself into a long row of women in dark kimono. They were mopping their foreheads with little paper squares and the *tenugui* of the workmen opposite were damp with sweat. They all had a good look at me and began questioning Tonosho, who quickly told them my story. They were very friendly but made it quite plain we could not catch the boat. Tonosho now suddenly began displaying his watch with resignation, shrugging and saying of course we could not catch it but – with a careless shrug – there was another at eleven.

I had a rush of blood to the head at the thought of spending an hour and a half on some ghastly hot foodless wharf in his company. I said bitterly, 'This is your fault. If I'd got the train I'd be there now!'

One of the great joys of Japanese travel is the almost complete absence of the slow baffled stare of utter incomprehension that goes with more leisurely minds. Tonosho did not understand the words but he got the message. He looked guilty; then became very masterful and went into conference with the conductor. The passengers were speculating, comparing their watches, calling questions to the driver, who kept turning round to shout out what time we should reach certain points along the route. The bus trembled with tension and excitement; then the driver suddenly put his foot on the gas and began blasting his horn. Bicycles swerved out of the way, pedestrians shrank back. We turned a corner and there was the boat drawing out from the quay.

I began to laugh helplessly; but Tonosho grabbed up his possessions and snarled ferociously at me to get ready. As the bus hurtled up to the gates – onlookers shouting and waving as at a regatta – the ticket officer on the wharf sent out a cry through the public-address system. The *funé* stopped, backed in, came alongside. Without tickets or gangway we leapt. Hands reached out and dragged us aboard. There were more shouts and laughter. The steamer hooted. Those on the quay waved and cheered.

Shodashima was visible long before we reached it, stretched out across the grey sea with a mountain at one end. The island has great quarries; the stone for Osaka castle was dug from its mountain but it is not bleak at first sight. There are terraces all down the graceful slopes, green trees against white earth, and in the foreground the floats of pearl farms.

I hoped to fade from Tonosho's life when we landed. He had put me into a stuffy cabin full of smoke and curled up beside me, hat over eyes, clearly not a good sailor. I left him and went on deck; but he bore no grudge and as we approached the port came to find me, all ready to organise me to his friend's house. I said No no, thank you, thank you, but he didn't listen. He was in a frantic hurry to get me ashore, pushing and shoving down the crowded gangway, turning back to shout in a very exasperated way. He beckoned like a South Sea Islander, as though waving me away, in between plucking at my sleeve, saying urgently *'Basu'* and *'Gohan'* – (rice, food) – that he was taking me home; but now I struck. I wanted to be alone. I wanted to look round. I wanted coffee and *croissants*.

He listened, like a small hopeful ape, then took my arm and rushed me across the town square, pausing only to point at a stone group of children clustering round a young woman, saying *'Firimu'*, which I took to mean I should photograph them.

When I saw he was leading me to a tourist office, with buses drawn up outside, I stood still and refused to move. He tugged and dabbed and jerked his head but I was adamant. If I would not go to his house I was certainly not going on a bus tour with leaders and flags. He looked at me in despair; then ran ahead to the tourist office and quickly returned with a pleasant young man who spoke English.

I felt ashamed. Poor little Tonosho, doing all he could for me, befriending me, offering me hospitality, dragging me here because the young man spoke English. I thanked him remorsefully, shaking his little dark claw among the bundles and fishing-rods. He snickered and grinned but I glimpsed relief in his eyes. We bowed and he scampered away to jump on a departing bus.

After all the trouble he had taken to get me there I suppose I should have stayed longer, but in a couple of days I became restless. Shodashima is beautiful but it lacks intimacy. It is not like an island at all: one might as well be on the mainland. It is also very popular with holiday-makers from Kobe and Osaka and is well supplied with look-outs and tourist attractions. But away from the coast the country is unspoilt. Along the dusty road by the sea olive groves go up the hillsides, gnarled, silver-leaved in powder-pale earth. It is like Greece, with its fine filtering dust and glaring sun, apart from the grey houses and occasional shrines, the straw hats and *mompei* of the women working among the olives and citrus orchards, helping build embankments. Men cut the stones, the women, their hands gloved, fit them into diamond-patterned walls. Here and there pilgrims in white, with mushroom hats, make their way with bells and staves from shrine to shrine. There are eighty-eight shrines to St Kobo on the island. Figs, persimmons, mandarins, pomegranates ripen round the tiered olive-groves; and from the mountain-top heroic views unroll, over terraced slopes to the indented coastline, to far-off little islands. At night the towns, bays, islands, distant ships are alive with lights.

In these ports Hideyoshi built his navy. I picture this little monkey-faced Shogun as a cleaned-up Tonosho.

They make a great fuss of the island's olives and the stone figures – which I saw down in Tonosho – of a schoolmistress with her twelve pupils. These are characters from a novel called *Twenty-four Eyes*, by a woman of Shodashima, which was filmed (*firimu*). The figures are stamped on biscuits, souvenirs, printed on postcards, made into little replicas. The olives – small, green, delicious – are in bottles and boxes, and used as decorations on everything from head-towels to wrapping paper.

But the greatest attraction, adored by the Japanese, is a fearful gorge called Kankakei. It is reached through exquisite country of rice terraces, large ponds and pine trees, and crossed in a ropeway, a yellow cable-car with a little white-gloved female attendant with a microphone, who behaves as though you are taking a turn round the block instead of a journey into space. As soon as you start she begins to talk and continues all the time you are swinging out over the appalling valley, which reaches up at you with jagged peaks. It is better to look back upon the superb unfolding view of plains, bay, islands and sea, but there is a compulsion to look down, to stand up and peer out at the horrible sight. Ahead, miles away, is a grim wall of rock into which, from the way the line sags, you are going to crash. Metal towers holding the cables rise from the valley floor, and approaching each one the little car slows down sickeningly, almost slithering back.

Unperturbed, the conductress continues her commentary, about the view, the statistics, the magnificence of the valley in autumn when the maples turn red. She will still be at it when your mangled bodies are flung to the floor of the ravine, thanking you for your gracious attention and patronage.

Shodashima seemed 'Inland Sea' only in name, not in spirit. Where were the opalescent clouds, the small terraced islands, the floating rocks with crooked pines standing out at odd angles? The sea was misty, the landscape muted, with a hazy quality never found in the Mediterranean. At night on the mountain a great gale blew.

I crossed to the mainland in a boat full of proud white goats and began to make my way along the spoiled coast.

17

'Well-come, Nancy-san!'

I HAD PROMISED Hiroshima-san that I would visit her family at
Matsunaga, near Fukuyama, on the Inland Sea. She had written
out the names and ages of her parents and sister, the name of
the temple, the full address, the telephone number, what train
to get to Matsunaga, where to get off, where to take a taxi, the
distance from station to temple and how much the taxi would
cost. She had also drawn careful Japanese maps and charts
with coloured arrows.

'My . . . family . . . I . . . write . . . My family . . . say . . .
Well-come, Nancy-san. My sister Yoshiko . . . very good English.'

But when I telephoned Yoshiko there was a paralysed silence.

'Did my letter come?' I asked very slowly.

A breathless whisper said '*Hai.*' There was a long pause. I
did not know if I should mention my visit or just pretend I was
ringing to say Hullo. Believing Yoshiko spoke English, I wondered if I had embarrassed her by ringing at all.

The pause had become informed with anguish that transmitted itself down the wire. At last a small voice said, 'Well-come, Nassi-san.'

But did that mean I was welcome to go to Lange-ji? I said tentatively, 'Your sister Yoriko is my friend. She is a very good girl.'

'*Hai.*' Another agonised pause; then faintly, 'Well-come ... Nassi-san ... Lange-ji.'

I said with coarse western directness, 'Please may I come to see you and your parents, and tell you about Yoriko at Itto-en?'

There was a little burst of relief.

'*Hai hai.* Please. Well-come Lange-ji.'

I asked 'When?' and since she seemed to be struggling, suggested 'Tomorrow?'

She said '*Hai,*' and as though waiting for such a cue to read a prepared speech, 'Tomorrow-busy-day-temple.'

Did that mean I shouldn't go tomorrow?

'Yes yes, well-come Nancy-san Lange-ji tomorrow. Busy day. Like you see.'

I found Lange-ji just outside Matsunaga, at the top of a steep narrow lane. The gates and temple are eyelash-roofed with grey tiles and inverted gold fish on the ends of the ridge pole. Today the buildings were draped with white curtains printed with purple chrysanthemum crests. Coloured flags of all nations were strung across the courtyard and from a tall white post covered with black calligraphy, a narrow white banner stretched, like a bandage.

In the hot clear light a young girl was sweeping before the Master's house. Slender, sweet-faced, with a sad droop to her graceful neck, she gave an impression of gentleness and resignation.

'Yoshiko-san?'

'Oh!' She put her hands to her face in confusion. She was very pretty but otherwise quite unlike her sister. There was none of Hiroshima-san's dash or pent-up devilment. She said, blushing, 'Well-come. Well-come Nancy-san.' She seemed to be terribly shy.

208

She took me through the great temple kitchen where women in kimono were talking as they cooked, stirred, set out trays. In a cool quiet room Mrs Hirota came and knelt to welcome me. She and Yoshiko were both run off their feet, preparing for an enormous influx of people, but showed no signs of impatience or agitation. Yoshiko brought tea and cakes and gave me an envelope inscribed 'Nancy Theran San' in English and Japanese.

I was glad to rest in the shaded room, drinking o-cha and reading Yoshiko's letter:

> You are wellcome, Nancy Theran San.
> This temple names 'Rengezi.'
> Rengezi was opened by Kobo Daishi 1150 years ago. Kobo Daishi is one of the greatest Buddhist monks of Japan. He opened Koya-san, too. The teaching (instruction) of him is telling true words to everybody anywhere. So named 'Shingon shyu' (Shin means true, Gon means word). But the teaching is deep, so somebody call it that is opened but has a great secret.
> Why is that called so?
> The reason perhaps exist the point that the deep and inner part of this teaching takes up the deep soul, moreover if everybody (the both man and woman) makes efforts always, he (or she) will be able to become to be Buddha in this world (no Heaven or Hell).
> I cant understand the whole teaching of Kobo Daishi. But I will make efforts to understand the teaching.
> Today is the day that the virtue of Kobo Daishi is admired and advertised.
>> Yoshiko.

For a couple of hours people trickled into the temple grounds, buying bentos from a great stack that had been delivered by carriers, finding shady places to sit. A number of soberly dressed gentlemen had arrived and now sat cross-legged in the main temple building. There was an air of peaceful expectancy and from time to time, as I prowled and watched in the grounds, Yoshiko would appear to reassure me that something wonderful would shortly happen. Such an occasion might only come once in fifty years, she said, and she wished me to see it, to share it.

Towards midday she came out hastily and beckoned me to the gate. Outside, people had gathered on each side of the lane and I heard a rhythmic chanting, a delicate intermittent tinkling. Presently a procession with banners appeared from the street at the bottom of the hill; men in dark suits, women in dark kimono with purple stoles. Chanting, they came up the lane, in one hand carrying a rosary and a small long-handled tasselled bell, in the other a tiny hammer with which, all in unison, they struck the bell. At the temple gates they separated and lined the lane, still chanting, still striking their bells, and almost at once there appeared a procession of human dolls with whitened faces. The little girls held pink gold-stemmed flowers, and wore golden crowns with tinkling bells, surmounted with gold flowers and phoenixes; the boys wore gold caps. All had gorgeous kimonos in brilliant colours and over them *hakama*, divided skirts, purple with white medallions, or with purple medallions on white. Over this again was a kind of sleeveless surplice of gold, green, scarlet and blue brocade with chrysanthemum flowers. Beside them walked the mamas in their best kimono and each child pulled, or at least had its hand on a long red rope.

Behind came priests in dark robes, blowing on conch shells; behind again more priests in silks and brocades of purple and orange and gold. The bizarre combination of superlative colours, the luxurious textures in the bright sun, the primitive mournful note of the conch, the chanting and tinkling of pilgrims' bells was wildly exciting, an excitement now intensified by a strange new rhythmical beat.

A group of young men sprang into view, wearing short black coats with black and white stripes round the neck, white

210

gaiters with black leggings, white shorts, and round mushroom hats on their backs. Some carried long poles ending in flaxen mops, some carried red-and-black boxes, like old-fashioned cabin-trunks, on their shoulders, some had long-poled mops covered with scarlet cloth and streamers. They moved in a strange graceful rhythm – one leg forward, the other foot raised to the knee, then pouncing forward with a springing movement, at the same time turning right round and reversing their mops and cabin-trunks, as though tossing and catching them again. A cat-like step forward, a pause to raise the other foot, then the sudden pounce again, the tossing and turning, all to the rhythmical accented chant. Behind the dancers, grave young boys in black kimono, with gaiters and swords and huge pilgrims' hats preceded and followed a sedan-chair carried by monks. Inside the chair, gorgeous in high golden cap and brocade, sat O Cho San, honourable Mr Priest, Jiko Hirota, master of Lange-ji, father of Hiroshima-san.

'*Odori* . . . Boys dance *Daimyo Gyoretsu*,' Yoshiko whispered.

'It's wonderful! Is it old?'

'Yes. Now boys carry a principal monk in *o-kago*.'

'The chair?'

'*Hai. O-kago* is old in history. *Odori* is old too.'

'How old?'

'Heian period. *Keisan-Hoyo* is the name of the ceremony you will see today.'

'Are the children's costumes old?'

'Children's costumes oldest of all.'

The *Daimyo Gyoretsu* was now circling and pouncing its way round the courtyard. The monks bore their *o-kago* to the temple steps and O Cho San got out, mounted the steps and bowed. Meanwhile two clowns carrying comic baskets on their shoulders and *saké* bottles, with blackened faces and long wild hair, had followed the monks, gnawing bones and imitating the dancing boys. After them the crowd surged in.

The little children, now hot and tired, had dispersed and

211

were starting to fight, cry, fidget and go to sleep, though parents and relatives persuaded and pleaded for one more photograph. With crowns and caps askew they raced round the courtyard licking ice-creams. There was a raid on the *benjos*; faces were hidden in parents' knees and small shoulders shook with exhausted tears. *Saké* bottles and *bentos* were unpacked. The solemn festival became a big family outing.

In the temple kitchen I ate with the family and friends, Mrs Hirota and her helpers, Yoshiko, a married sister with a baby. O Cho San came and asked in English if I had enough, if I were enjoying it, if he could do anything more to please me. He was young and good-looking, like a happier, handsomer version of Daito Kokushi, in Sansom's *Short Cultural History*. This was his great day, he was the most important figure, there were dozens of people waiting to see him, not to mention high church dignitaries come specially for the festival; yet he had time to be friendly and welcoming, to play for a minute with his baby grandchildren.

We ate from magnificent *bentos* and drank warmed *saké*, which, with heat and excitement, made us all drowsy. I marvelled that I, an absolute stranger, was now sharing with this family one of their most important occasions, made so welcome that I did not feel out of place.

After lunch there was a somnolent pause in the temple, where bodies reclined in every room. On the shady veranda by the mossy enclosed garden Yoshiko and I talked quietly. I had grown very fond of Hiroshima-san but this gentle sister evoked immediate affection. She was so humble, so guileless, so innocent and so vulnerable.

'When you get married ...'

'Oh no, I shall not marry. I shall stay here and try to help my parents. I have so much to learn. I am trying very hard to understand the religious teaching.'

'But you *will* marry ...?'

She looked very sad. Later, she wrote that she had lost a

sweetheart and I remembered her wistful expression; but she said nothing and I could not ask.

When not helping her mother Yoshiko sat with me to explain what was happening. There were more superb processions, with conch shells and cymbals, and purple and scarlet and gold robes with rich plaited cords and tassels, embroidered with phoenixes and mountains floating above clouds. In the prayer hall the worshippers assembled for the long afternoon service, the chanting of *sutras* and burning of incense and rhythmical striking of bells. When I saw the gorgeous priests, the children in their brilliant kimono, I suddenly thought of the Buddha's *Sangha*, the homeless medicants who gave up all and lived with one robe and one bowl, under a tree and on a stone. It was like remembering Christ and his ragged followers in St Peter's.

It was very solemn and grand, yet during the chanting and praying the congregation carried on their own conversations, gossiping, playing with their babies or holding them out over the edge of the veranda. The children had become restless and ran about rather noisily, eating Mickey Mouse toffees handed out by the priests. Infants in arms, wearing splendid kimonos, dribbled and hiccupped and snored.

An exceedingly handsome man with grey hair came and sat with us. His beautiful features and ivory skin looked perfectly healthy.

'But he is ill,' Yoshiko said, when he had gone. 'He comes from Hiroshima. He was badly burned by the bomb. He has terrible scars. And he must go all the time to hospital because of his sickness.'

'After all these years?'

'Oh yes. It is the bomb sickness. He will never be better.'

The late sun glinted through the trees and shone in the prayer hall, on the dark-kimono'd women sitting back on their heels, on the black and the red, the purple and gold, the hangings and lacquer and gold-fringed banners, the offerings of

213

scarlet apples, cakes, chrysanthemums and piles of bulb-like tubers. In the garden, cicadas and crickets sang; in the temple a tenor solo chant had risen. Cymbals clashed gently; then there was quietness, only the sound of rosary beads rubbing together.

'Yoriko tells me you are a writer,' said Yoshiko, presenting me with an exercise book and a pen. 'We would all be very honoured if you would write your impressions.'

My head was full of impressions, I was half-dazed and blinded; but did she expect me to write a *haiku*? Educated Japanese toss off these poems with no trouble at all.

She said timidly, 'You know about our poetry?'

I said bleakly, 'You mean *haiku*? Seventeen syllables?'

'*Hai*. Seventeen syllables. Complete experience. Immediate impression...'

Embarrassed, I had to say, 'Please excuse me. I'll try to write one and send it.'

She was too well bred to show surprise. Some of the other guests had already written their poems. The beautiful little characters looked up at me from the exercise book, reproaching my barbarism.

'Aye-*ah*! Aye-*ah*! Aye-*ah*!' the pilgrims chanted, marking time – one – two – three – with their bells, then striking with the hammers. 'Aye-*ah*! Aye-*ah*! Aye-*ah*!'

18

'Nothing There'

YESTERDAY, while I was at Lange-ji, Seto Naikai sparkled;
today it was pallid and colourless with so thick a haze you
could hardly see any islands. It was early still, so I hoped the
haze would lift. I sat on the deck of the little boat and thought
about fishing fleets coming in, nets drying, walks in hills terraced with flowers, a simple inn with wonderful meals of fish.

All these I expected to find at Innoshima, the island I should
soon reach. Everyone at Onamichi said Innoshima was beautiful.

The boat hooted. I looked up and saw docks, ships, cranes,
tin sheds. We were approaching a wharf.

'Innoshima!' said the deck boy.

But it couldn't be! Innoshima was an island, it must have
fishing villages. This was a port, hot, ugly, noisy.

'Innoshima,' said the deck boy again, and added that if I
didn't get off quick I'd be taken on to Shikoku.

On the wharf an archway said WELCOME TO INNOSHIMA.
Nearby, a map of the island showed tourist attractions, tourist

215

bus routes. The buildings were new and ugly and there was a hot dusty street. There were no little *ryokans* by the water.

I should have known from the way the Japanese raved that it would be awful.

Trying to make the best of it I went to the ticket office and asked about the other side of the island. The woman in charge shook her head. She offered taxis up the mountain for seeing the view, boats to Setoda ('The Nikko of the West'), hot springs, hotels right here in the port or a bus tour to somewhere or other. She had infinite patience and kindness but she was utterly baffled. Though she assured me repeatedly that there was nothing at all on the other side of the island I went on asking for buses and fishing villages, for when the Japanese say there is 'nothing there' they are usually saying what they think you will think. When they say *beautiful, wonderful, interesting* they mean hot springs and western hotels, yawning abysses, boiling mud, craters, hissing jets of sulphur, immense panoramas or Nikko-type monstrosities. So I persisted; and at last she left her office, her telephone, her queueing customers and led me to the bus stop.

'*Koko!*' (here), she said, but with a worried look added, 'Nothing there ... nothing there.'

'Shigei!' said the conductor as the driver released the doors.

I looked at the small hot fishing-town, half-asleep by its harbour, and got out. The bus groaned away down the street and on round the island. Heat, silence, fine white dust closed in on me. I was almost afraid to look Shigei in the eye lest it vanish. The water-front was deserted and most of the shops shut but two boys talking quietly in a little store came forward to take my bag. As they led me through the narrow streets to the inn people came out to look, shyly, curiously. *Shoji* slid back, revealing dark eyes, bright with amusement.

The *ryokan*, in a hot back street, was not grand, but hostess and maid, unusually flustered, welcomed me kindly and gave me a large room with a splendid gay painting of Genghis

216

Khan's fleet being driven off by the *Kamikaze*. There was a great deal of padding and rustling and thumping and childish voices, and as I drank my *o-cha* the scuffles came closer. The *shoji* edged open and dozens of little black eyes glinted in at me. The hostess appeared, flushed and embarrassed, and said her daughter was having a party. When I said Bring them in, she giggled and put her hand over her mouth but opened the door. The children stared in, thunderstruck. I said 'Konnichi wa' and after a startled pause there was a wild explosion; then a very shy chorus answered 'Konnichi wa.'

Shigei seems so cut off from the rest of Innoshima that it might be a separate island. On one side, high hills enclose the little town and on the other a long low point running out into the sea hides the view down the coast and increases the feeling of isolation. Though a bus rattles through now and then the sea is the real focus of life. Distant hydrofoils dash about like birds of paradise flying in feathers of spray; passenger boats come and go, tooting politely in hail and farewell. A little car-ferry glides to the landing-stage and releases a yellow truck. Even in the dead hours of midday when everything swoons and disappears in the heat-haze there is still the faint sound of invisible fishing boats.

I was the only guest at this humble *ryokan*, living in great comfort. Though the appointments were rather eccentric – the bathroom in a grotto of ferns, the *benjo* down a precipitous ladder – they worked well enough, and the food was a gourmet's dream...lavish *sashimi*, fish *consommé*, steamed and grilled fish of every kind, prawns with marinaded mushrooms, large dishes of *tempura*, whole crayfish, all straight from the sea, and salads and fruit and vegetables fresh from orchard or garden.

Since this was the village inn it was the centre of local revels. When there was a bucks' party in one of the rooms, with merrymakers howling, singing, thumping, shouting, dancing and roaring with drunken laughter, the people on the other side would turn up their television in competition. Though the *shoji* rattled, I slept through it all.

In the evenings, when at last I came indoors, the host, who spoke a little English, would come to my room bringing Japanese pears or fresh pineapple and sometimes a very small child like a toy. We would sit on the floor round the low table and he would draw maps and tell me about the islands. The gardens on Innoshima's hills are planted with vegetables and a scented flower used for mosquito incense. Among them are orchards of citrus, what he calls 'little oranges'. In spring the hills are white with blossom and the scent is like paradise. It drifts out over the sea. I think of boats becalmed at night, paper sails held upright with heat, and the scent of flowers on dark water.

'Come back in early summer, before it gets too hot,' the host says. 'I will find you a fisherman to take you to little islands where the passenger boats don't go.' Though terraced and cultivated many are uninhabited. People go there each day to work but every drop of water must be carried from other islands or from the mainland.

Each morning I wake early to the temple bell; then at six o'clock a siren sounds. If you go down to the port at this time you find some shops already open and men at work on their boats in the inner harbour. The sound of hammering echoes clear and flat. A low mist smothers the water and the mountains all round are shrouded. The water lies unmoving, like silk, the sun is an orange disc behind the heat-haze.

The houses round the boat-harbour, below the terraced hills, are old and beautiful, many with upper stories and handsome grey-tiled roofs, ornate oval windows and criss-cross decorations. In the farmyards, hay ricks are built up round central poles – half pillar-box, half overstuffed Christmas tree – covered with tarpaulins. There are piles of red turnips, white goats, well fed dogs and cats.

During the night the mist descends, cutting us off from the world. With daylight it drags itself up, lingering, reluctant,

218

and little fishing boats, rocky islets start to show black. Then, as the sun advances, the sea comes back, ghost shapes feel their way through the vapours till the big far-off islands float round us once more.

All day this giving and taking goes on between the sea and the islands, but on shore the sun shines steadily. Heat cuts through the morning veils and flares back from the harbour. By midday it is intense. Boats lie listlessly, moored to un-moving reflections; the road sweeping out of the town throws painful white brilliance up into the eyes. Ripe pomegranates and persimmons hang motionless, powdered with chalky dust; the grey tiles of the houses seem to sweat.

Up in the hills there is shade under the pines and sometimes a little breeze. In a local straw hat bought for Y60 and a *furoshiki* full of cheese, Shodashima olives and Japanese pears I climb the hill to a shabby shrine with a Jizo in a little hut sheltered by pines. Here I lie among vast crooked roots, reading or dozing, doing nothing. Sometimes children play at the shrine but mostly I am alone, with yellow and white butter-flies and a cricket. Occasionally there is a tinkle, like sheep-bells or wind-chimes.

To the west is the sea, glimmering under its haze; to the south, across a hollow of grey tile roofs, a high hill with shrines and two great cemeteries. I go up there to watch the sunset. Buddhist cemeteries are usually friendly, not macabre or mouldering or full of wild regret. Here everyone is tucked in neatly, hundreds and hundreds, row upon row of grey stones and Jizos and *boddhisattvas*, with paths and wide steps up to the pines and bamboos at the top, where crickets chirrup and trill; and below, the divine view opens out over the sea to the western mountains.

Life is busy without hurry or urgency. Fishing fleets go out, people mend nets, repair boats, deliver truckloads of vege-tables on the quay.

At evening this everyday life becomes poetry. All round, mountains fold into soft mists, line upon line, as in clouds or dreams. From high on the terraces snatches of voices echo down. There is the barking of crows. Far away someone is playing a pipe. A little bell tinkles. There is the rustle of water, the mutter of fishing fleets coming home. Boats towed in line cross the sunset.

Then they are all gone and the sea is deserted but for islets and buoys. As the sun goes down behind the western islands, mountains across the water emerge as through smoke, outlines grow sharper, distant houses, even the pattern of fields and terraces become visible.

At this time, as in all sea towns, people come out to stroll on the quay, to stand with arms folded across stomachs, nodding and smiling. Men tinker with boats, children play on the steep-stepped harbour walls. It is the hour for knocking-off, taking a breath, pausing before supper or evening chores.

From the farthest end of the sun-warmed stone breakwater you look down as through glass to the sea-bed, or up to the slopes where the white earth and all the greens are now gilded. The evening is dove-coloured; a boat with two men and a long steering-oar drifts across a glittering path and the mountains fade and die beyond the sea.

The mist never quite leaves Seto Naikai. All day a haze hovers, sometimes wistfully, sometimes jealously, constantly changing, fainting as though to dissolve; brooding; descending possessively; smothering; then again melting, growing tenuous, vapouring away, revealing phantom mountain-tops and pine islets and plateaux of satin water.

I no longer minded the hazy light. With bare legs and thongs, a shift and a straw hat, I moved about the islands, free as a bird. I got on and off ferries, hired fishermen, took lifts in rowing boats. I explored waterless islands like ice-cream cones, trailed my hand in the sea from bleached silver-grey hulls with little awnings, heard the rattle and creak of the long oar over the side.

220

Climbing on clean brown rocks, basking on white sand I remembered identical moments on other white beaches and other brown rocks in quite other parts of the world. Old rotting boats, wheeling sea-birds, rock pools are universal, like the dry seaweed matting the shore, which as the tide advances takes to the water in green bird's-nests, a floating fine froth of lace.

One morning, on my way to Oshima Island, we touched at an island so beautiful I jumped off the boat. I did not know its name, only that it had orange groves on its slopes, rice fields and gardens cascading down to white inlets and headlands, almond-green bamboo, pine-green forests and above, mountain peaks piercing the mist. I could see fishing villages, fishing boats, people working in fields and orchards and close by, all round, little islets.

Convinced I was mad, the deckhand distractedly wiped a palm across his eyes as the boat moved away. I waved to him reassuringly and he quickly waved back, with the rest of the passengers.

On my beautiful island, with no idea how to see it, where to stay, how to get off again, I waited for what would happen. Almost at once a voice said beside me, in English, 'Good morning. Can I help you?'

The young man had a roundish agreeable face and slightly standing-up hair. His smile was pure Japanese.

Yes, there was a bus that went most of the way round the island; there were boats to Shikoku, to Oshima; there was a *ryokan*. But why had I come to Hakata? No one ever came here, except to work, not even Japanese tourists, certainly not foreigners.

I said I had left the boat on impulse because the island was so beautiful.

He said rather dubiously that there was 'nothing here', no tourist attractions. At the *ryokan* there were only Japanese beds, Japanese food. Only local country buses...

I said I liked Japanese food and beds and country buses;

liked to climb hills and lie under pine trees, sit on the harbour wall and watch the sunset, the fishing boats coming home.

He understood.

'*Ah so*! Hakata is my island, my home. Of course I think it is the most beautiful, though people say it has nothing. If you just want peace and beauty and ordinary island life you will stay here. And here is the most excellent *ryokan*.'

'Could I hire a boat to take me to that island over there?' I waved at the green terraced hill floating out in the sea.

'Maybe; but no one lives there. There is no water. They carry it there. Why do you want to visit such an island?'

'It is so beautiful.'

'Ah! But perhaps more beautiful seen from Hakata than when you are on it. This often happens with islands,' he said consolingly.

The young man proposed I should go with him. He would take me to the *ryokan* and the bus-stop. We began to walk round the curving bay towards Kinori, the little town. Women in *mompei* looked out from their cottages, smiled, said good morning and quickly questioned my friend.

I asked his name. He was already calling me Nassi-san.

'You will please call me Mike. That is my English name.'

'Where did you learn to speak English so well?'

'At school and university. I am graduate of Kyushu University. You have been to Kyushu?'

'I am on my way there.'

'Ah!' His cheerful face looked wistful. 'Kyushu is very wonderful!'

'Better than Hakata?'

He raised his hands.

'Hakata is beautiful; but it is only a little island. But Kyushu . . .'

We seemed to have walked for miles. I asked about the *ryokan* and the bus but now he had a better idea.

'You will come with me. I am going now to my office. I work in local government at the town hall. This morning I am going to drive to the mountain and climb to the top to inspect a road being built. The view from there is very wonderful... all the islands of Seto Naikai.'

It was already exceedingly hot. When he said it would take three hours to climb the mountain I declined. I stopped at a little shop to buy rolls but when I asked about coffee Mike urged me along.

'Coffee later. Come with me now.'

The streets of Kinori were narrow and winding and the town hall was somewhere at the back, a large squarish cement structure. Mike led me down the side and into a room where a kind-faced woman was talking to a young man. They did not seem surprised to see me. They bowed and murmured and the woman at once went out to get *o-cha*.

'Please take a seat,' Mike said. He went out and came back with a sort of ordinance survey map which he spread on the table. He and the young man leaned over it, talking earnestly. From time to time the woman also made a comment or dabbed at the map. I drank my *o-cha* and felt slightly restive.

'If you could just tell me where I catch the bus...'

'Yes yes. I will show you,' Mike said in a *Chotto matte* voice, but continued discussing the map with his colleague as though I did not exist. At last he said, 'Please wait, I will take you to the bus,' and went out of the room with the others.

He was away so long I started to eat my rolls, studying my own map. I wondered if I were to be kept here all day till Mike's work was finished; if I had misunderstood him and should just wander off; if there were in fact a bus. Heat was already glaring outside and the air was humid. I was sleepy and rather sticky. I longed for a shower, to lie down in a cool shaded room.

Mike came back and said, 'Let's go.'

I followed him meekly. A car was parked at the front.

'Oh,' I said, as he opened the door. 'But I don't think I want to go to the mountain... it's so hot for climbing...'

'No no...we are not going to the mountain. We will go along the coast.'

'But the bus?'

'The bus doesn't go all the way. You would miss the most beautiful part so I will take you to see it, then you may pick up the bus.'

It was in the opposite direction to his mountain, miles out of his way. He waved my thanks aside.

'So long as I'm back here by ten o'clock it is all right.'

The road was rough, the car springs eccentric, but the views were exquisite. Mike glowed at my reactions. He was slightly baffling. He loved Hakata but longed to travel, to see the world. He was clearly intelligent, had graduated with honours in economics. I asked, 'But why do you stay on Hakata, if you want to see the world? Couldn't you try for a job abroad in a trade commissioner's office perhaps?'

'Ah. That's what I should love to do more than anything. That is my life's ambition and this is work I could do very well.'

'Is it so hard to get?'

He shrugged. 'That isn't the point. I am an only son. My father was killed in the war. I cannot leave my mother. I must stay here.'

It was said with complete lack of bitterness.

At the terminus – a little port where boats were being built – an antique bus stood by the road like a patient old horse. Mike, all apologies for deserting me, renewed his invitation to climb the mountain and said he would get me a room at the *ryokan* as soon as he returned to Kinori; then he was gone along the white dusty road.

The bus girl showed me her watch. Twenty minutes to wait. I wandered into the valley behind the road where people were cutting rice, and Mike's mountain, misty and blue, dreamed against the pale sky. The rice-cutters waved; a girl leaned from an upstairs window and said *Ohayo!* I waved and smiled back.

224

I had taken my seat in the bus when the girl who had called from the window ran down the road and thrust a large newspaper bundle into my lap, smiled, bowed and rushed away. The parcel was full of magnificent figs.

Like Innoshima, Hakata is for afternoons under the pines, for slow walks and long idle sessions on sea walls; for picnic lunches of olives and cheese and figs, and seafood dinners at the *ryokan*. Ingredients are the same ... the scent of pines, the distant bark of crows, drumming cicadas, the miraculous cricket, the temple bell from the opposite hill ... yet they are different. In its essence Hakata is unique. The busy unsynchronised companionable hammering down at the shipyards by the small crescent harbour, the sweet-voiced town clock, the lunch-hour cries of children in the school grounds all have their own special character. The serenity, the subtle richness of the air comes from deep country lanes, warm scents of sweet-cut hay, bees droning lazily, glutted, in orange groves, persimmons, pomegranates splashed on black branches, dark leaves with yellow and red.

The winding road up the hill leads through clove-scents and lavender-smelling grass, the cool smooth fragrance of ripening oranges, along a spur from which terraced hills and slopes cascade in an immense amphitheatre to long white deserted beaches far below. Out on the sea, spectral islands appear and vanish; a fisherman's sail is suspended against the haze; there is the faint throb of an invisible boat.

I lie in a cypress copse on a promontory jutting out into the valley, absorbing sound and scent. It is so quiet I can hear the distant sea lapping and washing the sand; pigeons coo in the woods. From far hillside gardens the voices of old men come through the afternoon torpor, sounds unrelated to speech, existing as separate entities. A muffled tractor is no more alien than the droning of bees.

I breathe the heavy scents of late summer, of orange groves and the seven grasses of autumn. I drowse. Dragonflies, yellow

225

and white butterflies, little birds swoop low across me. The sea, a glimmering line of light between my drooping lids, is pale, calm under its haze. Are the islands real? – the white sand and black rocks, the scent of the pines?

Early afternoon is the time for hilltop siestas, or lying flat on the *ryokan* floor, with *shoji* half-closed against the glare; but when the heat declines people are out in their orchards or gardens, calling from hill to hill, spraying their trees or clipping or turning the earth. Girls in *mompei* and headscarves like bonnets, their hands gloved, pick still-greenish oranges, small, delicious, with a mandarin flavour.

'*Dozo dozo*,' they cry, piling fruit into my hat; and '*Domo domo*,' when I take their photographs.

As I walk in the deep lanes the rattle of small trucks and cars, the voices of unseen workers beyond high hedges have a strange unreality, give a sense of eavesdropping, of being a ghost passing by.

Early evening, when the worst of the heat no longer flares from the sea, is the time for water trips. The tiny boat weaves among red or white dolls' lighthouses, black petrified cones with arthritic pines against a persimmon sky. Evoked by the dying light, more and more islets unfold from the mist. On the white beaches of green waterless islands, the day's heat lingers in sand and rocks, round sheltered hyaline shallows.

A little car-ferry goes to Oshima, from Oura, outside Kinori, a secluded cove of lovely abandoned hulks and fishing boats. When the back of the vehicle section is open the ferry leaves a wide wake and you feel you are on a raft. With a cargo of schoolgirls and *obasans*, trucks, cars, goldfish in large plastic bags and men who vainly trail lines from the stern, we churn through a channel of currents and Siamese-twin islets to a high green mountainside where men are making a road. At the moment of impact the ferry slows down and rams the cliff gently. With typical Japanese nonchalance towards vehicles the front drawbridge is lowered and a couple of trucks trundle off to the road.

226

Near Oshima, the wide calm bay is dotted with whirlpools, small sinister circles where the water goes round and down exactly as in a drain.

The sunset is lingering. Fishing boats glide across it and purple mists steal over the water. The mountains fade or deepen all round. It is cool on the sea, which lies very still, like a Highland loch.

Walking home to the inn in the twilight you meet the local men returning from work, women and children meandering dreamily, enjoying the last of the sunset, the soft air honeyed with evening scents – hay and oranges and a fragrant white hedge flower. There are roses, Michaelmas daisies, zinnias, phlox, sunflowers, golden lilies and clover in cottage gardens by the roadside.

Through the dusk the deep temple bell vibrates. A young moon shines very white above the hills. Friendly voices come from dimly-seen figures... *Komban wa. Komban wa. Komban wa.*

19

A Night with St Kobo

I HAD looked at Shikoku doubtfully on the map. Apart from Takamatsu, no one talks about this island. If you ask, people say they are always meaning to go there but....Furthermore it was pouring with rain when I landed at Imabari, on the Inland Sea coast.

By the time I reached Kochi, many hours, trains, tunnels and kindnesses later, I knew Shikoku to be an island of ravishing beauty. There is endless variety in its strange combination of volcanic luxuriance and vernal innocence, freshness and unexpectedness. Coming through the misty drenched central mountains there was a moment when we emerged dramatically into a smiling land in full sun and the whole air smelt of the south, a moment as sharp as walking through the door of a dark house into a summer garden. I felt high-spirited, and it seemed that the people were also gay. It may have been the clarity of the air, the brilliant yellow sun, the great lobelia Bay of Tosa, after Seto Naikai's diffused lights and monochrome sea.

228

This is the ancient land of Tosa, where they still breed white cocks with tails like long streamers and tough fighting Tosa dogs. At Kochi, where the sun shines and palms grow, a bank opened after hours to cash my travellers' cheques; people ran about finding *ryokans* and working out train and bus connections and seeing I got to the station on time.

The Japanese, whose country must be about the world's easiest to move in, have comic ideas of difficult travel. *'No transport'* means you might have to wait a few hours, at worst that there is only one bus a day. They are so cushioned with good railways they cannot envisage survival beyond the end of the line and warned me I would have trouble getting from Kubokawa ('nothing there') across the mountains to Uwajima, on my way to Matsuyama. Since I had plenty of time I took a very small train from Kochi down the south-west side of Tosa Bay and up into high hidden harvest fields and streams and bamboo groves, above hook-shaped coves. Below was the flat blue sea where the ship in the tenth century *Tosa Diary* sailed on its way to Kyoto, with coloured flags streaming and people composing poems, drinking *saké*, making offerings to the gods for protection against storms, pirates and shipwreck.

Now the light was tawny and shadows were long. Workers were coming home from the fields. Our own moving shade ran beside us. The scent of wood-smoke drifted from villages. All the way up into the hills we looked down on small secret valleys, flowing like checked rivers to the black sand beaches, glimpsing islets of crooked pines and dark rocks with white lighthouses. A green smell, a scent of earth and trees came into the carriage and leaves touched my face as I leaned out, reluctant to let it all go.

Feathers of dusk were floating among the hills and fields, the mountains dark against the fading saffron sky. In the carriage a gentle peace lay over the tired peasants, the giggling school-girls.

A hand touched my shoulder. A small tree-creature in black leggings with cloven hoofs was shelling cooked eggs. There was a pile wrapped in newspaper in his *furoshiki*. He held out a quivering ovoid with such earnest good faith I could not refuse. I bowed and bit into it. It was lukewarm and the yoke started to run. Food offered in Japanese trains is usually pleasant, apart from dried squid and a sort of fish jam sold on stations, but this was an exception. Since he was eagerly peeling another egg I offered a mandarin but he was not deterred. The second egg was tendered. I smiled, bowed, put my hand on my heart, on my stomach, made gestures of repletion but he continued to hold it out, watching me keenly with bright little animal eyes.

This time the white was also runny. I felt slightly sick. He was peeling the third when the train stopped.

'Kubokawa! Kubokawa!' The peasants and schoolgirls woke up and joined the cry on the station. They sounded gently put out, as though having brought me here with their own hands, at my request, I was refusing to get off.

I thanked them and snatched at my bags. As I got out the egg-peeler, with friendly grunts, thrust his last offering at me.

At Kubokawa no one spoke English, not even the station officials. It was growing dark by the time I established the fact that there was a bus at six-thirty next morning through the mountains to Yoshinobu, and a train from there to Uwajima, but I could not find out if the little town had a *ryokan*. People said *E-to*, and *Anoné* and *Ah so!* and *So desuka!* and pushed back their caps and stroked their chins gravely and simmered with suppressed excitement and finally decided to take me along to the temple which is also a youth hostel.

The railway man put my bag on his bike and led me down the main street. The evening was cool, with the last of an orange sky beyond the mountains and purple clouds gathering round the dark peaks. Country smells of earth and growing crops drifted in from the fields, small flat distant country sounds were held in the sharp air. As we walked through the town a child pressed its face against its mother's knee and

230

wailed with fear, while others stared with astonished eyes and mouths.

When we came through the temple gates in the dusk I saw a courtyard surrounded with buildings – on the left the main temple, on the right several smaller structures, one with broad steps up to a narrow veranda, a huge bronze incense-burner, a great covered bell, a washing-trough.

Though a light shone at one side of the temple there was no sign of activity. I noted with relief only two pairs of shoes outside the *shoji*. If the hostel was empty I could count on a bed.

'*Chotto, chotto matte, kudasai.*'

My escort made 'down Fido' movements at me and crunched across to the kitchen. The *shoji* opened; he vanished within. Immediately a head popped out of a small building beside the kitchen and a tiny man skipped forth. He was a perfect Chinese sage, in brownish robes, with shiny bald head, smooth ivory cheeks, a little white straggly beard and a childlike expression of interest and curiosity. He scampered across the courtyard, like a dry leaf, bowing to me with a cackling laugh, and entered the main building. I wondered if I had imagined him. There was a feeling that anything might happen here. At this hour the temple had an air of being sealed off from time and the world.

My railway friend was taking so long in the kitchen I wondered if he were dining; but presently the *shoji* opened and he backed out, bowing. A woman in kimono and overall followed and they stood murmuring together. He approached, looking distressed, and announced I could not stay at the temple after all. It was full. Forty people, coming tonight. Booked ahead.

At first I did not take it very seriously. I thought it must be a party of schoolchildren. They would make room for me; I had often slept with them before. But they weren't children; they were pilgrims, men and women. The whole temple had been reserved and they would be here any minute. The suppers were all ready...

Though hungry, I said I could do without supper. I only wanted somewhere to sleep. I didn't take up much room and I didn't need a *futon*.

The servant was very distressed. She and the railway man pondered, stroking their chins. There was no other sign of life. The little sage had dematerialised.

'Well,' I said at last. 'I had better go back to town. There must be a *ryokan*. If not, I can sleep in the station waiting-room.'

They shook their heads vehemently. The servant said to *Chotto Matte* and rushed out through the gates to ask the woman next door. She came back looking downcast. Next door was also full.

I was very much touched by their concern for this stray *gaijin* who had turned up without warning.

'Anoné ...' said the railway man, grasping his bike where my bag was still perched. 'You will come to my house ...' But the maid, clapping her hand to her forehead, began to gabble.

'*Jinja! Jinja!*' She gestured across the courtyard to one of the buildings, conferred with the railway man, pointed again, then turned to me. Would I mind sleeping in the shrine?

They watched me anxiously, as though asking an outlandish favour. When I nodded and said 'Yes,' they looked relieved and hustled me across and up the steps to the shrine veranda. The maid pulled back two sets of doors. As she opened the inner *shoji* there was a delicious scent of fresh wood. She switched on the light.

'Oh!' I cried, dazzled by the gorgeous brilliance. 'I like it! It's nice!'

They were delighted.

'Naice, naice,' they cried, chuckling, bowing. 'Naice-naice.'

'Whose shrine is it?'

'Kobo Daishi.'

'St Kobo? Koya-san!'

They beamed and nudged each other. It was like an introduction from an influential friend. '*Hai hai*; St Kobo.'

232

When the railway man had gone the servant hastened away to get my bedding before the pilgrims arrived.

My bedroom was big but more than half was occupied by a gold pagoda with many dangling bells and filigree ornaments. There were scarlet and orange and gold brocade hangings, tassels, drums, lanterns and shrine-lamps with turned-up hats; little tables of red lacquer and gold; purple, red and gold cushions and in the background a scarlet frame with a roof, containing portraits. I could not see who they were, away there in the shadows, if it were St Kobo or the founder or perhaps a past abbot. In any case I was too taken up with the pagoda to care. It was so audaciously splendid, so superb and outrageous. As well as its gilt and bells and red lacquer, in each of its four corners were bunches of plastic tulips...red, green, yellow and darkest purple. All round were little gold *saké* cups. My scarlet shirt and trousers fitted in beautifully.

I was prancing about in delight at the thought of sleeping in this gay, dashing, exotic room when the maid reappeared in the courtyard, shouting and beckoning me for *o-furo*; and just in time, for as I emerged a bus drew up in the temple lane and the first load of pilgrims pelted in through the great gate, chattering, tinkling their little bells. They made straight for my building; the courtyard was suddenly full of figures in white, stout men and women in white leggings, white knee-length kimono and narrow navy blue stoles round their shoulders, printed with white characters. The women's enormous umbrella hats were lashed on over white head-scarves, giving a medieval appearance. They all carried staves and little long-handled bells like the pilgrims at Lange-ji.

I was caught on the shrine veranda. Smiling and bowing, they clustered at the foot of the steps round the great bronze cauldron where their leader was now lighting incense. Offerings were thrown into the big slatted box; then they lit incense sticks, tinkled their bells, put their hands together and bowed. The leader began chanting, the others joined in. Grey coils rose in the dusky air, the sweet familiar scent drifted up. It was moving and beautiful, the white figures in their shadowy hats, the light of the little incense flames flickering upon their faces.

But the maid was now signalling distractedly. I edged cautiously along the narrow platform and wriggled down to the ground without disturbing the ceremony on the steps. No one seemed to mind me or my scarlet pants. Several female pilgrims turned to watch me, sidling up to take my arm, asking sympathetically if I were all alone.

With excited cluckings, impressing upon me that I must hurry, the maid led me through the great kitchen where forty red trays were being loaded with goodies. I took an express bath, washed out my smalls, pulled on my clothes and emerged with wet hair.

In the temple, screens had been moved to make two great connecting rooms where long low tables were set end-to-end. In a corner a TV set flickered.

Suddenly the corridors were full. The pilgrims flocked in, hungry and eager for their bath. The temple thudded with *tabi*'d feet, voices laughed and shouted, bells tinkled.

I was directed into a smallish room, adjoining and slightly above the kitchen, where at a low table an old priest sat looking rather peeved. His thoughts were obvious. Why had the maids let this damn foreign woman in? Can't speak the language, won't like the food, nothing but trouble and all these damn pilgrims. . . . But he was courteous, if a little aloof, till he saw that I ate with enjoyment, using chopsticks; then he began to thaw and offered me *saké*.

Futons and bedcovers were piled up behind him and odd garments hung about so there was a slight feeling of eating in an airing-cupboard. There was a fearful noise . . . shouts and clatters in the kitchen, thumps and bangs from the pilgrims, a loud TV commentary. Loaded tray after tray, rice containers, tea-kettles, *saké* bottles went down the corridors. People cried 'Hai dozo . . .' The television bellowed above all.

A very old man had seated himself in the passage where

234

dozens of trays and small tables were piled. I could not leave the airing-cupboard without stepping over him or putting my feet in the trays. I dared not descend to the kitchen, where people were whirling round, dishing out food; I must stay with O Cho San and the *saké*, struggling to keep awake and converse politely in fragmentary Japanese.

When the trays thinned out in the corridor I stepped over the ancient man, now sleeping, and found the two great rooms a sea of *futons*. The pilgrims were spreading them end to end, packing them in like parts of a puzzle. Stout ladies in different stages of undress pounded across to help with unrolling and making up. In and out of the bathroom plump wet men and women wandered in towels or nothing at all, pink, steaming, fat stomachs, bouncy buttocks, sloppy bosoms, all in excellent humour, full of food and *saké* and human kindness, clean and relaxed from *o-furo*, blissfully, healthily tired.

It was pure Chaucer – the gusto, the lack of self-consciousness, the rather bawdy good humour, the white robes, staves, tinkling bells and straw sandals, the white-coiffed heads and umbrella hats of these middle-aged Japanese pilgrims doing the rounds of the eighty-eight shrines of St Kobo by bus.

The only drawback to my bedroom was that I could not turn in till after nine. Pilgrims were trailing across in *yukatas* to pay their respects; so I took a turn round Kubokawa in the dark and came back to find the temple office open for business.

Inside, the light shining off his bald yellow head, was the little sage with the white beard. In one tiny hand he held a brush. He was very busy with a pile of books covered in gold and silver, vermilion and scarlet brocades – the pilgrims' records of the shrines they had visited – inscribing black characters down the white pages, stamping with large red seals. He worked quickly, smiling his childlike smile, chattering to himself or whoever was handy. He was the only person I have ever met who really laughed *tee-hee-hee*.

There was an exceedingly colourful pilgrim at the office

window. He wore robes and a little embroidered skull-cap. His hair was drawn into a pony-tail at the back of his head. He carried the biggest pilgrim mushroom hat I have ever seen, covered with plastic. He had a long staff, wispy beard, hollow cheeks, large dark eyes, and was hung round with rosaries, some made of beads, some of crystal. Even the sides of his spectacles were threaded with crystal beads. He carried a small oblong chest, like a deed-box, and told me he had just arrived by train.

He was very friendly. He showed me a map of Shikoku with the eighty-eight shrines, pointing out his route. Since the conversation was in Japanese the finer points escaped me and I do not know if this were a special journey or if he spent his life in perpetual pilgrimage. He would finish at Koya-san, which, I gathered, earned extra merit.

He then opened his deed-box and presented me with some coloured tourist brochures of Shikoku in which he appeared, posed alone by the sea or with a group of children. It was hard to tell if he were a genuine innocent, naively pleased at having been photographed, or a self-advertising professional holy man. He gave me a little ticket with St Kobo's portrait, joined his hands in prayer, bowed his head, then vanished across the courtyard and out through the temple gates.

When I proposed paying for my supper and bed the little sage fished out a pair of incredible glasses with circular gun-metal frames, set them ritually upon his nose and peered at me over them with his bright yellow eyes.

'Sheeto?'

His voice was a high, cracked, fluttering pipe. He squinted at my youth hostel card. I said I had no *sheeto*. He calculated, sucked in his breath, cackled delightedly. He made some squiggles, stamped my card, announced the price and gave me the change. Then he patted the *tatami* beside him.

'Dozo...'

I longed for bed, but business was brisk in the shrine, so I edged through the kitchen where people were still washing

236

up, climbed up to where O Cho San sat with his *saké*, watching television and arguing with a friend, and picked my way round their legs, over the piles of spare *futons* to the office.

The sage's hands were the size of a child's, with long talon nails. I watched, fascinated by the sureness of his strokes, the beauty of the characters down the china-white page among the scarlet seals. When he saw this, without interrupting his work, he instructed me to get down a packet of paper from a high shelf, rejected several sheets, called for another packet, selected a page, held it up to the light, hissed approval, inscribed, stamped and presented it to me.

I was a prisoner. Each time I tried to escape he dabbed at me with his little paw and pointed to an antique pocket watch. Though it was not yet quite nine o'clock most of the pilgrims were sitting up in bed watching TV, so at last I said I must go to the *benjo* and furtively sneaked across the courtyard to the brightly lit shrine.

My bed was made up in a corner before the pagoda. I lay down in my clothes and pulled up the covers.

Presently there was a tap on the *shoji* and two gentlemen in *yukatas* came in. They bowed to me very politely, knelt before the altar, took out their rosaries and chanted a *sutra*. Afterwards they sat quietly talking together, admiring the pagoda; then they bowed to me again and withdrew.

I put out the light and was dozing off when the *shoji* rattled, a torch flashed, the light was flipped on. The sage put his head round the opening, came in, bowed to the shrine, looking at me reproachfully. He pattered about, prodding cushions, twitching plastic flowers, then approached my bed and asked if I were comfortable.

I had got up sleepily and assured him I was all right. He nodded, waved at the pagoda and assured me St Kobo would keep me from harm; then he wished me good night, cackled and made a sudden dive at me, patting and squeezing. It was such a naive kind of pass I could not be annoyed but I shook my head and frowned, just in case. He slid away, bowing and hissing and smiling, then scampered out, shutting the *shoji*; then tapped and put his head in to tell me to keep the doors closed while I slept.

I wondered if sleeping in the shrine put me into the category of temple maidens and if he were the forerunner of other devotees.

Since it was now after nine and officially the shrine was shut, I fixed up my little clothes-line, pegged out my towel and washing, got undressed, put cream on my face and lay down. Lights were out in the temple; voices were subsiding, the pilgrims settling down like a flock of birds. Moonlight flooded the courtyard, a distant dog moaned; then the kitchen *shoji* rattled noisily open, feet crunched across the yard and blundered up to the shrine. With much clanking and tinkling, the offertory box was emptied. The steps clumped round the platform, heavy shutters were slammed into place, the outside light switched off. St Kobo and I were shut in for the night.

I had wondered if I should feel nervous, alone in this out-house; not of human intruders – anyone opening those shutters would wake the whole temple – but there was a touch of claustrophobia now all was sealed up. It was hot and stuffy; the scent of wood and incense, though delicious, had become rather heavy. I edged apart one of the inner *shoji*. A little draught ventured in. I got into bed and lay listening to my washing releasing gentle drips down on the polythene sheet I had spread to protect the *tatami*. I wondered if corpses were left here overnight before funerals; if spooks would disturb me, if St Kobo might suddenly pounce.

But soon a gentle benevolent sleep descended. I sank into a velvet well, drowning in peace and contentment. I woke once in the night to a sense of comfort and companionship. Even in the dark the gay gold pagoda gave out enormous kindness and cheerful good humour. I felt protected and drowsily happy, sinking back again into the well.

I think I should always sleep safe and happy in Buddhist temples, but not in mosques, not in Christian churches; not, above all, in Shinto shrines. They frighten me, for all their vermilion paint and lanterns and scarlet *torii*, their wonderful costumes and dances and *saké* barrels and jolly good times. Nothing quite shuts out the invisible eyes, the sense of being surrounded and watched, of never knowing what They will do.

At five o'clock I came out of my sleep as though floating to the surface, every nerve and muscle completely relaxed and refreshed. I felt calm and serene and strangely grateful, as though a kind healing hand had rested all night on my head.

Assuming it was St Kobo – who now seemed like an old family friend – I put my best apple in front of the shrine, bowed, got dressed, rolled up my bed and packed my bag.

Dim lights showed across the dark courtyard. Above, the sky took a lingering farewell of the night.

There were heavy thuds and poundings from the temple where maids rushed about with breakfast-trays, half-dressed pilgrims wandered with toothbrushes sticking out of their mouths, *futons* were being rolled up. Since the bathroom was locked I had to clean my teeth in the gentlemen's *benjo* where male pilgrims, some quite without clothes, were using the urinals. Complete unselfconsciousness creates complete innocence.

Then out to the shrine with their bells, lighting incense, joining their leader in chanting. Again little flames flickered upon pale faces and threw moving shadows into the depths of mushroom hats. Beyond the courtyard an ashen light was spreading and above the temple the sky grew red. The scent of incense rose in the fresh dawn air. As the medieval white-robed forms prayed their bells chinked absently, like sheep grazing high on the mountains.

In the background the little sage pattered about, wearing a knitted topknot.

Several lady pilgrims approached. When you go on a pilgrimage to the eighty-eight shrines of St Kobo, they said, you get an official record from each one you sleep at...they waved their brocade-covered books; but there was also a certificate. Since I too had slept not only *at* but actually *in* the shrine, not to mention having been to Koya-san, I was entitled to have one of these. A motherly creature tore a ticket from a kind of receipt book and presented it, bowing and patting my hand. They all patted me very kindly and looked at me with compassion. They seemed to find it pathetic that I had had to sleep alone in the shrine, to feel responsible for driving me out of the temple. I had no doubts who had fared best.

20

The Shadow on the Steps

SOUTHERN SHIKOKU is the Japan of the scroll paintings, the land of the graceful flat-bottomed boat where the fisherman, in straw hat with short ragged coat, leans on a long pole, gazing up at the high narrow gorge, the peaks emerging from swirling mists.

Sometimes mist fills these deep valleys to the tops of the mountains, as though flooding them with water. The sun glares through like a white disc; then the veil lifts and the river is so still and clear that each tree has a separate reflection. It lies in pools or rushes over stones and down into little cascades, here and there netted, or set with winding barricades of criss-crossed stakes, for trapping fish.

Harvesters go out to work in yellow fields while the sun comes over the eastern mountains and a full moon moves slowly down a clear pale western sky. Gold and orange splash the endless greens ... orange lilies, persimmons, yellow dahlias, drying rice laid out in bundles, corn, golden grain spread on straw mats round cottages and farms.

Beyond the mountains and the lyrical valleys are wide flat basins where the little train, up to its knees in ripened rice, creeps through the fields. People are harvesting all round with sickles and here and there small one-man machines like lawn-mowers that cut sideways. When the train stops the scent of grass and flowers comes in. Under their big hats the women wear their *tenugui* pinned so the ends hang below the chin like a bearded wimple. Everywhere groups are beating out grain with a kind of foot-pedal threshing bag. It is a rich, peaceful, idyllically beautiful land.

'Are you going to Hiroshima?' asked a young German at Matsuyama.

'Yes. Are you?'

He looked superior and disapproving, as at someone rushing to gape at a street accident.

'No. It is morbid to go there. I think best it should all be forgotten.'

'But you don't even *remember* it! You weren't born when it happened!'

'That is true,' he said complacently, adding dismissingly, 'Before my time.'

I met a number of such youths, German, Swiss or Swedish, born since 1945, who regarded Hiroshima as some kind of old-time vulgarity kept up by reactionary sensation-loving squares. I preferred the tourists who said they had come to Japan to enjoy themselves and had no intention of looking at depressing sights.

At Ujina, where I landed from the Shikoku boat, everything seemed grey...the streets and houses, the clothes, faces and hair of the women; but the people were gentle and friendly and by the time I reached Hiroshima's large, grand, modern station the sun had cut through the haze and the sky was blue above the mountains.

As I left the street-car two pretty schoolgirls bounced up

242

and asked in charming English if they could help me, be my guide, take me to the Peace Park, the museum...'We have many foreign visitors,' they said. 'People come from all over the world to see Hiroshima'; and like gay little parrots they chanted together, 'NO MORE HIROSHIMAS!' Strangely, it seemed neither phoney nor irritating. I felt rather mean to be asking only for directions to the post office when they were offering me international peace.

The city, all very new and spaced-out, with wide streets and open places, emanates a brisk sort of cheerfulness. The people do not look specially smart or prosperous but show a practical kindliness. The atmosphere is so light-hearted it is a shock to remember, as you do all the time.

Coming to Hiroshima more than twenty years after does not mean there is no impact. Though the fires are out, the dead cremated, the chaos cleared away, what happened is still imprinted invisibly in the air of the bright sunlit town. You keep looking up at the blue sky and mountains all round and thinking, 'This sky... these mountains saw it happen... the cloud, the fires, the black rain'; looking round at the older people in the streets and realising some of them had lived through it.

The city's sensible getting-on-with-life only emphasises the thought of those still suffering, still dying, out of sight, the maimed ones struggling to live. I remembered the handsome man at Lange-ji who still goes to hospital, the children, babies when the bomb fell, who died years later of the Sickness.

In the same way the busy streets emphasise the effect of the Peace Museum. You approach it all unsuspecting. Though you know what to expect you have not yet had the visual experience that makes all the difference. Outside in the sun people dawdle or hustle across the bridges; on the calm river coloured boats float end to end with a holiday Maidenhead touch. Flocks of kindergarten children in yellow hats are herded along with whistles. Postcards, ice-creams, fizzy drinks are bought and sold in the park. The familiar iron parrot-cage above the trees is silhouetted against the sky; strings of paper cranes sway in the Children's Memorial, and at the Cenotaph, parties form into groups for each others' cameras.

From this sunlit normality you ascend the stairs in a queue and having bought your ticket a young lady accosts you earnestly, offering for Y200 to hire you a little ear-plug with an English explanation of the exhibits. When you ask Why? she says that without it you will understand nothing. When you ask Are there no captions? she says, 'No. Nothing.'

It seems strange, but since it is only Y200 you take the disgusting little deaf-aid and go in and find there are perfectly adequate captions in English. The petty swindle seems out of place in a Peace Museum; but is quickly forgotten as you are sucked in with the rest of the silent crowd to the orbit of horror. Like the watch with hands marking the hour it happened, time in this hall has stopped at 6 August 1945.

It is set before you without comment. There are no arms raised in imprecation or hands stretched out for pity, and perhaps this is the secret of its terrible power... the detachment, the almost laconic captions... 'A *dying baby*...'; the businesslike presentation.

No one speaks. Those who had chattered on entering have become silent. There are only the sounds of feet moving quietly and the flutter of birds. Through open spaces in the walls they fly in and perch on the beams, on the glass cases containing the tattered clothes of the dead, cooing and muttering, flapping and balancing above the dark significant stains, the charred edges.

It was eight-fifteen in the morning, a hot sunny day like today. People were going to work, to school. Here are two of them at the station, a long way from the epicentre. They stand, shockingly life-like, in the remnants of the clothes they were wearing – one, in a blue summer dress, blasted off frizzled skin, exposing the seared breast. One woman is burnt on one side, the face is red and purple, the eye scored open, the swollen veins seem about to burst. The body is raw, boiled,

244

roasted, plum-coloured to the state where the flesh is ready to fall off the bones. It is awful, but what of those whose skin did fall off, just like pulling off gloves, when rescuers tried to take hold? Those whose whole skin hung from them like rags; the ones who swelled up to three times their size and turned black and lay moaning in their own ghastly stench while flies crawled over them; whose eyes were burned out and ran liquified down their raw putrifying cheeks?

The models and photographs do not show these. They show some terrible sights but they are *silent*, they don't *move*, they don't *smell*. These blackened bodies don't vomit and scream, they don't grovel and crawl, you can't smell the pus that oozed from the burns; they don't show the colours of raw skin or the blood and vomit and diarrhoea that ran in streams. They give no hint of the silent deep-seated destruction by invisible rays, of cells dispersed in apparently untouched bodies, of whole human mechanisms eerily blasted with no visible burn or scratch. They cannot even suggest the mental and spiritual damage.

Although there was individual heroism, compassion, self-sacrifice there was also destruction of human status, loss of human values. The mind cannot stay horrified for ever; if it does not break, it adapts. Children became so used to seeing dead bodies, even of friends and relations, they spoke of them 'like dead ants'. People became so callous that they could shovel up the dying and burn them together with the dead; they made jokes about the thousands of bloated corpses out in the fields 'like watermelons in a patch'. They said, 'If only they were watermelons you could eat them.' Do these minds ever recover? Could such children ever understand the solemnity of death? Could people ever be quite the same after such inexplicable terror? No visible human agency, just a flash, a blinding white light, then darkness, blasting wind, buildings collapsing, fire, bodies burned to death or dying for no apparent reason. A Nagasaki survivor wrote, 'In an atom bomb war, I realised there were just too many dead people; there weren't enough living ones to take care of the dead. They had to leave the bodies where they were. People got used to seeing corpses lying about, they came to take it as perfectly natural, they came to joke about it.'

In 1946 Her Majesty's Stationery Office published the report of a British mission sent to Japan to investigate the results of atomic bombing. It is curious to read this together with a book called *We of Nagasaki*, by Takashi Nagai, a Nagasaki doctor. The first is a detached account by chiefs of staff, made several months after, with lessons for home defence in mind, in which everything, including people, is reduced to figures; the other is the record of some who lived through it, a book by a Japanese, which describes the dead, injured and survivors as people not statistics. The mission's account, reporting with controlled optimism that if proper steps are taken British cities could escape annihilation, refers to *exaggerated horror stories of survivors*. It is hard to know how you exaggerate the ultimate horror... like the woman in Dr Nagai's book who found there was nothing left in the pumpkin field but a human head:

> A gold tooth gleamed in the wide-open mouth. A handful of singed hair hung down from the left temple over her cheek, dangling in her mouth. Her eyelids were drawn up, showing black holes where the eyes had been burned out. The head had come right off at the neck. There was not much blood. She had probably looked square into the flash and got her eyeballs burned, then the blast must have taken her head off at the neck and sent it flying with the blood gushing out behind!

And the scene at the hospital:

> I had to hold my nose...regular streams of filth were pouring down the stairs and I had to hop from one clear spot to another. Some of the people on the second floor were on the point of death, and had no control over their functions; many had been sick on the concrete floor, and the whole place was one foul pool. The patients lying on the

floor were bathed in it. It poured over the floor and down the stairs. I just had to get Hatsue out of there. The woman lying on her right was dead, the body already cold, and the woman on her left was unconscious and about to die.

Hatsue was a young mother in the last stages of pregnancy, whose unborn child was already dead and who died soon after.

There are any amount of such horrors from Nagasaki and Hiroshima but the worst must be that the official document takes it for granted, *only three months after,* that there will be more bombs. Dr Nagai was dying when he wrote his books but he lived long enough to see attempts to outlaw the bomb come to nothing, to hear the very words he had predicted ... *not so bad after all ... not everyone dies ... radio-activity dissipates ... It is just another weapon with greater physical effects. ...*

Do they understand, have they investigated what it does to the heart and conscience and mind of those who survive? Do they have any knowledge of our society of spiritual bankrupts, now striving lamely to function as a community?

We of Nagasaki, who survive, cannot escape the heart-rending, remorseful memories ... we carry deep in our hearts ... stubborn unhealing wounds. When we are alone we brood upon them and when we see our neighbours we are again reminded of them; theirs as well as ours.

It is this spiritual wreckage, which the visitor to Naga-saki's wastes does not see, that is indeed beyond repair.

We moved round silently, past the burns, the preserved keloids – big pink rubbery growths, like fungus on trees – removed from the skin, the deformed limbs, the depilations, the photographs of dead and dying, of agony and despair, the liquified roof tiles and glass, the fused crockery, melted granite. People stood and looked at the paper crane, the page with the pencilled figures of Sadako Sasaki's blood-count. Sadako was four when the bomb fell. At the age of twelve she suddenly became desperately ill. Because she wanted to live she be-gan to make paper cranes, in her hospital bed, for there is a

Japanese belief that if you could make a thousand you could recover, even at the point of death. She also recorded her blood-count every day. She lived long enough to make six hundred and forty-four cranes. Her death started the Paper Crane movement, now a youth peace movement. This story has been told many times, but the paper crane, the pencilled figures have lost none of their power. All Hiroshima's stories have been told many times and they are no less terrible.

'Sorry.' 'Sorry.' 'Terrible.' 'Ashamed and sorry.' The comments in the visitors book repeat over and over again. 'Shocking.' 'Tragic.' Joypol Sartoro had written: 'We must struggle for peace and against imperialism'; someone else: 'What about Pearl Harbour?' But all the rest say . . . 'Sorry.' 'Sorry . . . ashamed.'

Who was the man who sat that morning on the steps of the Sumitomo Bank? He was probably poor and humble if he was sitting there at eight a.m.; perhaps a beggar who had slept there, perhaps a peasant with feet aching from hot city pavements, one of those merry simian little men in black clovenhoofs I was always encountering in rural trains and buses.

He was there when the bomb exploded and in a sense he is still there. Round him the surface of the granite steps and wall were blasted. His body disintegrated but his shadow remains on the stone. The bank has a new façade and new steps but he is still crouching, with a railing and a plaque that tells his story. All these years he has sat there reminding us; now he is growing faint, as though discouraged by the world's refusal to listen.

At *O-Bon*, when the dead come back to their families and friends, Hiroshima glows with welcoming lanterns. When it is time for the spirits to leave again, thousands of lighted boats are set sailing down the rivers to guide them back to the shades.

This morning the shrine at Miyajima was floating. At the foot of the dark mountain, red-railed galleries lay on the

248

limpid water, thrush-coloured roofs curved like velvet tents over buildings hung with scarlet-splashed white melon lanterns. In the foreground, bronze lions and lanterns, stone lions and lanterns, black pines, the powdery pink of faded scarlet; behind, high brooding disembodied peaks rising from moving mists.

Against this perfection of shabbiness, mossiness, greyness and dampness Shinto priests with black and white robes move about the wide platforms. On the hill to the left, a red pagoda looks out from the woods; and in the grey sea a great vermilion tree floats with upturned branches, as unexpected, as fresh as the day it was set there.

As afternoon fades the island changes. The tide has gone out and the *torii*, reflecting the orange sunset, stands revealed to its roots, growing up from a stretch of wet sand where people are walking. Far off, across the straits, a yellow dragon-faced boat comes and goes. The shrine on its encrusted columns is now poised above the water. Mist shuts us off from the mainland. I begin to understand how Miyajima, the symbol of Japanese tourism, the subject of countless posters, photographs, book covers, has preserved its virginity. Accessible only in one sense, it has the power to retreat, cut itself off, withdraw completely.

Tonight is the Autumn Rite, the offering of the chrysanthemum to the gods. The floor of the dais before the main shrine has been covered with brilliant green damask. Striped banners with chrysanthemum crests are hung round little enclosures on the open platforms.

When darkness comes a bluish floodlight turns the *torii* to pale terracotta pink, insubstantial against the starry sky. The red pagoda, obliquely lit, hovers half-seen, half-imagined above the trees. The tide has turned; it is silently, slowly creeping up, lapping gently at the pillars, catching the lanterns and throwing long white spindles on its black shining surface.

At the shrine, workmen are setting out rows of benches. Priests in white gauzy kimono patter about in the shadows bringing candles. I hear fugitive phrases of music, the measured

249

banging of drums; then a priest says, '*Dozo* ...' and indicates a seat in the front.

The few stray watchers move closer. There are no dignitaries, no tourists, no crowds. It is strange music, strange dancing. In the candlelight, archaic male figures move slowly in gorgeous robes, mustard-yellow with one vermilion-lined sleeve, emerald and scarlet and gold, trains and helmets, brocades and embroideries, monstrous masks, magnificent headdresses. Slow, slow and deliberate ... sliding, half-squatting, a foot raised and lowered in a soft stamp; swooping; challenging the sky; raising a lance; then the foot brought forward and down, heel first, the arms stretched at the sides, two stiffened fingers raised, hands brought together and separated as though parting water. Grotesque shadows fall in the candle-light. In the background, light shines up into faces, as white ghostly forms bend over lanterns.

Behind the shapes of these *bugaku* dancers, black against the stars, is the floodlit *torii*. From time to time swooping car headlights shine out on the bay, revealing greenish shadows of trees. White mists begin to move down from the mountain, enclosing pagoda and pines.

Now comes the High Priest, in a robe of rich white brocade, led by a young priest with a round white paper lantern held low to light the feet. On the green dais the brocade figure kneels before the white chrysanthemum in a slender white vase; then carries it to the main altar in the shrine and offers it to the gods.

The weird music, the strange dances continue, the drum and pipe, the masks and robes. Faltering red reflections float under the shrine building, the white spindles rock and shatter as the tide once more begins to retreat.

Going out very early next morning I find the *torii* changed again. Its ethereal quality gone, now it is gay and light-hearted and orange-red, its roof green with moss, with coloured fishing boats floating round its tree-trunk posts.

250

21

Kuma is far from the Sea

I SHOULD not have been surprised or disappointed at Kyushu. I knew already that in Japan distance does not guarantee freedom from crowds, and places close to big centres may be more isolated than northern Hokkaido. When one of my Japanese friends went to visit in-laws in a village fifty miles from Tokyo she caused a stir by wearing shorts.

But I had not expected crowds so big, so all-pervading. I seemed to have been fleeing for weeks down exquisite coasts, over stretches of opal sea, across beautiful islands, in and out of historic towns just one jump ahead of tour leaders with their flags and whistles. These were not the only disillusionments. Northern Kyushu is mainly industrial; Sasebo said WELCOME U.S. NAVY. STEAM BATHS. MASSAGE; Hirado Island, an old trading port, was thick with Japanese tourists; the Ninety-Nine Isles, of which there are a hundred and seven, hidden in fog.

The biggest blow had been Nagasaki, to which I had gone so eagerly. As well as being intensely hot a hard dry wind was blowing grit and dust through the air; traffic stormed down the streets with appalling speed and noise; people fell over each other in their frenzy to move along pavements, get on and off vehicles. The city itself depressed and vaguely frightened me, less physically than spiritually. Under the noise and bustle I sensed decay, as at Sasebo, and something worse...I still do not know quite what...almost desolation; yet it is a fascinating town, the oldest port in the country. Spanish, Portuguese, Dutch, English traders came and went till the seventeenth century. It still has a cosmopolitan population. Ships from all over the world lie in the great harbour at the foot of beautiful mountains. There are fine views and fascinating little streets and a lively Chinatown; but something moulders beneath it all.

Dr Ogata had warned me the Kyushu people would be different...very blunt and direct; but they also seemed rude, coarse, unfriendly and stupid. They are ugly, specially the Mongol type, with a surly, almost brutal expression. The nose is a negroid blob, the skin coarse, lips thick, teeth large and bad, eyes very small and deep-set, head square with flat top and low forehead. They could model for anti-Japanese war posters showing bestial grinning apes.

Unlike Honshu and Shikoku, there are no answering smiles. To my astonishment, station officials were unhelpful, uninformative, unco-operative. They showed impatience, even irritation. The men in the luggage *deposito* were curt and unsmiling; and at the information office directions were given out rudely and grudgingly.

In the street, when a foreigner approaches, possibly seeking directions, people look the other way and walk past. If you persist they may brush you aside and move on, though occasionally, unexpectedly, they may be very helpful in a rough way. When spoken to they stare, either through slowness of wits or bloody cussedness. You soon reach the stage where you ask all friendly intelligent civilised Japanese if they are from Honshu.

In the Oura quarter – a favourite with tourists – the narrow streets seemed chronically crowded. Parties of badly behaved schoolchildren pushed, shoved, shouted and pointed. Red-faced male groups reeking of *saké* staggered about making wolf-calls and whistles. Men and boys came up and tapped my shoulder or took my arm saying 'Hi baby', or 'Hi sweetheart'. The souvenir-sellers clotting the roadside were rude and arrogant. I wondered where I was. It did not seem like Japan. Even the buildings were different, these charming old painted houses with European windows and superb views out over the harbour.

Friendly cheerful Chinatown, where I went often to eat, could not lift my depression, nor the wonderful early prints of Europeans in the Oura museum. Here we are as the Japanese first saw us, every feature, weakness, absurdity – pomposity, heaviness, prominent noses, big stomachs, bulging eyes – recorded with subtle and devastating accuracy and wit.

This museum also has relics of concealed Christianity. Since the sixteenth century, when St Francis Xavier landed in Kyushu, Japan has had Christian converts. At first all went well but during the seventeenth century the Shogun Hideta set out to exterminate the new religion. Foreign missionaries were expelled and native converts persecuted and massacred. Those who would not recant died under terrible torture. They were hung by the feet for days over pits of filth, boiled alive, raped by crowds, thrown into

> tubs of Snakes and Adders, which crept by several passages into their bodies, suffered them to perish after unspeakable miseries ... they thrust hurds into the Mothers privities, and binding the Sons about with the same combustible matter thrust and forced them, as also the Fathers and daughters, to set fire to each other whereby they underwent unconceivable torment and pains ...

By the middle of the seventeenth century it seemed Christianity had been stamped out; but in 1865 it was found that hundreds of Kyushu families had remained faithful Catholics. For two hundred years they had worshipped in secret, using concealed crosses – in buckles, cups, books, designs – and Maria Kannons. These are figures of the Virgin Mary disguised as the goddess Kannon (Kwan-yin) with an almost imperceptible cross, hidden among the necklaces, jewels or robes, to which the Christians addressed their prayers. The effect of a Maria Kannon with a baby is curious. Most western madonnas are sweet simple girls with mild placid faces suited for maternity; but babies are quite incongruous in the arms of oriental goddesses with patrician features and cool haughty expressions.

During the persecution, suspected Christians were ordered to tread on *fumi-e* – pictures, plates, tiles showing Christ's image or the cross or other sacred symbols. These relics must be steeped in vibrations of the faith, fear, devotion, misery, torment, courage they witnessed. Looking at them the feeling of desolation increases. The past seems horribly close in the silent museum room, where apparently no one comes. All the tourists are down the hill, at the ugly nineteenth-century Oura Church, the oldest Catholic church in the country, built in honour of twenty-six Christians martyred at Nagasaki. There is also a new, more pixylated church to the Twenty-six Martyrs, closer to the city centre. It reminded me of the Walt Disney buildings in the Guëll Park at Barcelona.

Nagasaki seems more interested in the Twenty-six Martyrs and Christian persecution than the atomic bomb. I had trouble finding the Peace Park, for no one was quite sure how to get there. One does not blame them . . . the park is bleak, scruffy, sterile; the Peace Statue unspeakably ugly. A bronze monstrosity, ten metres high, with pin-head and colossal legs, sits with one arm up and the other outstretched like a traffic cop. The legs are vaguely attempting the yoga *Pose of a Hero*, the face on the end of the prize-fighter's neck is blandly complacent. It is hard to believe it came from the sculptor who made the sensitive figures of Tenko-san and Sogetsu-san at Itto-en. It is only surpassed in ugliness by the pair of incredible figures at Lake Towada.

Across the narrow grey valley of Urakami, above which the

bomb exploded, the hillside is now covered with mean little houses. There is a fine new Catholic cathedral, several glass matchboxes standing end-up, an atomic museum and new Culture Hall. It was on this hill that Dr Nagai lived in his little hut, called *Love-thy-neighbour-as-thyself*, and wrote his books while he was dying of leukemia, accelerated by the bomb.

I had moved on and on. Now, returning from Hondo, in the Amakusa Islands, the boat was approaching Misumi, on mainland Kyushu. I opened my map and saw a train line from Yatsushiro along the Kuma River to Yunomae. The last name was printed in very small type. Letters so insignificant could only mean 'nothing there'. No little triangles denoted mountains to be climbed, there were no *onsen* (hot spring) symbols or N.P. for national park. I would take a chance.

Almost at once I entered a different Kyushu. The exquisite Kuma River rises at the foot of the sacred mountain Ichifusa and flows through plains and valleys to the sea at Yatsushiro Bay, winding between high, higher, highest hills where red leaves now splashed the dark cypress forests. Like southern Shikoku, it is scroll-painting country . . . flat slender boats, fishermen with long poles, lonely sages, rapids and little grey villages.

The small friendly *densha* follows the river all through the valley to Hitoyoshi, the capital of old Kuma County, seat of the Lords of Sagara. Before the railway was built, in the twenties, local rice was taken from here to Yatsushiro by water; but now the river left us and we entered a broad gold plain where beautiful houses stood among rows of drying-racks. Rich lion-coloured walls of rice marked off the fields; little streams ran under willows; in the distance a far crown of purple and blue mountains changed colour as the sun moved. The air smelt of earth and dry straw, the warm dusty universal scent of harvest.

Yunomae seemed to consist mainly of a street with shops on both sides. At one end of the town a big timber-yard gave out a wonderful smell of fresh wood. Buses passed through from time to time, on their way to Yatsushiro. Strange sirens went off in the night and early morning as they do in some small country towns.

The inn was humble, small, very clean; its people simple and friendly. For about 12s 6d I got dinner, o-furo, bed, breakfast, frequent plates of fruit, cups of o-cha and cake, bags fetched and carried to and from the station, shoes cleaned and much kindness. When I came in tired from a walk the motherly maid brought me tea or a pleasant hot drink, which tasted like Bonox, made by pouring hot water over a seaweed-like substance. Then she would kneel and massage my shoulders. O-furo, which I had alone, since it held but one at a time and I was the only guest, was a wooden tub with a fire underneath. The meals were good, with beautiful sashimi and delicious little black-eyed shellfish and ayu from the Kuma river.

The Kuma locals are not only more friendly than those round Nagasaki, they are better-looking, less coarse, negroid and stupid, with pleasant smiles and often with good teeth. Kyushu people are rather a mixture. The original natives were hairy, in this district were called Hairy Kumaso, but many Koreans settled in the island and now there are also types with smooth faces, arms, legs, and chests. Since Kuma is far from the sea, less accessible to raiders, it seems largely to have escaped Mongol influence. Its remoteness from western tourism has no doubt helped preserve the people's agreeable manner.

All day I stayed out in the fields, walking, talking to peasants, looking at scarecrows, dozing under trees. I ate fruit for lunch and returned to the inn for dinner. The whole countryside had changed since I arrived in Japan. It was now alive, enriched in colour, deepened in texture and peopled not only with scarecrows but moving figures in wide hats and mompei, working alone or in groups. Parties sat together for refreshments; little children in red ran about; babies crawled. There was the swish of sheaves hoisted into trucks, the whirr of threshers, an odd tractor. Stacks, stubble, sheaves spread out to dry, the weird hobby-horses of loaded hurdles in rows of orderly knots and fringes, sometimes in straight lines, sometimes curving and winding, make an entirely new landscape. Beyond are dove-grey thatch and tile roofs among dark trees and bamboo, and the mauve *murasaki*, one of the grasses of autumn.

With all this beauty on their doorstep the locals keep wanting to know why I don't go to Mount Ichifusa or Hitoyoshi.

It was late afternoon when I walked down the road that leads out to the rice fields. This plain is a shallow basin surrounded by exquisite changing mountains. Now, with sunset approaching, the western ranges grew dark while those still in the path of light turned from blue to Byzantine purple. Mists floated up from shadowed crevasses and foxtails of smoke hovered above farms and cottages. The smell of burning wood joined the scent of earth and rice-grain and sweet cut grasses.

A few people passed on the rough country road...school-children on bicycles, a man bringing cows in for milking. They all said *Komban wa*. Coloured cosmos, little daisies and zinnias grew by the roadside. Among the high tawny plush fields, bright shallow cut-out patches showed, with fine spring-green grass sprouting through stubble. Round about were the rows of golden tassels, the long-haired lion-skins hanging over the racks.

An old wooden building with gothic church windows rose from the rice. In the yard a small Shinto altar stood among orange dahlias and purple Michaelmas daisies.

Dying slowly behind the western mountains, the sun bled, crimson, orange, pink, gold. The stains lingered on in the sky and the last shafts of light enriched the ripe fields, intensifying their colour. There was the sound of a crow.

The world here is surrounded by mountains. The old women of Kuma used to say that after the sun sets in the west it goes secretly during the night, round behind the mountains to the east where it climbs again in the morning.

I walked on. The sky faded. I passed a dusky farmyard with cows; pigs squealed away on the right. Through the scented stillness came small distant voices, invisible late workers out in the fields. Soon lights appeared in windows and I felt a chill in the air. A crescent white moon, a few stars sparkled in the dark blue sky.

I walked without destination or purpose, in fact without thought. Such peace, such completion left no room for awareness of time or direction. I had become part of the evening, the rich harvest scene, the moon and the stars. I felt no fatigue, no desire ever to stop, to leave the beautiful night, go inside, let people close *shoji* and shut it out.

When I finally looked at my watch it was half-past eight. I had been walking for hours and had no idea where I was. The lights of Yunomae seemed very far off across the plain and, strangely, in the wrong direction. I had left the main road to explore the wooden church and gone on from there through little lanes; now I realised I had lost the road.

I was terribly tired. I longed to sit down, better still, lie down, go to bed. I wondered, without much concern, how far I had come, where I was, if there were buses to Yunomae. I had seen none on my walk and it was most unlikely one would come along now, in this lane through the rice. I supposed if the worst happened I could sleep under a hedge; but the crisp air was cool and there was a certain dewy dampness about the ditches along the road.

I began moving towards the light of a house across the fields, sliding and slithering on long grass, frequently stopped by thick walls of rice. It seemed to take hours to feel my way round by the little foot-path and by the time I reached the farmyard I had lost some of my evening serenity; but only on the surface. I was not deeply worried nor was I nervous out there in the dark, though I knew the scarecrows were all round. It may have been the open atmosphere of the wide tranquil plain, the absence of forests, but I did not feel the *kami* here, as on Kinkazan or Sado. No one watched, no one minded. Benighted travellers had nothing to fear.

There was a side entrance by the road and a dim yellow

light through *shoji*. At the back, in a small courtyard, dimly I saw haystacks in ballerina skirts and a large machine covered over with matting, on the edge of an open linhay. In the dark I smelt flowers, straw-dust, earth and *benjo*.

A little dog reared up and yapped.

Remembering Yasou on Sado, I knocked at the *shoji*. The voices inside ceased and after a pause a shadow moved and the *shoji* was pushed aside. A little monkey-man peered out at me. Beyond, in a large dark-walled room people were eating.

I said, 'Dozo . . .'

He seemed paralysed; but a plain kindly woman with protruding teeth, bundled up in a *tanzen* with an apron tied over it, got up and came to join him. She bobbed her head and said 'Komban wa,' and made gestures inviting me in.

I took off my thongs and entered.

The family were up on the *tatami* tucking into their evening meal. Though it seemed very late a small child was propped up beside a young schoolgirl in uniform. Apart from the monkey-faced farmer and kind-looking wife there were several bullet-headed young men with gold teeth, and an ancient *obasan*, smudged and blurred like an ink-drawing left out in the rain.

I offered the key words . . . 'Yunomae . . . *ryokan* . . . *basu*?' They understood at once, but turned to the schoolgirl to give the reply. She said bashfully, 'Excuse me . . . no *basu* Yunomae.'

I said 'Ah so!' and asked *where* was Yunomae, pointing enquiringly in different directions. They all pointed together in the one direction I had not guessed. They had begun to smile, as though at a game. I asked if it were far. They said Yes, it was far.

There was a pause. No one jumped up and offered to show me the road and not liking to ask, since they had all been working late at their harvest, I was about to bow and withdraw proudly into the night when the mother said 'Gohan? Yushoko?' and offered the rice pot.

It was warm in this rather rough farm kitchen, which smelt

of bonito stock. I was tired; it would not hurt to sit down before I began the walk home. I bowed my thanks and at once
the little girl, Michiko, moved to make room. The grand-
mother's faded lids flipped up and down and she leant across
to peer at me. A large container of rice was plonked beside me
on the floor. On the low table were pickles, a big tea-kettle,
the remains of boiled vegetables.

In a corner, rather lower than the floor where we sat, was a
square sink and a chopping board. Baskets hung on the dark
walls, in the middle of the room a bare electric light globe
with switch. There were empty *saké* bottles, Coca-Cola bottles
and hideous souvenirs from Beppu and Mount Aso. Enlarged,
sombre, slightly spooky photographs of dead-looking people
were hoisted high on the walls.

The family watched me intently as I worked through soup,
boiled pumpkin, rice, pickles and *o-cha*. They seemed amused
that I could use chopsticks.

'American?'

'Australian.'

'*So! So desuka!* Australia!'

This was marvellous news. It was relayed to the *obasan*, who
quickly asked a question. The giggling Michiko interpreted,
'How-many-babies?' And when I had answered, 'What-is-
your-age?'

There was more nodding and sucking of breath and *So!*
and *Sah!* We exchanged names. I drew a map of Japan and
traced my journeys, drew a map of Australia and showed the
ship route across the Pacific. I dug out and presented the last
of the discontinued Australian pennies with kangaroos, even
found a couple of Qantas kangaroo pins for the men. No
doubt these Kuma peasants are still wearing FLY QANTAS
badges.

Then I said '*Anoné* ...' and began bowing and making signs
of leaving; but the farmer's wife, who had been whispering
with her husband, now spoke. Michiko translated, 'Sleep here,'
and went into hysterics, hand over mouth.

Mother spoke again. Michiko said, 'No sleep...Yunomae,' indicating her father.

I asked if they had a car. There was no *kurama*.

It was my own fault if I had to walk back to Yunomae but I did not see why the poor little monkey-man should have to turn out and escort me, then walk home, after his long day's work. When I bowed and said 'Thank you, I'd like to stay,' he looked relieved, though a slight unease crossed his wife's face.

But she quickly forgot her fears and took from a cupboard a padded gown like the one she was wearing. I was given a little towel and led by Michiko across the starlit yard to the bath-house. It was a country bath with a fire underneath and small wooden tubs for preliminary washing. It was bare, dark, primitive and exceedingly clean and though it seemed the family had been in before me the water was still hot.

In the *benjo*, a folk art model, a flower in a little basket hung on the wall. A persistent wandering scent suggested a nearby cesspool. I almost reeled with fatigue, intensified by the bath. Wrapped in the heavy gown I stood in the courtyard, dizzily wondering how soon I could get to bed; if I should have to sit up and let Michiko practise her English on me.

I was relieved to find her reading a comic with the wireless going full blast. The young men, the baby had vanished, and *obasan*, after blinking at me with her little black eyes, crawled away into her hole. She was bent almost at a right-angle.

I sat in my *tanzen* thanking God it was not winter, for there was no sign of heating beyond the *kotatsu* hole in the floor, and presently Mama, kindly exposing her fan of teeth, spread a *futon* in a far corner of the big room. I lay down gratefully, and despite wireless, conversations and glaring light, went to sleep. I was vaguely aware of a screen being pulled across to shut off the other room.

I woke in the night, wondering where I was. The sealed room was black and stuffy. Somewhere in the darkness sleepers droned and puffed but I could see nothing. I was hot under the heavy covers and longed for fresh air. I also thought of

261

the *benjo* but could not face making my way over unseen bodies and battling with *shoji* and shutters. I concentrated on the countryside out in the dark, the flayed lions hanging limp on their hurdles, the stubble squares softened with young grass. I thought of the mountains leaning back against the blue-black sky and the crisp little crescent and stars. I wondered again how and why the Japanese, who love nature and keeping fit, immure themselves at night.

A gentle snuffle came from outside where an animal moved in the courtyard. There was a sleeping grunt from behind the dark screen. I slept again.

When I woke, just before dawn, people were up and moving beyond the screens. Presumably everyone had slept together next door to allow me a room to myself. I dimly perceived the god-shelf, the family altar, and assumed I must be in the parlour.

I pulled on my clothes, rolled up my bed and went out. They were all there, except *obasan*, getting ready for work. Mother was hovering over a charcoal fire with a pot of soup and one of rice which she shortly set out with a kettle of tea. There was the same bonito-stock smell, suggestive of tarred ropes.

Out in the courtyard the covered-up form I had stumbled against last night was grinding and churning. As the rice was fed in one end the grain came from a spout into sacks which the women held ready. The full sacks were quickly lifted and stacked beside the ballerina haystacks and work went on smoothly. There were several people I had not seen before and I wondered if they were neighbours come to help. I wanted to ask if the farmer owned the thresher or if it were borrowed round the district but they were all so busy I did not like to ask questions.

As it was, I had no way of showing my gratitude for their kindness beyond smiles, bows and repeated thanks. They bowed, smiled in return and *obasan*, now creeping about in the garden with the baby, so bent that her head was not far above his, drew back her yellow lips and showed blackened Heian-period teeth. While we made our farewells, Michiko, instructed to put me on the right road to town, skipped about on one foot, holding the other ankle.

Mists were still among the mountains and dew thick on stubble and grass. After the stuffy night the air was exquisite, scented with hay, flowers, early morning. All the population were out . . . children playing before school, women washing clothes in the stream, men and women cutting, drying, threshing in fields and farmyards. They all smiled, they all waved cheerfully and those close enough screeched questions at Michiko. It was easy to guess what they asked, what she replied.

Round the harvesters large crows waited hopefully, serious, intent. Small birds twittered in the tall rice. The sky was pale with autumnal warmth and now I could see the country I had walked through by starlight last night.

22

Volcano and Mist

To REACH Kagoshima from Yunomae I had to take the little *densha* back to Hitoyoshi, then a very slow wandering local train through the mountains. This wonderful journey ends dramatically. Suddenly, after day-long mountainous country, you emerge on the shores of a great bay where across the pale water a superb volcano sends up white smoke. It is called Sakurajima.

At the station I took a taxi to Isohama youth hostel, a little way out from Kagoshima centre. My first glimpse of the town was of hot dusty streets, shabby buildings and plenty of traffic; but as I drove to the hostel there was an extraordinary feeling of going back in time. Isohama, on its headland, far from street cars and noise, basks in afternoon sun. High stone walls, stone stairways, stone European villas in deep green gardens look out tranquilly on the wide bay, the lazy volcano. Magnificent trees, bamboo, bananas cluster by curving drives with azaleas, rhododendrons and everywhere, filling the warm air with scent, the cream trumpet-bells of *brugmansia*, drooping heavily upon diamond-patterned walls overgrown with moss and tiny ferns.

It was beautiful but it was sad; when you looked closely it was all in decay – the grey walls and gateways, the mansions now run as hostels or *ryokans*, restaurants or boarding-houses, the mossy stairs and walks overgrown, the lush gardens choked with weeds. It was out of date, beat-up, completely romantic. Though buses and cars drive round the coast road and youth hostellers rush about on motor-bikes and drinking parties shout at the restaurant over the road, Isohama still hears carriage wheels, even sedan chairs on her drives; Meiji beauties still bow to officers in splendid uniforms, foreign ladies waltz in egret feathers and diamond chokers. Fleets still come and go, receptions are held, there are chandeliers in the great stone houses and Japanese lanterns out in the scented trees, and across the water Sakurajima sends up red smoke against the stars, throwing a red reflected path on the bay.

I left the taxi at a high stone wall where wide steps mount the ramparts. There was also a low gate through which you entered half-crouching, as though in a tea-house. I wondered if it were for serfs or security. At first sight the house on the ramparts was pure European. Solid, substantial, vaguely Italianate in the South Kensington manner, there was no trace of Japan beyond a stone lantern in the overgrown garden.

Inside, a high-ceilinged room with long windows and great tarnished mirrors was festooned and littered with a bizarre east-and-west mixture – low Japanese table and *zabutons*, European bookshelves up the walls, youth hostel banners and photographs, Italianate plaster arches, a modern stereo. Despite the disorder the room was noble, dignified, a gentleman's library, faintly sad and disturbing beneath the cheery groups and views of Sakurajima, the pop music churning out from the player.

A maid took me to a Japanese annexe where I left my belongings. No one asked for cards, registration or payment.

The hostel parent was running another hostel up in the mountains at Kirishima and this one – the family home – was managed by his sons and daughters when they came back from work, school, university or wherever they spent the day.

Kagoshima is rather nondescript and wide open, like most cities that have been rebuilt more than once, but its amiable easy-going, up-to-date appearance is deceptive. Though there are modern bars and coffee shops, *depatos* and universities, prefectural offices and fine apartment houses, the real focus of its inner life is the nineteenth century.

Two personalities dominate the town – Sakurajima, the living volcano, and Saigo Takemori, a dead nineteenth-century general. Sakurajima, over the water, takes the place of the weather in local conversation, all talk, all life coming back eventually to it and its moods. 'The volcano is angry today.' 'The volcano is quiet today.' 'Last night the volcano sent up many flames.' 'The smoke from the volcano goes so many metres up into the air.' 'The volcano causes the dust...' The dust is good for endless discussion. 'When the wind blows this way we are *covered* with dust,' the locals say happily. 'You must excuse the dust' – waving at the fine ash powdering the furniture – 'It is from the volcano.'

Sakurajima erupts from time to time but people continue to live at its foot and cannot be persuaded to move. It is strictly forbidden to climb the mountain beyond a certain distance or venture at all on some sides, for it frequently tosses out red-hot rocks. It is unpredictable and cantankerous and this seems to endear it even more to the townspeople. They speak of it as of an eccentric beloved grandfather who bullies and browbeats but must be indulged.

'Kagoshima is called the Naples of the East,' they tell you. 'And Sakurajima is the Vesuvius of the East.'

General Saigo's personality and deeds overshadow even those of the great Lords of Satsuma, the local *daimyos*, and Admiral Togo (the Nelson of the East), hero of the Russo-Japanese War.

266

After the Meiji Restoration, when power was removed from the Shoguns and given back to the Emperor, there were many reforms and changes. One was the destruction of the *samurai* class. For centuries the *samurai* had lived as privileged warriors; now they had to exist on tiny pensions and were not even allowed to carry a sword. Their status as fighting men was denigrated by conscription, which showed that anyone, even a peasant, could become a good soldier with appropriate training. General Saigo, a Satsuma man, who was in the Government, objected to this reform. Since there were many dissatisfied *samurai* out of a job he proposed leading them on an expedition against Korea. The plan was rejected, Saigo withdrew from the Government and eventually returned to Kagoshima where he had followers among the Satsuma *samurai*.

In 1877 he led them in an armed rebellion against the Government. Fighting lasted for several months, thirty thousand men were killed and the new despised conscript army won. Realising he was defeated, Saigo, lying wounded in a cave on Mount Shiroyama, behind Kagoshima, asked a close friend to kill him. The friend cut off his head.

It was not only Saigo's courage, the manner of his death that stirred the romantic imagination of the local people. He was a great man, in size as well as in strength of character. He had *panache*. He was blunt, outspoken, independent, defiant, impatient of petty restrictions. He personified everything the Satsuma people admired, for they had a long local tradition of defiance against the capital. He must have seemed a kind of safety valve, a vicarious outlet for all that the ordinary man could not express; and though his martial influence, fanatical patriotism, dreams of military supremacy in Asia are not quite in line with modern Japan's renunciation of war, he is still a great hero in Satsuma. His admirers call him the Garibaldi of the East.

In Kagoshima he is everywhere. His large angry eyes glare beneath heavy eyebrows, like a martial Daruma, on biscuits, on china, on postcards, on trays; he has a tomb in a temple; he is venerated at Nanshu Shrine; notices tell you that here he stood, here he lay, here he asked his friend to cut off his head. He became so much a part of my life that seeing his figure in Tokyo, at Ueno Park, where he stands with his dog, was like meeting an old friend.

Kagoshima has twice been razed to the ground, the second time during the Pacific war, but when the residents speak of The War, which they frequently do, it is Saigo's war, Saigo's revolt.

'Have you seen the sights of Kagoshima?' a kindly man asked at the bus stop. 'The tomb of the General? And on Shiroyama, the cave where he died?'

'Have you seen the General's memorial?' the young lady in the craft centre enquired solicitously. 'It is a very fine shrine and the view from Shiroyama is very beautiful, you can see the volcano. Kagoshima is the Naples of the East. And there is a statue of the General on Shiroyama . . . and the cave where he deceased during The War.'

'You have heard of The War, of course?' said a little patrician old gentleman on a street-car, bowing and presenting his card. 'Kagoshima very important in The War. General Saigo. He is the Garibaldi of the East.'

Yet for all its prolonged love affair with the past, Kagoshima is not dreary or moribund. Streets and shops are lively, though the old port's great days are gone. Its main traffic now consists of small ships going south through the outer islands to the Ryukyus and Okinawa or Taiwan. Tramps and cargo ships put in, but no great liners come to the magnificent bay, where the Japanese Navy carried out its secret training exercises for the attack on Pearl Harbour.

In 1862, during the anti-foreigner campaign, an Englishman named Richardson was attacked on the Tokaido highway by retainers of the Lord of Satsuma, pulled from his horse and killed. In retaliation Britain sent a naval squadron to bombard Kagoshima and burnt most of the town. Instead of rousing Satsuma's hatred this started a friendship between the two countries. Japan's navy became largely modelled on the Royal Navy and when the Nelson of the East defeated the Russians at the Battle of Tsushima, during the Russo-Japanese war, it was with ships mainly built and fitted out in England, with English-trained Japanese officers.

Like Saigo, the volcano quickly took over my life. All day I was aware of it across the bay, changing colour, with its pale straight plume that turns white as the sun sinks and the sky grows grey, or shoots out in black blasts like an angry engine.

I sat in the garden for hours watching it; the maid approvingly would call me sometimes to see flames licking, rocks being hurled in the air. Strangely, these fireworks were less sinister than when the mountain sent up black, rather stern, charcoal smoke, slow, steady, vertical, as though getting up steam.

White ferries come and go to and from Sakurajima and at weekends they are crowded, mainly with schoolchildren and businessmen on the spree.

I am told that there is a leper settlement somewhere across the bay but no one talks of it. I think they feel it a social blot.

At close quarters, Sakurajima is perfectly vile . . . like Beppu, another famous Kyushu natural phenomenon. But whereas Beppu is all jets of steam shooting up in the air like express trains, Sakurajima's big attraction is lava. I never saw, never wish to see again, so much lava, fields of it, miles of it, black, sinister, sterile, hideous. The mountain was once an island – 'Cherry Island' (*Cheery Island* in a local brochure) – but lava now joins it to the mainland. Beppu has a slightly more homely appearance – from the sea it resembles a town cooling off after bombardment – but Sakurajima does not belong to this planet. It is about as attractive as the face of the moon and I could not get away from it quickly enough nor feel right till distance had once more restored its beauty.

Isohama hostel is offhand, ramshackle, easy-going, completely delightful. Meals are noisy, informal and good. There is no *o-furo.* You have to go to the public baths, some little distance away, a merry rowdy place where you bath with a great many women and children while the men shout on the other side of the partition, walking back afterwards in the dark with your little wet towel along the scented road. Crowds of hostellers came and went and were all squeezed in. One night when our *futons* were literally cheek-by-jowl I slept out on a tiny veranda near the *benjo* which perfumed my insomnia. In the untidy garden water hyacinths grow in a pond, stone lanterns and crooked pines stand among lines of washing and there are stone benches for sitting and watching the bay and volcano.

Sometimes I walked up the mossy stone stairs to a small park where Admiral Togo looks out on the bay he loved. There was rarely anyone in these gardens, he was usually all alone, a little straight man with moustaches. I would sit with him and think of his times. In the Russo-Japanese war both sides behaved like *samurai*. The victorious Japanese general gave his own white horse to the defeated Russian commander and Japan's humane and generous treatment of her prisoners-of-war stirred the world's imagination.

The sunsets were lingering. In the long blue evening birds twittered round the little bronze Nelson. Sakurajima's feather glowed orange against a hyacinth sky and lay reflected on the dusky bay, where boats were coming home through gentle mists.

Down the hill is a big kiln set about with beautiful blue-and-white Spanish-looking tiles. At the back, in a simple building, I found men painting on china – roses, pheasants, peonies, wistaria – outlined in gold; and though I do not care for Satsuma's ornate decoration and heavy cream crackle it was right to find it there after watching the sunset with Admiral Togo. Satsuma-ware and dogs called Togo were as much a part of our grandmothers' lives as the buttoned plush chairs in their drawing-rooms.

When the men beckoned me in and patted the ground among the paints and unglazed pots I sat down and watched

270

their careful and delicate movements, their calm patient faces and sensitive hands. As they worked they referred to great dog-eared books, taking a peony here, a pheasant from over the page. It was peaceful and restful in the fading light, with Sakurajima glimpsed through the window.

The owner of the potteries, a handsome youngish man painting with the others, told me his family had owned this Satsuma kiln for two hundred years. They had never changed their method, he said, showing me round a big room where men were throwing; they still use only pine wood for firing.

The shelves were full of pale pots, jars, incense burners, vases, so much more beautiful without glaze and decoration. In a dark corner I saw a Maria Kannon. I asked if I could buy her.

He shook his head. 'It is very old. We must keep it as a sample. Besides, it has never been finished, never been glazed.'

She swayed in a typical Kwan-yin attitude, elegant, with a little crown, holding a rosary, impregnated with love and faith, a different breed to the rather pedestrian figures in Nagasaki. She might have been two hundred years old, for Kagoshima was Japan's earliest contact with Christianity, when St Francis Xavier landed here.

All Satsuma ware is not ornate. The main kilns in this part of Kyushu were started by Koreans for making tea-ceremony utensils in the Korean tradition, and two – Ryuomonji, on Kagoshima Bay, and Naeshirogawa, in the Satsuma peninsula – still produce simple and beautiful pottery of the Korean type. The Naeshirogawa potters, brought here by the Lord of Satsuma, were forbidden to marry Japanese and this isolation helped preserve their traditions and culture.

You may buy black-glazed Ryuomonji and Naeshirogawa pottery in Kagoshima shops, along with decorated Satsuma, lacquerware, red wooden *mingei* Kagoshima fish on wheels and portraits of General Saigo.

✻

There are buses from Kagoshima, south to Ibusuki and round the Satsuma Peninsula, which has another volcano. There are also boats to Takeshima Island, where the first Europeans landed in Japan, Portuguese merchants on their way to Macao, blown ashore in a storm. They brought the first gunpowder the Japanese had ever seen.

I could not bear to leave Isohama for long enough to go to these islands but I went on the local bus down the beautiful coast, past where St Francis landed. It is said that he brought an organ which so intrigued the Japanese they started schools for studying this and other western instruments brought by missionaries. The Kagoshima people were also fascinated by the naval brass bands of the British who had bombarded them, and bands became all the rage.

Ibusuki, at the end of the peninsula, is a holiday resort but on the way there are miles of deserted beaches and small sheltered coves with fishing boats, crooked pines, rotting hulks and drying nets. Here and there, women work at some marine activity, by an Aegean Sea strewn with ghostly blue islands and mountains.

The locals claim this coast is like the South Seas. It has a tropical lushness of fruit and flowers; there are bananas, *brugmansia* and bamboo, which was here first introduced to Japan; but in the Islands no one cuts rice by the sea or lives in thatched houses with *shoji*.

The people are very agreeable.

'*Banjulo*,' said a friendly girl in the bus, giving me a strange fruit, smiling when I said I liked it. She took my arm. 'Have you seen our volcano? It is called Sakurajima. Last night it was very angry. Flames.'

I had seen the flames. I said it was a beautiful mountain.

'Oh yes, it is beautiful. We say the volcano changes colour seven times a day. Sometimes the smoke from the volcano goes hundreds of metres into the air. The volcano sometimes explodes!' she offered eagerly. 'Many times it explodes. Once a whole side blew out! And often there are stones and flames.

And ash! So much ash! There is so much fine dust!' She laughed delightedly, proudly. 'Everything in Kagoshima is always covered in dust from the volcano!'

North of Kagoshima, at Hewa Park outside Miyazaki, there is a *haniwa* garden. Here, clay Sun Kings sit cross-legged among bushes and shrubs, patient clay horses stand, ready harnessed, for clay soldiers to mount; cheerful clay peasants in jesters' caps rollick home with hoes on their shoulders; strange Thurber figures with round eyes and mouths dance in perpetual astonishment. The Thurber touch is very strong in the animals – faithful hounds peering round shrubs, melancholy unidentifiable creatures turning in mild reproach. All, even the warriors, are gentle; some of the disembodied heads have a sad haunting beauty. The biggest is no more than two feet tall; the smallest, planted out as in garden beds, a few inches.

Set in grass, unexpectedly glimpsed among branches and leaves, dappled with sun and shade, these relics of proto-historic Japan are startling and wonderful. They come from Kyushu grave mounds, but there are many others in parts of Honshu. They are so primitive they are utterly modern. Some of the more grotesque might have come from living sculptors but for their innocence. Some look Japanese; others could be European or Eskimo, but all are Japanese in the sense that they say everything that need be said with complete economy. They are the essence of human emotions, the essence of animal life.

At Itto-en, Yoshio Harakawa had talked to me of Takachiho, in Miyazaki Prefecture. Kyushu has two Takachihos; one, which I had skirted coming through the mountains from Yuno-mae to Kagoshima, is the peak where the grandson of Amaterasu, the Sun Goddess, descended to begin reigning over Japan; the other is a small mountain town, where, Harakawa-san told me, some aspects of life have not changed for generations. Much work is still done by hand, ancient songs are still sung.

273

He had given me introductions to friends who live there, pictures of women wearing strange and beautiful baskets on their backs and records of traditional songs, some merry, some mournful.

One is a thatch-cutting song, the *Kariboshi Kiri Uta*, which they sing in the autumn when all the slopes have turned scarlet. The villagers, working together with sickles, sing as they cut the thatch for roofing and animal feed; and in the winter they give thanks for good harvests with ancient sacred dances, wearing masks, at night, round the Iwato Shrine. The *Kagura Seri Uta* is the song which the onlookers sing, standing with arms locked, watching the dancers.

It was these haunting primitive chants that were taking me to Takachiho. Such spare, taut, lonely, disturbing music could only come from a strange land.

I left my boxes of *haniwa* replicas at Nobeoka station and took a local bus through a valley of unsurpassed loveliness, along the edge of an olive-green stream. Houseboats like gondolas lay moored by shallow grey half-moon beaches. As the road climbed the coastal heat faded; cool air moved down the fantastic gorge; terraces became forests of yellow and scarlet; chasms, cliffs, vast rocks rose ahead. Curves were hairpin bends, dizzy bridges arched immense gulfs. When an occasional car approached we drew in to a bay to let it pass. Rural tranquillity turned to drama as we mounted and mounted, the air acquired a new sharpness.

Though we seemed to be literally among clouds, we came out suddenly into a valley, swung high between peaks, like a hammock, rich, secret, beautiful. It is not a Bach landscape, like Koya-san; cultivated terraces, farms and cottages give a softer domestic air; but it evokes an extraordinary combination of excitement and gentleness ... the thrill of the totally unexpected, the soothing familiarity of harvest scenes.

The little town itself is an anticlimax. Though mainly one street, it is bigger, more sophisticated than I expected. Tourists and hikers are catered for; shops sell *haniwa* figures; there is a

274

youth hostel and more than the one *ryokan* described by Hara-kawa-san. Since the road goes on to Mount Aso National Park, cars and buses pass through in the season.

At close quarters there was no hint of the strange *isolated* quality of the songs. People were friendly and after the first shock of surprise the beautiful valley lost its high hidden Tibetan mystery. I went to my *ryokan* feeling faintly let down. I wondered how long it was since Harakawa-san had been here; if I had come too late.

The inn was busy with a male party, servants were rushing and people were laughing and it was all very merry and brightly lit; but by the time I had taken *o-furo* and dinner there was a sense of change. I realised something was going on outside. We seemed to be withdrawing, a warm cheery island, into a sea of silence.

It was happening to the whole town. As darkness came on, drifting sheets of mist united and pressed down upon the mountain, sealing us off from the rest of the earth, from the stars, enclosing us in a great ghostly bird's-nest of eiderdown. When I opened my *shoji* a pale cold smoke billowed in, but without aggression or threat. This fog was neither sinister nor claustrophobic. If one were lost in it out on the mountain it would be cold, wet, unpleasant but without terror; if one died in it of exposure, death would be quiet and peaceful. Indoors, enjoyment of comfort and warmth was only increased by awareness of the grey presence pressing so lightly against the *shoji*, deadening the sounds from the streets.

When I woke next morning, in a diffused light, the gentle jailer was still outside. There were faint easing creaks of damp-beaded slithery tiles, moisture dripping from leaves, branches that stirred as melting liquid lightened their load, the almost inaudible runnelling of a gutter or stream; and supporting, intensifying all, yet utterly separate, the heavy dense silence that pressed on the eardrums.

In the streets, phantoms emerged and vanished through a soft opaque wall. Footsteps were deadened, voices muted. As in a dream, movement was slow, without direction; and just as the cheerful townspeople about their morning chores had been transmuted to disembodied presences, hearing had become distorted. School bells, children's cries, distant machines could not be located. Released from their origins, sounds wandered, rootless, seeking no destination, in absolute being.

No wind disturbed the curtain; it hung, thick and moist, almost tactile. A high dim radiance suggested a continuing sun, a possible sky.

I set out for a walk, almost feeling my way, up a flight of steps above the main street to where a droning chant indicated a school. Later, each time I passed here, little red-cheeked dolls would cluster to stare, some astonished, some appalled, some eager to touch and see, others flying in terror. At the bigger school, teenage boys and girls rushing out to go home would be brought up short by my unexpected appearance; but they never gave whistles or calls of 'American!' as in more progressive areas.

The path became narrow and steep between high grassy borders and weighted-down trees. It led to the edge of an amphitheatre where wide horseshoe terraces went down into the mist. Close by, harvested rice was stacked in pale bell-tents on shallow descending shelves of stubble.

When would the mist disperse? It was now ten o'clock and beyond our grey capsule the sun must be strong. There were dim tree-shapes and a fainting and weeping all round, as liquified vapours dripped into bushes and grass, but valley and town were invisible. In eighteen hours I had seen nothing of Takachiho's surroundings beyond the first dazzling glimpse.

Visually, I was alone on the earth; but people were around somewhere, bafflingly untraceable. I could hear snatches of conversation, thin muffled calls, the rhythm of small machines. Where were they? How to get to them? I began to shuffle down a steep hillside, seeing only my own feet before me. I might suddenly walk over a cliff; yet though confused and un-

276

certain I had no fears. This fog was still gentle, devoid of menace.

There was a movement in front, so close I seemed to step on it, a faint scuffing plod, the hint of a swish. I stopped abruptly, my foot almost touching a girl who was leading a cow. She wore blue-and-white *mompei* and *tenugui* and on her back one of the beautiful Takachiho baskets, a more elegant version of those worn by some Nepalese tribes. Unsurprised by my silent intrusion, she smiled showing beautiful teeth in a round rosy face and said *Ohayo*. I slowed down to let them get ahead and in a couple of seconds they had ceased to exist.

If I went on walking this way I should end up at Mount Aso, a volcano I had no desire to see. I left the road and followed a track and again stopped abruptly. Again people were near. I felt like a spy, hidden and silent; and suddenly, there they were, a child and two women wearing baskets, in a stubble-field, bending and gathering among crinolined haystacks.

For a moment the mist was wispy and thin, though it walled us in all round; then it thickened again and I groped away from the once-more invisible workers.

I seemed to have pushed through unseen forests and fields for hours when I sat down on wet earth, among smooth rounded bolsters of tea, to rest and think. I loved the mist but I wished it would lift; and immediately it did. Without vapourings, reluctant trailings or dwindling it was suddenly gone and a hot sun shone out of a clear noonday sky and all over the mountain red-cheeked families, groups of neighbours in wide floppy hats, were having lunch in the fields by their little threshing-machines. They called me to join them and I sat drinking *o-cha* and eating *Inari-sushi* and laughing and photographing their babies.

Behind them were gabled farmhouses with thatch held down by heavy poles and gardens bright with simple flowers. Everywhere black trees were splashed with persimmons and on the terraced hills, armies encamped in little bell-tents.

For a few hours this bright busy normal world existed. Harakawa-san's friends dropped their work and devoted themselves to showing the sights, gorges and waterfalls, rivers and autumn forests where buses come and people buy postcards and colour-film; then all was gone again and might never have been. Once more the mist came down, the great soft bird's-nest, shutting us off from the world, and softly, insistently, silence pressed against the *shoji*, against the eardrums.

23

Land of Yamato

AUTUMN in Japan has a special quality. The light seems more luminous, there is the lingering radiance of a long slow sunset, yet softness and poignancy in the air do not destroy brilliance and clarity. When the Japanese autumn wind blows it is not just a wind from nowhere. It comes from the past; it brings a sense of far-away and wakes memories of lands one has never known.

At this time of year, at Hasedera temple, in the Land of Yamato, the worn stone steps climb up between crimson and yellow. Beneath the vermilion pagoda with golden bells, people eating lunch from *bentos* quietly enjoy the view down the autumnal valley. Higher up, the little cemetery, the grey-and-white buildings are soft against sudden stabs of scarlet, shafts of sunlight through orange lace. The tolling of bells, the chanting of *sutras* comes clearly through crystalline air.

How I shall miss the *sounds* of Japan...the clop and drag of *geta* on cobbles, the torn-silk trill of the cricket, the *bento* men on the stations dolefully crying 'Ben*taw* ... Ben*taw* ...' the harsh disturbing crows, the plangent *samisens*, the clappers, the chanting, the wind-chimes.

Further along the valley, the steps at Muroji wander through moss and fallen leaves, pause to rest, to look down on a scarlet drum-bridge or up at pavilions or at a pagoda. Muroji in autumn is almost too beautiful, with its maples and a little chill creeping as vapours rise from the river and dusk gathers under the trees. Drinking parties picnic on the banks; a group is part-singing from scores, people paint, take photographs, walk, recline, view the autumn leaves.

Out in the countryside, smoke drifts from bonfires, river scents join the floury smell of harvested fields. The narrow amphitheatres are full of sheaves drying on racks. Here and there a poor derelict scarecrow lies on his face. The toy trains quietly clicking their way through serene evening hills will soon clatter against bitter winds.

Over the wide plain the smoke-wreaths rise and rise,
Over the wide lake the gulls are on the wing;
A beautiful land it is, the Land of Yamato!

In Tokyo, *yukatas* have disappeared from department stores, wind-chimes are packed away, the annual Imperial Messenger has been led in procession down the avenues of Meiji shrine. In rural *ryokans*, heavy lined gowns are now laid out, and thick padded bright-coloured jackets and working trousers piled on the counters of village shops.

It is time to go home. At the last possible minute I finish packing, resentfully rope up cartons of books and *mingei* toys and pottery, stamp on suitcases and fling left-overs into the new bags I have had to buy. The very small taxi-man stares appalled and says '*E-to!*' then he smiles philosophically, says '*Anoné* ...' and begins to pack it all in. We move off, across Tokyo. In the fine afternoon blaze Sendagaya's crowded parks and gardens, Akasaka's empty affluent streets, the Emperor's walls and moats are all very sharp and clearly outlined. Down the long avenues, past tizzy Ginza to Harumi-dori and the docks, an unplanned tour of farewell.

As we drive, thought is blurred in a farewell glow, irritations and annoyances forgotten. Europeans who live here, even those who love the country and people, have cycles when everything Japanese exasperates them. At these times they warn the euphoric newcomer he would feel differently *if he really knew them.* Knowing another race, in this sense, means they are not so nice after all. Since I do not profess to know the Japanese I am leaving them with regret; but I wonder can anyone say they *really* know them?

We are at Harumi. Clouds have covered the benevolent sun, a bitter wind has come up and whips down the exposed docks. Because this is a national holiday the customs are to be open for only two hours. I hope it will be long enough for them to get through my effects, that I can quickly embark and go to sleep.

At the customs shed the taxi driver carried the bags from the car, then returned for those in the boot. This he had locked, for unknown reasons and now, taking his keys out to open it, he dropped them. They fell down a grating.

It was three forty-five. At four o'clock the customs men were going off duty. At five-thirty we were still waiting for someone from the taxi company with another key, for not only could the driver not open the boot, he could not start his car. Many people had come and gone, experts, advisers, observers, hangers-on had gathered and made suggestions; crowbars, pieces of wire, bunches of keys had been brought, telephone calls made. *E-to! Ah So! Anoné . . .* had been said endlessly, fruitlessly. I grew colder and colder in the bleak twilit customs shed. The staff had gone home, leaving one unfortunate to wait and inspect my luggage. He was not cross with me for spoiling his holiday, he showed only sympathy. I longed to get aboard the ship, where lights now shone and I could smell dinner cooking, or go back and have *sushi* in Kanda, but I could not leave the shed. The driver, rather a hero to start with, had begun to look pinched. I supposed he was thinking of all the customers he was losing on this public holiday and felt so sorry for him I gave him an extra Y1,000. He bowed five times and rushed off to try once more to force the lock.

At six o'clock, in darkness, the customs official came and said, apologetically, as though depriving me of a promised treat, that I would have to go on board without inspection since unfortunately he must now close the office. Two minutes after he drove away, the new key came. The boot was opened and my luggage carried aboard.

Cold, hungry, exhausted, I lay down in the warm cabin to restore myself before dinner. There was a gentle knock. Outside, a worried Japanese official bowed.

'Mrs Phelan? I am sorry, your luggage has not been through customs...'

I explained. He regretted...I protested. He gently insisted. Unfortunately it was the law. The customs official should not have gone away. 'But it was six o'clock,' I said. 'He had waited two hours overtime. It was not his fault. It was not my fault. It was not anyone's fault. It was an accident.'

He was sympathetic but firm. He rustled papers and said, 'Unfortunately...' and 'How many pieces...?'

I waved at the mountains stacked round me. I said, almost tearfully, '*I can't!* I'm frozen...I've waited three hours in the cold; I'm exhausted. I simply can't open all those things and pack them again.'

He gave me a kind look but repeated, 'Unfortunately... Well...I must have a word with the purser.'

He bowed and went away and I sat down to prepare for his return. Now I understood why people said what they did about Japanese officials, why they raged at Japanese bureaucracy. I forgot the sympathetic customs officer, the little man yesterday at Yokohama who had left his work to drive me, in his own car, round in circles to find the immigration authori-

282

ties; the endless help and kindness people had given me all over the country. I hated them all.

When the knock came I got up, took my keys from my bag and opened the door very coldly.

The official, still looking worried, bowed, rustled his papers and said, 'Mrs Phelan...'

'Mrs Phelan,' he said. 'I have spoken to the purser. Mrs Phelan...your luggage has not been inspected...' Then hastily, 'You are very tired. You have had a long wait in the cold wind. I am sorry. We will not ask you to open the bags.' He said pleadingly, 'You will promise me you have nothing in your luggage...no firearms...no drugs...?'

'Come in,' I said, ready to embrace him. 'Come in and have a look. I'll open it. I don't mind.'

He smiled and said, 'I hope you will have a good journey back to your country. *Sayonara.*'

Index

Nonomurta, Mrs, 34–7, 82

Obi, Shodashima Island, 200, 201

Ofunato, Chap. 2, Chap. 3

Ogata, Abbot (O Cho San), of Chotokuin, 113, 114, 116–118, 120–7, 129, 131–5, 143–144, 252

Ogata, Mrs, 115–16, 120–1

Ogi, island of Sado, 96–7, 98

Ojika Peninsula, 12, 15, 27

Okayama (on the Inland Sea), 201, 202

Okhotsk, Sea of, 72, 73, 74

Omoto, 54

Onagawa, Ojika Peninsula, 20

Oniwaki, island of Rishiri, 62

Osaka, 184, 185, 204; Castle, 203

Oshidomari, island of Rishiri, 62, 63–6

Oshima Island, 221, 226, 227

Otaru, 60

Oura, island of Hakata, 226

Panino-san, Elder of Itto-en, 169, 175

Rebun Island, 63, 67, 68

Rikuchu coast, 50

Rikyu, tea-master, 135–7

Rishiri Island, 61–6, 67, 69

Ryoanji garden, Kyoto, 117, 125–7

Ryotsu, island of Sado, 91, 96

Ryuomonji pottery kiln, Satsuma, 271

Sado, island of, 82–99, 258

Sagara, Lords of, 255

Saghalien, 63, 68, 72

Saigo Takemori (General Saigo), 266, 267–9, 271

Sakurajima volcano, Kyushu, 263, 264, 266, 269, 270–1, 272–3

Saroma Lake, Hokkaido, 73

Sartre, Jean-Paul, 173, 248

Sasaki, Sadako, of Hiroshima, 247–8

Sasebo, Kyushu, 251, 252

Satsuma, Lords of (samurai), 266, 267, 271

Satsuma Peninsula, 266–72

Seki, Hisake, 165, 181

Seki, Tetsuya, textile designer, 165

Sendagaya, Tokyo, 102–4, 106, 281

Sendai, 11, 12

Seto Naikai (the Inland Sea), 199, 207, 215, 217–20, 223, 228

Setoda, island of Innoshima, 216

Shigei, island of Innoshima, 216

Shikoku Island, 215, 221, Chap. 19, Chap. 20, 252

Shimo Yûbetsu, Hokkaido, 72–3, 77

Shingon Sects, 193–4, 197

Shinmachi, island of Sado, 97

Shinto gods (kami), 25

Shiraoi, Hokkaido, 77

Shiroyama, Mount, near Kagoshima, 267, 268

Shodashima Island, 199, 200, 201, 202, 203–6

Shokokuji temple, Kyoto, 113–14, 121, 122, 139

Shuko, fifteenth-century tea-master, 128

Siberia, 61

Sogetsu-san (wife of Tenko-san), 162; statue of, 254

Sohodoro-na-Kami (gods of the scarecrows), 84

Somekawa-san (O-furo-san), healer at Itto-en, 151–5, 159–61, 177, 179, 181, 182–183

Sotan, founder of Urasenke School, 135, 136–7

287